Frontispiece: Portrait of Rev. Isaac Nicholson, President of Cheshunt College 1792–1803
(Cheshunt archives, C9/14/4)

Hertfordshire Record Publications Volume 6
(Hon. General Editor: Richard J. Busby)

CHESHUNT COLLEGE

THE EARLY YEARS

A Selection of Records
edited with an introduction by
Edwin Welch

Hertfordshire Record Society
1990

Hertfordshire Record Society

The publication of this volume has
been assisted by generous grants from:

The Cheshunt Foundation, Westminster College,
Hertfordshire County Council,
Hertfordshire Local History Council,
The Robert Kiln Charitable Trust,
and The British Academy

ISBN 0 9510728 5 4

Printed by
E. & E. Plumridge Ltd.,
High Street, Linton, Cambrdige, England

CONTENTS

Illustrations

Acknowledgements

I am indebted to

(1) The Governors of Cheshunt College Foundation for permission to print these records,

(2) Two Presidents of Cheshunt, the Rev Jack Newport and the Rev Dr Stephen Mayor, for their assistance, encouragement and hospitality,

(3) Dr Geoffrey Nuttall who has supplied much information and commented on my draft,

(4) The Cheshire Record Office which searched for and copied Nicholson's ordination records for me.

Lantzville, B.C., Canada
Oct. 1989

Introduction

In 1768 Selina Countess Dowager of Huntingdon founded a college at Trevecka in the parish of Talgarth in Breconshire[1] for 'the education and instruction of truly pious and well-disposed young men whom the Lord should call to the Work of the Ministry of Jesus.' In 1782 she seceded from the Church of England and formed the Connexion which still bears her name. Because of concern about the continuance of the College after her death a number of her supporters formed the Apostolic Society to take future responsibility for it. From then until her death in 1791 they collected and invested funds for this purpose. In 1792 they removed the College to Cheshunt where it remained until 1905. Cheshunt College then moved to Cambridge in order to benefit from proximity to the university. From 1905 to 1920 it occupied Cintra House while its new buildings in Bateman Street were being completed. After two centuries of independence the College merged with Westminster College, Cambridge in 1968 and the Bateman Street buildings were sold.

Until 1791 Lady Huntingdon was responsible for all the expenses of the College and students, and she also made most of the decisions. For this reason there is no continuous record of the College before 1792 and information about it must be gleaned from her voluminous correspondence.[2] She allowed the Apostolic Society no part in running the College and even their fund raising activities languished, more especially after dissensions arose within the Connexion. After her death the trustees and the assistant committee of the Society continued to run the College very much as she had done, but fortunately kept minutes, the earliest of which are printed here. The information in these minutes has been supplemented with the college plan drawn up in 1787 and other records kept by the secretary.

The Early Methodists

In the eighteenth century, the word Methodist was used either as a term of condemnation or to indicate a person who believed in evangelical Protestant Christianity. It did not refer exclusively to the followers of John Wesley, and in the early years was more often used of George Whitefield and the Moravian Brethren. Until almost the end of the century there was no organised Methodist denomination, and most Methodists were nominally at least members of the Church of England. The Countess was one of the first Methodists to form a separate Church; this was followed later by the Wesleyans (after John Wesley's death), and the Welsh Calvinistic Methodists. However from the middle of the eighteenth century those describing themselves as Methodists split into two groups on doctrinal grounds. Some, led by the Wesley brothers, were Arminian, and others, represented by George Whitefield and Howell Harris, were Calvinists.[3] The distinction (and the controversies which developed between them) is complicated and obscure, but Calvinists believe that those chosen by God could be saved, while the Arminians accepted that anyone could be saved. The Arminians accused the Calvinists of the heresy of Antinomianism, while the Calvinists replied with charges of Socinianism. They also disagreed over the value of good works, and more heat than light was generated by their innumerable pamphlets. Those who believed in unity, in particular Howell Harris and the Countess, maintained an uneasy truce between the two until about 1770 when the difficulties became so great that the two sides separated. This eventually resulted in the establishment of several Methodist denominations - the Welsh Presbyterian Church, various Connexions in England, and the Wesleyan Church[4].

Lady Huntingdon (1707-91)

Selina, Countess of Huntingdon was converted, by her own account, in 1739 and the principal agents in this were her half sister, Lady Elizabeth Hastings of Ledston (West Riding), and the Rev. Thomas Barnard, a Leeds schoolmaster. As a result she met many of the leading Methodists over the next few years. Charles Wesley, Howell Harris, Benjamin Ingham and George Whitefield all became her friends, though John Wesley can hardly be described as more than an acquaintance. For the next thirty years most of her time was taken up by family affairs and her opportunities for evangelism were limited. Until her husband's unexpected death in 1746, she was responsible not only for his household but also for much of the administration of his estates. From 1746 to 1758, she was her husband's administrator and responsible for their surviving children and the Hastings estates. Even after her eldest son, Francis the tenth Earl, came of age, she supervised the renovation of the family home at Donnington Park in Leicestershire while he made the Grand Tour. During all that time Methodism was only a part, though an important part, of her life. It was not until 1768 that she was able to devote all her great energies to the cause with which her name is associated.[5]

Until then her efforts for the Methodist cause has been in response to some immediate need or crisis. She encouraged the formation of Methodist societies; she protected them from hostile incumbents and she supported evangelical ministers against their diocesans.[6] It was after 1760 that she was able to begin building meeting places for some of the societies.[7] In all these activities she acted with the approval, and often at the instigation, of the Methodist leaders. It was in 1768 that she began to take the initiative and then discovered that it was impossible to please all the Methodists at the same time. Early in 1768 she brought to an end a scandal involving the evangelical clergymen, Martin Madan and Thomas Haweis, by buying the advowson of Aldwinkle All Saints in Northamptonshire. This was the action of a clear-sighted, practical person to bring to an end a pamphlet war which brought discredit to both sides. However it annoyed Madan and did not please some of the other Methodists.[8] The establishment of her College at Trevecka later in the same year did not immediately arouse disapproval, but was later to be a sore trial to John Wesley and others.

The College at Trevecka

As early as December 1765 Lady Huntingdon had plans for founding a college and tried to recruit Francis Okely, the Bedford Moravian, as its president.[9] She planned to establish it at Trevecka in close proximity to the community which Howell Harris had founded in his home there. It was also her intention to allow Harris to decide on the curriculum. As early as 1749 Harris had

> 'especial freedom to try for a school at Trevecka to train young men for the Lord. If He would bring one there that He would make it a blessing to all God's Church, and bring His Catholic Spirit on them all'[10]

However, Okely refused the offer of the presidency and opened a boarding school in Bedford instead. Nothing further was then possible, because Lady Huntingdon seemed unable to find a suitable person to preside over the College. However less than three years later, in March 1768, a sense of urgency was added by the expulsion of six students of St Edmund Hall, Oxford for being enthusiasts 'who talked of regeneration, inspiration, and drawing nigh unto God.'[11] Within a few months Lady Huntingdon had acquired a lease of College Farm, Trevecka (Trefeca Isaf) about half a mile away from Howell Harris's home. In June 1768 she visited John William Fletcher (1729-85), the vicar of Madeley (Shropshire), a prominent Methodist, and persuaded him to become the first President.[12] The College opened on 24th August - the Countess's birthday[13] - and two of the first students were from St Edmund Hall.

Since she was still a loyal member of the Church of England, Lady Huntingdon's intention was to provide training for an evangelical or Methodist ministry, but even then she had no intention of excluding dissenters from its benefits. The College was not to be, as Dr Nuttall has already made clear, a dissenting academy of the old kind.[14] Neither was it an Anglican theological college. The first Anglican college was founded in the next century.[15] It was, therefore, a completely new departure in training. However it was not entirely without some precedents, especially in Wales. A considerable number of the clergy were not graduates of Oxford or Cambridge in the eighteenth century.[16] They had obtained their education in one of the better grammar schools, which could on occasion provide better training for ordinands than the ancient universities.[17] It is noteworthy that the Rev. Isaac Nicholson, the first President of the College after it moved to Cheshunt, was a non-graduate whose education was from a Cumberland grammar school. The Countess's college provided a similar education in the classical languages and mathematics, but added to them instruction in preaching and practical experience in evangelism. The former was particularly important since many of the students were Welsh-speakers with a poor grasp of spoken English.

The new college was well suited to provide training for Anglican ministers. Neither Oxford nor Cambridge gave similar instruction, even though the bishops preferred to ordain graduates. At both universities the study of classics and mathematics led to a degree, election as a junior fellow to ordination and a college benefice, with very little commitment to religion and a clerical life being required. The College was also a very inexpensive alternative to the universities. George Whitefield might graduate cheaply as a servitor at Pembroke College, or a patron might pay for a promising student, but Welsh students in particular found the road to graduation very difficult. Neither did the universities welcome evangelical undergraduates. Howell Harris's stay at Oxford lasted less than a week. William Delamotte left Cambridge without taking a degree. Hostility to Methodism had been limited to petty harassment. The *testimonium* needed for ordination would be refused them: they would be passed over when junior fellowships were being awarded.[18] But in the second half of the eighteenth century the universities began to expel or reject known Methodists. This probably reflects a hardening of the attitude of bishops. Martin Benson, Bishop of Gloucester, who had urged Whitefield to be ordained in 1736, was firmly opposed to Methodism a few years later.[19] So Lady Huntingdon's alternative to the universities was not very successful in getting its students ordained in the established church, and some sought ordination from dissenting ministers instead. When in 1782 other events convinced Lady Huntingdon that she must leave the Church of England, the difficulties of ordination for her students may have helped the decision. The following year six students from Trevecka were ordained at her chapel in Spa Fields.[20]

Until her death in 1791 the College was very much the Countess's creation and the object of her affections.[21] The great love which she had for her husband and for her children, all but two of whom were dead by 1763, was now transferred to her students. They were recommended to her by evangelical ministers, but she made the selection. Their progress was closely monitored by her either in person or by letters from them and their tutor. They were sent out to preach, and returned to College, at her command.[22] All their expenses while at College, and many of those when on preaching tours, were paid by her out of her own income. She *was* the College and the two other strong characters which she associated with it were eventually overwhelmed by her energy and authority. Howell Harris continued his interest in the students until his death in 1773, but gradually spent less time at the College.[23] John Fletcher only lasted as President until 1771 when he resigned as a result of the Calvinist controversy with John Wesley.[24] After his departure no other President was appointed during her lifetime. The Master, assisted by a senior student, provided the education. The Countess, who spent part of each year at the College, was her own President in fact if not in name. As Fletcher had been a part-time President, dividing his time between Madeley and Trevecka, this was not an important difference.

The Countess of Huntingdon's Connexion

While the College continued to train evangelists for almost any Protestant church, the Countess was gradually forced into establishing a separate denomination for her chapels. She always refused to register them as dissenters' meeting houses, which would have provided protection from persecution under the Toleration Act. Instead she had used her privilege as a peeress to appoint some of her Anglican ministers as her personal chaplains, and to describe her chapels as private chapels within the Anglican Church. In 1779 she took over Spa Fields chapel in Clerkenwell to protect the ministers officiating there against the Anglican incumbent of St James' church. He promptly challenged her privilege in the ecclesiastical courts and won. In 1781 she abandoned the appeal to the Court of Arches and, with three of her ministers, seceded.[25] The establishment of a separate denomination alienated most of the Methodist ministers, who wished to retain ties with the Church of England. The Connexion continued to grow throughout her lifetime with the help of her students, but she made no attempt to link the work of the College with that of the Connexion. Her 'plan' for the Connexion was rejected before she died, and in her will she left it in the hands of trustees.[26] Her College, however, became the responsibility of the Apostolic Society as she intended.

The Apostolic Society

Since almost all of Lady Huntingdon's income died with her, the subsidies which she provided for the College and Connexion would end with her death.[27] This was of considerable concern to some of her adherents, and they began to plan for the continuance of both. There was a small group of Anglican clergy associated with her, but they had little money. Two of them, Walter Shirley and Thomas Wills, were her poor relations. There was also a group of prosperous London merchants and tradesmen who were able to find the money needed when she died. Most of these were members of the Spa Fields chapel in Clerkenwell, but they were supported by members of the Countess's other London chapels - Mulberry Gardens, Holywell Mount and Sion. The former favoured a form of clerical government for both College and Connexion: the latter supported lay control. It was on this division that proposals for the future foundered. The 'Plan' for the Connexion was abandoned because of lay control, but the merchants in the Apostolic Society in accordance with their 'Plan' were successful in taking over control of the College in 1791.[28] Although from 1787 to 1791 it was merely an organisation for collecting and investing money for the future, and nearly collapsed from lack of practical role, the Society was ready to take action as soon as Lady Huntingdon died.

The subscribers to the Apostolic Society were almost all from London. Of the 382 persons who subscribed between 1787 and 1799, eighteen gave no address, either paying through another subscriber or anonymously. Only thirty-three of the remaining 349 lived outside the City and its suburbs. Most of these subscribers can be identified. Some, such as John Lloyd of Swansea and Thomas Charles of Bala, were old friends and supporters of the Countess. Others, such as W.F. Platt, were old Trevecka students. The seven from Cheshunt and three from adjacent towns were recruited after the College moved. The Connexion's chapels outside London provided remarkably few subscribers:

Bath	2
Brighton	3
Bristol	1
Bodmin	1
Hull	1
Newcastle on Tyne	1
Norwich	1
Plymouth	1
Reading	1
Swansea	1

It is possible that some chapels may have organised an annual sermon and collection for the College, but for most of the period donations of all kinds formed a small proportion of the Society's income. As late as 1812 when a collection for the travelling, college and provident funds was made in twenty chapels outside London a total of £267 18s. 6d. only was raised.[29] The overwhelming number of subscribers whose residences can be identified lived within a mile of Spa Fields chapel - 115 in all - and many within half a mile. Sixty-five lived within a mile of Sion chapel in Whitechapel.[30] Most were successful merchants and tradesmen. Eighteen subscribers designated as esquire lived in the same area, and some like James Oldham, were retired merchants.[31] Twenty-four clergy were subscribers, but most lived outside London.

The income obtained from these subscribers varied from £33 in 1789 to £469 in 1797, but eventually settled at about £500 a year. Expenses were usually very close to annual income, and the trustees were careful to avoid a deficit.

The College at Cheshunt

The above figures help to demonstrate how much the College became linked with Spa Fields chapel. The chapel was the only one to have an annual collection for the College. College meetings were often held at the chapel, and chapel officials acted for the College too. At a slightly later date it is possible to find College trustees' minutes in the chapel minute book.[33] During the period from 1791 to 1804 this helped to promote co-operation between the College and the Connexion because Lady Anne Erskine, now head of the Connexion, resided in the chapel house and a delegation could easily 'wait upon her ladyship'. After her death in 1804, the Rev. Thomas Haweis succeeded to the title, but as he was still vicar of Aldwinkle and lived mainly in Bath for his health, the link was broken and the two organisations gradually drifted apart.

Seven of the eight College trustees were active members of Spa Fields chapel:

James Oldham Oldham of St Andrew Holborn, esq.
Mathias Peter Dupont of Aldersgate St., innkeeper
Thomas Weatherill of Cold Bath Sq., gent.
William Hodson of Lothbury, merchant
William Langston of Gutter Lane, wholesale haberdasher
Henry Batley of Seward St., druggist
William Astle of Portpool Lane, leather seller[34]

The eighth was John Lloyd of Swansea included by the Countess, it was believed, as a compliment. He was old and did not attend meetings. The other trustees were supported by an assistant committee chosen each year at the October quarterly meeting of subscribers. The trustees kept a tight control over the assistant committee and the quarterly meetings of subscribers. The latter was allowed to choose only two new assistants each year (unless there had been a death or resignation) and these were probably nominated by the trustees. No clergyman, Anglican or dissenter, was allowed to serve on the committee. Senior clergy, Charles of Bala or Haweis, were permitted to act as assessors when applications from students were considered, but the committee and trustees interviewed them all both as probationers and full students and made the decisions. Even when clergy were present at meetings, the lay chairman sometimes insisted on his privilege of opening or closing the meeting with prayers.

The trustees also carried out the negotiations for the appointment of the President. On this first occasion they advertised for candidates, but finding that this only produced applications from Anglican clergymen seeking to improve their stipend or status, they asked known evengelical clergymen for nominations. Even this was not particularly successful as the records printed here show. Eventually Rev. Isaac Nicholson was proposed by the Rev. Richard De Courcy, vicar of St Alkmund in Shrewsbury. De Courcy was always a minor character in the work of the Countess and only a few of his letters to her exist.[35] His principal contribution to the College and Connexion was probably his nomination of Nicholson. Nicholson was then the curate of Coddington, a small village near Chester. He was born at Woodhow in Netherwasdale in Cumberland and since he did not graduate at Oxford or Cambridge was probably educated at St Bees Grammar School.[36] He was ordained deacon at Chester Cathedral on 28 September 1783 and probably served a curacy in that part of Cumberland then in the diocese of Chester. On 17 July 1785, after explaining his beliefs to the bishop, he was ordained priest in the Cathedral with the title of Coddington and a stipend of £40 a year. According to Urwick it was here that he was converted by reading De Courcy's sermons, and was subsequently removed for Methodism by 'an old squire'.[37]

No hint of this appears in these minutes and the sermon preached at his burial says that he was unregenerate, playing cards with the squire and dancing.[38] What is certain is that after he left Coddington some of Nicholson's congregation formed a dissenting meeting at nearby Tattenhall. Nicholson was expected to teach all the subjects required - Latin, Greek, Hebrew, mathematics, history, geography, English and elocution - but was given the assistance of a senior student when the numbers exceeded twelve. Since the students were at different levels of competence and knowledge this must have been a gruelling task, and some years later another tutor was appointed to help the President. Nicholson was not assisted by the continuous inspection of the trustees, who expected to be consulted and to decide quite minor matters about furniture, linen and the property. However since they had to manage on a tight budget their concern is understandable. They even attempted to recover their costs if a student left the College without completing his course. They also changed the Countess's policy by refusing to send out students before they were fully trained.

The strain which this régime placed on the President is illustrated by the subsequent career of Isaac Nicholson. In the spring of 1801 he was 'much indisposed' but recovered.[39] Twelve months later the trustees allowed him to take a sea voyage on the advice of his physician, and he went to Newcastle upon Tyne.[40] The students were given a vacation during his absence and sent to various Connexion chapels. Nicholson's wife had died in December 1801, and he now married Miss Broughton of Enfield, but returned from his honeymoon in October "poorly in his Health".[41] It soon became clear to the trustees that he could not continue in office, and the College was made the temporary responsibility of the senior student, George Gladstone. On 20 January 1803 he agreed to retire, but difficulties arose about his income. The trustees later made him a present of £40.[42] He became minister of Pell Street chapel, Ratcliff Highway, but died four years later at the early age of 46.[43] Meanwhile his successor, Andrew Horn, a former student, was seriously ill by 1809.[44]

The acquisition of the house at Cheshunt is well documented in the Cheshunt records. After the trustees had decided to move the College nearer to London where they could supervise it, the search centred on the towns immediately north-east of London. Their immediate intention was to lease rather than buy, and in this they were following the example of the Countess who usually leased her chapels. They were persuaded to purchase it by James Oldham after the Cheshunt house had been chosen. This was in existence as early as 1701 when it was known as the 'house at Churchgate'. In 1784 it was bequeathed by Mrs Sarah Gwilt to her brother William Shaw. It was Shaw's widow Ann, then living at Inglewood in Berkshire who sold it to the Apostolic Society.[45] On 29 February 1792 she and the other executor conveyed it to Thomas Long Sheen, who was acting for Oldham.[46] The trust deed whereby Sheen transferred it to the trustees was dated almost a year later, 1 February 1793, and it was not enrolled in Chancery to give it legal validity until several months later.[47] Subsequently the trustees bought more land and in 1820 issued an appeal for funds, which led to an almost complete rebuilding of the College.[48] After the move to Cambridge, the buildings were bought by the vicar of Cheshunt in 1907 and opened as Bishops' College, an Anglican theological college, two years later.[49]

The Students

So few students attended the College between 1791 and 1799, that it is impossible to draw any firm conclusions about their origins and recruitment, as has been done for a later period.[50] As we have seen at this time, the College was closely linked with the Connexion and most of the students entered its ministry. It was not until later in the nineteenth century that most of the Cheshunt students went to congregational churches.[51] Then the Connexion found its ministers elsewhere - either from other congregational colleges or by less academic routes[52] - and Cheshunt trained evangelical ministers for other denominations.

For various reasons, Cheshunt differed from the other Congregational colleges whose students have been described by Dr K.D. Brown. It provided sufficient financial aid for even the poorest students, whereas other dissenting colleges appear to have charged a fee.[53] The social class of students at this early period was probably lower than that of other colleges. In addition Cheshunt was willing to take Welsh-speaking students who were rejected by other colleges.[54] Although the trustees preferred students, in their early twenties, they did admit older students. A list prepared at the beginning of the nineteenth century shows that two students were thirty one and thirty four when they entered Cheshunt:

Under 20	10
20 - 22	32
23 - 25	27
26 - 28	10
29 & 30	3
Over 30	2[55]

Inevitably, only the bad behaviour of students found its way into the minutes, but it would sometimes seem that theological college students of the nineteenth century behaved like university students of the 1960s. In these minutes there are brief references to their sexual misbehaviour, but there is also the example of William Jones who objected to the Connexion's itinerant ministry.[56] In the nineteenth century students became more vocal still. College rules were criticised and the use of Anglican services in some Connexion chapels were found objectionable.[57] In 1855 student unrest led to the appointment of a committee to investigate the running of the College, and other Cheshunt examples might be quoted.[58] However individual students did not cause problems in Cheshunt. Instead they preached in the surrounding towns and in some of them Connexion chapels were eventually erected as a result.[59] In these early years there was some local opposition to the existence of the College - arson was threatened and shots were fired. However the chief difficulty was probably relations with the neighbouring landowners. Isaac Nicholson twice exceeded his authority in dealing with these and was duly reprimanded by the trustees. All these problems became less important when the College became part of the Cheshunt scene.[60]

Editorial Note

All the records transcribed here are from the archives of Cheshunt College Foundation (Westminster College, Cambridge).[61] The first minute book (C1/ 1) is a small volume (6″ x 7 3/4″) bound in a stiff vellum cover. It has a contemporary inscription on the front board - 'College Minutes from AD 1787. A.' The second minute book (C1/ 2) is similar but slightly larger (7½″ x 9½″) and has the remains of two clasps. It is described on the front board as - 'College Minute Book B'. The list of subscribers (C5/ 3) resembles the first minute book and is described as 'Subscribers to the College'. Other items are either taken from larger volumes or files of papers. The handwriting of all the documents is good and they are in excellent condition so that very few difficulties have arisen in transcription. In places missing dates have been added and repetitive sentences omitted, but these are all indicated by notes.

FOOTNOTES

1 The correct Welsh spelling is Trefeca (E. Davies, *A Gazetteer of Welsh Place-names,* Cardiff, 1957), but Trevecka is now traditional and is used throughout this introduction. It should be noted that in 1842 the Welsh Calvinistic Methodists opened a second Trevecka College - in Howell Harris's buildings

2 Many of these letters are to be found in the Cheshunt College archives

3 E.Welch, 'Andrew Kinsman's Churches' *Trans. Devons. Assoc.,* vol. 97, 1965, pp. 212-236

4 The Wesleyan Church also subsequently split into separate denominations

5 This brief account of Lady Huntingdon's life differs from the traditional account and is drawn from a new biography which I am writing

6 Leics. Record Office, 14D32/ 4, 6 & 24, 1. Methodist Archives Centre, Drew Univ., Hunt. A 96

7 Only two chapels - Brighton in 1761 and Bath in 1765 - had been opened by her before the College was founded

8 For a correct account of the Aldwinkle affair see the contemporary pamphlets in the Congregational Library (now at Dr Williams's Library, Gordon Square, London). The account given in [A.C.H. Seymour], *The Life and Times of the Countess* (London, 1844), vol. 1, p. 413 is very inaccurate

9 National Library of Wales, Trevecka Letter 2616, printed in G.M. Roberts (ed.) *Selected Trevecka Letters (1747-1794)* Caernarvon, 1962), p. 106. For Okely's career see E. Welch (ed.), *The Bedford Moravian Church* Beds. Hist. Rec. Soc., vol. 68, 1989, pp. 6-9

10 T. Beynon (ed.), *Howell Harris's Visits to Pembrokeshire* Aberystwyth, 1966), p. 158

11 [R.Hill], *Pietas Oxoniensis* (London, 1768), p. 2. S.L. Ollard, *Six Students of St Edmund Hall* (London, 1911)

12 The deeds of College Farm are not to be found. W.P. Jones *(Trevecka College 1842-1942,* Llandyssul, 1942, p.59) states that the lease was secured 'by the help of Howell Harris', which has been sometimes interpreted as his ownership. Gareth Davies ('Trevecka (1706-1964)' in *Brycheiniog,* 1971, vol. 15, p.45) says it was leased from Thomas Harris. However the correspondence of the Apostolic Society with the owner, Mr Hughes, suggests that the farm belonged to Howell's older brother Joseph, whose daughter and heir married Hughes. For the Countess's visit to Madeley, see Abiah Darby's diary (Friends House Library, London, MS. vol. 310)

13 She was born on 13 Aug. 1707, but added on the eleven days removed from the calendar in 1752 by the change from Julian to Gregorian calculation

14 G.F. Nuttall, *The Significance of Trevecca College* (London, 1969) to which I am indebted for the references quoted here

15 Lampeter, opened finally in 1827, was one of the first. See, D.T.W. Price, *A History of St David's University College Lampeter,* vol. 1 (Cardiff, 1977, ch. 1

16 See for example the institution lists printed in A.I. Pryce, *The Diocese of Bangor during Three Centuries* (Cardiff, 1929)

17 D.T.W. Price, *op. cit.,* p. 8

18 Nuttall, *op. cit.,* p. 4

19 *George Whitefield's Journals* (London, 1960), p. 66. Methodist Archives Centre, Drew Univ., Hunt. A 98

20 E. Welch, 'Lady Huntingdon and Spa Fields Chapel' *(Guildhall Miscellany,* vol. 4, 1972, pp. 175-183)

21 Many of the letters written by Lady Huntingdon reflect her feelings towards the students, which contrasts with the letters sometimes written to her by aggrieved students and ministers

22 G.F. Nuttall, 'The Students of Trevecca College' *Trans. Hon. Soc. of Cymmrodorion,* session 1967, pt 2, p. 252

23 National Library of Wales, Trevecka diaries. I am indebted to the Historical Society of the Presbyterian Church of Wales for permission to consult these diaries

24 Cheshunt Coll., E4/ 7. For the controversy see P.P. Streiff, *J.G. de la Flechere 1729-1785; ein Beitrag zur Geschichte des Methodismus* (Frankfurt am Main, 1984), section D

25 'Lady Huntingdon and Spa Fields', op. cit.

26 E. Welch, 'Lady Huntingdon's Plans' *Guildhall Studies in London History*, vol. 2, 1975, pp. 31-40)

27 Lady Huntingdon received L1200 a year from the Hastings estates after her husband's death (Huntingdon Lib, HAP 31 (7)). However, other sums due to her under her marriage settlement were not finally paid until long after her death (Huntingdon Lib., HAP 34 (31))

28 E. Welch, 'Lady Huntingdon's Plans' *Guildhall Studies in London History*, vol. 2, 1975, pp. 31-40

29 Cheshunt Coll., C9/ 1. *Annual Address to the Connexion, 1813*

30 Some of course lived within a mile of both chapels

31 For James Oldham Oldham see E. Kaye, *A History of Missenden Abbey* (Aylesbury, n.d.), pp. 31-32

32 See figures in Appendix, summarised from the College receipt and disbursement book (Cheshunt Coll., C9/ 1)

33 E. Welch, *Two Calvinistic Methodist Chapels, 1743-1811* (London Rec. Soc., 1975), pp. 86-87

34 These details are taken from the printed trust deed (Cheshunt Coll., C16/ 3)

35 For De Courcy see R.F. Skinner, *Nonconformity in Shropshire, 1662-1816* (Shrewsbury, 1964) where his quarrel with the local Baptists is described

36 These details come from the episcopal records - Cheshire Record Office, EDP 87/ 1/ 3 and Act Book 1771-90. T. Bennett, *Funeral Sermon ... for Rev. I. Nicholson* (London, 1807) pp. 24-26

37 W. Urwick, *Historical Sketches of Nonconformity in the County Palatine of Chester* (London & Manchester, 1864). p. 105

38 For example Urwick calls the squire 'a lay rector', but the incumbent was the rector and the patrons the Dean and Chapter of Chester. *Funeral Sermon*, op. cit.

39 Cheshunt College minutes (C1/ 3), p. 15

40 *Ibid.*, pp. 36, 38, 42

41 *Ibid.*, p. 54

42 *Ibid.*, pp. 62-67, 89

43 *Funeral Sermon, op. cit.*

44 College minutes, p. 130

45 Cheshunt Coll., C21/ 1

46 Cheshunt Coll., C21/ 3. Enrolled in Chancery on 10 Mar.

47 The original trust deed is Cheshunt Coll. C21/ 4, but it is more conveniently consulted in the printed version (C16/ 2)

48 Cheshunt Coll., C9/ 2/ 1

49 Cheshunt Coll., C9/ 12/ 5. The Anglican college has now closed. The buildings were used as a community centre for some years, and more recently as offices by Broxbourne Borough Council.

50 K.D. Brown, *A Social History of the Nonconformist Ministry in England and Wales, 1800-1930* (Oxford, 1988)

51 In 1884 it was stated that of twenty two ministers in the Connexion only four had been educated at Cheshunt and fifteen in other colleges *(Report of Proceedings at a Conference of the Ministers and Managers of the Connexion* (London, 1885), p. 37

52 *Biographical Records of Joseph Rawlings, Minister of the Countess of Huntingdon's Chapel, Bearfield* (Bradford on Avon, 1866)

53 Brown, *op. cit.*, pp. 26 & 73

54 Brown, *op. cit.*, p. 69

55 Cheshunt Coll., C9/ 9/ 2. See Brown, *op. cit.*, p.68

56 Itinerancy was gradually abandoned by the Connexion in the nineteenth century

57   Cheshunt Coll., C9/ 6/ 37. For the Connexion's use of the B.C.P. see A.E. Peaston, *The Prayer Book Tradition in the Free Churches* (London, 1964), pp. 66-69

58   Cheshunt Coll., C9/ 7, 3

59   Cheshunt Coll., C8/ 1 & 2

60   For the later history of the College see P.C. Archer, *Historic Cheshunt,* part 3, Ch. 14, and S.C. Orchard, *Cheshunt College* (Cambridge, 1968).

61   The List & Index Society published a list of the Cheshunt College archives in 1981 (Special Series, vol. 14)

I

APOSTOLIC SOCIETY

MINUTES

APOSTOLIC SOCIETY MINUTE BOOK,
1787 - 1793

[i]   The Minute Book of the Apostolic Society instituted A.D. 1787 under the Patronage of the Right Honorable Selina, Countess Dowager of Huntingdon, for perpetuating Her Ladyship's College in Wales after her decease as a Seminary for Young Men who, under the influence of Divine Grace, are desirous of directing themselves to the Ministry of the Gospel of Christ at home or abroad.[1]

[1]

At Mr Dupont's, the Castle and Falcon,
Aldersgate Street, Friday the 5th October 1787

In consequence of an Invitation to partake of a dinner given by the Right Honourable the Countess of Huntingdon, the following Ministers and Gentlemen were present:

Revd Mr Rowland	Mr Carr
Revd Mr Knight	Mr Fidler
Revd Mr Barnard	Mr Dupont
Revd Mr Jenkins	Mr Wontner
Mr Oldham	Mr Regnier
Dr Lyon	Mr Langston
Mr Hodson	Mr Best
Mr Wetherall	Mr Batley
Mr Towers	

When a conversation took place, relative to the plan lately submitted to Lady Huntingdon by some persons whose minds [2] had been impressed with the necessity of a Society being formed in her life time for the preserving and continuing (under Providence) the College of her Ladyship when it shall please God to remove her.

The same having previously met with the approbation of Lady Huntingdon was also very warmly adopted by the Gentlemen especially of the Committee present and a meeting recommended to be held at this place at five o'clock the Wednesday following and notice to be given thereof the next Lord's day at the Chapel.

[3]

Mr Dupont's, the Castle and Falcon, Aldersgate street, Wednesday the 10th October 1787

Present - Mr Oldham in the Chair
Dr Lyon, Mr Wilson, Mr N. Soames, Mr Butcher, Mr Carr, Mr Dupont, Mr H. Soames, Mr Tilney, Mr Banks, Mr Batley, Mr Langston, Mr Silver

Resolved that it appears to this meeting very expedient and necessary that a subscription be entered into for the purpose of supporting Lady Huntingdon's College after her decease to be appropriated solely for that use, but the Subscription was not begun as we had not her Ladyship's plan and rules of College.

Resolved that Four Gentlemen wait on her Ladyship for the same and that another Meeting be held here on Wednesday next, the 17th instant.

[4]

Mr Dupont's, the Castle and Falcon Aldersgate street, Wednesday the 17th October 1787

Present - Mr Hodson in the Chair
Dr Lyon, Mr Tilney, Mr Butcher, Mr Tripp, Mr Butterworth, Mr Weatherill, Mr Langston, Mr Best for the Countess of Huntingdon, Mr Banfield, Mr Batley, Mr Dupont, Mr N. Soames, Mr H. Soames, Mr Bond, Mr Newcombe, Mr Biggerstaffe, Mr West, Mr Winch

Read the Letter from the Countess of Huntingdon dated the 17th October 1787 from Spa Fields.

Read the Plan of the Institution communicated by Lady Huntingdon.[2]

1. Resolved unanimously that it is the opinion of this Meeting that we form ourselves into a Society for the purpose of supporting, after the Countess of Huntingdon's decease, her [5] College in Wales or in any other part of Great Britain where she should erect one.

2. Resolved that this Society be called and known by the name of the Apostolic Society.

3. Resolved that a Book be now opened for the purpose of receiving Donations and Annual Subscriptions.[3]

4. Resolved that the Trustees to be appointed by Lady Huntingdon be a Committee to conduct the Business of this Society and to receive Donations and Subscriptions; the same to be paid into Dr Lyon's hands till invested in the public Funds.

Mr N. Soames objected to the Trustees having the power of filling up vacancies in the Trust after Lady Huntingdon's decease and proposed that these vacancies should be filled up by a majority of the then subscribers or such subscribers as had been so for a certain time to be agreed.

This being contrary to the Proposals sent in by her Ladyship must be submitted to her consideration. 8 hands appeared for submitting it to her Ladyship's consideration, 10 hands against it. [6]

5. Resolved that a Circular Letter setting forth the nature and design of the institution be drawn up and printed and some copies delivered to every subscriber to disperse amongst his friends in order to promote the same, and that Messrs Dupont and Batley be desired to draw up such circular Letter against the next meeting.

6. Resolved that a Quarterly meeting of the Subscribers be held at such time and place as the Trustees shall appoint, when they shall lay before the Society at Large all their proceedings and the affairs of the Society from the last General Meeting.

7. Resolved that to promote Unanimity and to prevent any Disagreements in the Society it is understood and agreed that the Proposal and Plan receive from the Countess of Huntingdon and read at this meeting be the Rule by which this Society intend to conduct themselves and the affairs thereof.

8. Resolved to meet again Wednesday next at four o'clock at the same place.

[7]
Mr Dupont's, the Castle and Falcon
Aldersgate street, Wednesday 24
October 1787

Present - Dr Lyon in the Chair
Revd Mr Rowland, Mr Hodson, Mr West, Mr Biggerstaffe, Mr Tripp,
Mr Weatherill, Mr Langston, Mr Best for the Countess of Huntingdon,
Mr Batley, Mr Paynter, Mr Banfield, Mr Dupont

The Minutes of the last Meeting were read and confirmed.

A Circular Letter having been proposed, the same was read and approved of, and 3000 copies ordered to be printed.[4]

Resolved the Trustees to meet at the same place and time the first Wednesday in December, and the General Meeting adjourned to the first Wednesday in January next.

[8]

Meeting of the Trustees,
Castle and Falcon,
Aldersgate street, December 5 1787

Present - Dr Lyon, Mr Dupont, Mr Oldham, Mr Hodson, Mr Langston, Mr Batley.

Minutes of the last General Meeting were read and confirmed.

The Treasurer reported the state of the subscriptions which amount to £156 15s. - out of which £200 3 per Cents Consols have been purchased for the Society in the names of Messrs Henry Batley, William Hodson and cost £153 5s.

Resolved to meet on Wednesday next at 5 o'clock when the Secretary is desired to being the Plan agreed on at the General Meeting to be signed by the Trustees preparatory to its being printed and sent to the several Congregations.

[9]

Meeting of the Trustees
at the Castle and Falcon, Aldersgate street,
Wednesday December 12 1787

Present - Messrs Oldham, Dupont, Weatherill, Hodson, Langston, Batley

The introduction of the word 'Secession,' and the explanation thereof, into the Plan was considered and agreed to, as well as liberty granted for the admitting fit and able Men into the Church of England and other Churches where there shall be openings in Providence and giving the seceding Connexion the supply in all the Calls that may happen the preference to every other; some objectionable expressions in the explanation of the Secession, were of opinion, to be omitted.

Resolved to meet on Wednesday next at Mr Dupont's further to consider the above and to point out the objectionable expressions.

[10]

Meeting of the Trustees,
Castle and Falcon, Aldersgate Street,
Wednesday 18 December 1787

Present - Messrs Hodson, Langston, Wetherill and Batley.

Mr Best from the Countess of Huntingdon attended and informed the Trustees her Ladyship had consented to the expunging the objectionable words in the explanation of the Secession and the admitting of students to calls in the established or other Churches, but requiring those in the Secession always first to be attended to.

The Trustees considered and approved of an addition to the clause respecting the Master and Assistant as follows:

> But before their appointment to be examined and approved as to their Abilities and Qualifications by one or more of the principal Ministers of, or serving in, the Connexion.

and also considered it necessary on application for a student to be sent to any place the Trustees to have the sole nomination or appointment of such student. [11]

Agreed to meet on Wednesday next at 4 of Clock at the Committee room of the Chapel particularly to consider the clause that part of it which relates to the 'appointment of a General Management' and how far that will clash with the Trustees.

Meeting of the Trustees, Wednesday 26 December 1787, at the Committee room of Spa Fields Chapel

Present - Dr Lyon, Messrs Dupont, Langston, Hodson, Wetherill and Batley

Considered the clauses conferred on at our last meeting and a new clause received from Lady Huntingdon this evening relative to the removing of any of the Trustees for certain causes therein mentioned and resolved on:

> That in case either or any of the Trustees shall declare their dissent from all or any of the Doctrines contained in the said following 15 Articles (to be brought in at page 3 in the Plan after the words 'what is herein contained') or shall refuse to pursue the line of conduct laid down in the subsequent [12] part of this plan, he or they shall be removed by the Countess of Huntingdon in her life time and after her decease by the unanimous vote of the other Trustees for the time being, and another or others be chosen and appointed in his or their room by the Countess in her lifetime, and after her decease by the other trustees, and also resolved on the two clauses respecting the Master and Assistant examination, and the permission of students to go into and serve in the established and other Churches as considered on by them the Trustees the 18 December last.

[13]

At a Quarterly General Meeting,
Apostolic Society, Castle and Falcon,
January 2, 1787[5]

Present - Dr Lyon in the Chair, Messrs Langston, Hodson, Oldham, Dupont, Wetherill, Batley, Galpine, Hoppne, Walsh, Tilney, Butcher, Revd Mr Taylor, Revd Mr Bradford, Fielder, Ayre, Mr Best for her Ladyship, Revd Mr Ayre, Bennett, Whittaker, Chambers.

The minutes of the last meeting were read and confirmed.

The Plan of the Apostolic Society with the additions was read and approved.

The names of the Subscribers with the amount of their Subscriptions were read.

The Plan and Rules of the Society having been fairly copies in two Books, one for the Countess of Huntingdon, the other for the Trustees, and both sign'd by the Countess, the same were signed by the Trustees and Subscribers present. Messrs Galpin, Best, Eyre and Bennett did not sign.[6]

[14]

Mr Galpine proposed in case of a vacancy in the Trustees happening, to be filled up at the next Monthly Meeting or the second at farthest, and that the Choice should be by the majority of the surviving Trustees (page 2 of the Plan).

Mr Galpine further proposed this addition in page 10 after 'of them at least' of *approved by a majority of them* are to give, etc.

These proposals agreed to be submitted to her Ladyship.

Mr Batley proposed to send Mr Wills the plan for signing, in order to its being forwarded to the other Ministers for their signing, that the Plan might be printed; which was agreed to.

Resolved the Trustees to meet the first Wednesday in February at the Committee room, Spa Fields Chapel, and the General Meeting adjourned to Wednesday 2d of April at the Castle and Falcon, Aldersgate street.

[15]

Meeting of the Trustees,
Wednesday, February 6 1788, at
the Committee room, Spa Fields Chapel

Present - Dr Lyon, Messrs Hodson, Langston and Batley.

Mr Langston brought in two subscriptions this evening - £2-2s. and £1-1s.

The Treasurer reported he had received since the last monthly meeting two donations of £5-5s. each.

Resolved that three of the Trustees shall constitute a board to transact business at their monthly meetings.

Resolved that as the Plan of this Society is compleated and the arrangement thereof vested solely in the Trustees, it is the duty of the Trustees carefully to preserve the same in their hands and not permit any innovation or Alteration to be made by the subscribers at large at any of the Quarterly Meetings. Such meetings to be considered as meetings of information only and the minutes of the Trustees not then to be read.

[16]

Meeting of the Trustees, Wednesday 5 March 1788, at the Committee room, Spa Fields Chapel

Present - Dr Lyon, Messrs Weatherill, Hodson, Langston and Batley.

Read and confirmed the minutes of the last monthly meeting.

The Treasurer reported he had received a subscription of £1-1s. since the last meeting.

[17]

At a Quarterly General Meeting of the Apostolic Society, Castle and Falcon, Aldersgate Street, Wednesday 2 April 1788

Present - Mr Hodson in the Chair. Dr Lyon, Mr Dupont, Mr Weatherill, Mr Towers, Mr Langston, Mr Tilney, Mr Batley.

Read the Minutes of the last Meeting.

The Treasurer reported to have received £14-14s. since the last monthly meeting, and also £1-10s. being one year's interest of a Note for £29-13s. from the Revd Mr Wills, the Revd Mr Porter and Mr Field to Mr Thomas Weatherill and given by Mr Weatherill to the Society.

Received from the Right Honourable the Countess of Huntingdon a List of the Chapels and preaching places in the Connexion, being 116 in number.

The Secretary reported that the Proposals agreed at the last General Meeting to be submitted to the Countess of Huntingdon having been approved by her Ladyship were inserted in their proper place in the Plan of the Society.

The Meeting adjourned to the first Wednesday in July at the Committee room, Spa Fields Chapel.

[18]

Meeting of the Trustees, Wednesday 7 May 1788, at the Committee room, Spa Fields Chapel

Present - Dr Lyon, Mr Weatherill, Mr Batley.

Read the Minutes of the last General Meeting.

The Bill from Messrs Hughes and Walsh for Stationery, amount £10 6s. 9d., received and the Treasurer desired to pay it.

Meeting of the Trustees Wednesday 4 June 1788

Present - Messrs Weatherill, Hodson, Langston, Batley.

Read the minutes of the last Monthly Meeting.

[19]

Meeting (Quarterly General) of the Apostolic Society, at Committee room, Spa Fields Chapel, Wednesday [2] July 1788[7]

Present - Dr Lyon in the Chair. Messrs Weatherill, Hodson, Langston, Galpine, Best, Batley.

Read and confirmed the minutes of the last General Meeting.

The Treasurer reported to have received £6 5s. 6d. since the last Meeting.

Adjourned to the first Wednesday in October at the same place.

[20]

Meeting of the Trustees, Wednesday 6 August 1788, at the Committee Room, Spa Fields Chapel

Present - Messrs Hodson, Langston, Batley.

Read the Minutes of the last General Meeting.

Received a Letter from Dr Lyon intimating that he had resigned all future services in Lady Huntingdon's Connexion and that he is ready to deliver into the hands of the other Trustees the Money remaining in his possession on receiving a proper indemnification under the signature of her Ladyship and the Trustees.[8]

Resolved that Mr Batley be desired to enquire of Dr Lyon the kind of indemnification he expects, to have the same prepared against the next Monthly meeting, and to request Dr Lyon's attendance.

Resolved a vacancy being now made of a Trustee and Treasurer by the resignation of Dr Lyon, the absent Trustees be acquainted therewith and the whole of them be summoned to the next monthly meeting for the nomination of a Trustee and Treasurer.

[21]

The Secretary reported having in his hands a subscription from the Right honourable the Lady Dowager Viscountess Montague of £5-5s.

Meeting of the Trustees,
Wednesday [3] September 1788,[9]
at the Committee room, Spa Fields Chapel

Present - Messrs Dupont, Weatherill, Hodson, Batley.

Read the minutes of the last monthly meeting.

The Secretary reported Lady Huntingdon having nominated Mr William Astle to be a Trustee in the room of Dr Lyon resigned.

The Secretary desired to communicate the nomination to Mr Astle and request his acceptance thereof; the same being with the entire approbation of the Trustees.

Resolved unanimously that Mr Oldham be appointed Treasurer to this Society in the room of Dr Lyon.

[22]

Quarterly General Meeting of the Apostolic Society
at the Committee Room, Spa Fields Chapel,
Wednesday 1 October 1788

Present - Mr Hodson in the Chair, Mr Langston, Mr Tilney, Mr N. Soames, Revd Mr Rowland, Mr Omer, Mr Towers, Mr Butcher, Mr Batley.

Read the minutes of the last meeting.

The Treasurer (Mr Hodson L[ocum] T[enens]) reported to have received since the last General Meeting £15-15s.

The Countess of Huntingdon the 7th July having dismissed the Revd Mr Wills from her Connexion, Dr Lyon in consequence thereof resigned his Offices of Treasurer and Trustee to this Society. Her Ladyship has appointed Mr William Astle a Trustee and the [23] Trustees have nominated Mr Oldham Treasurer in the room of Dr Lyon, both which Gentlemen have accepted their respective appointments.

Adjourned to the first Wednesday in January 1789 at the same place.

Meeting of the Trustees,
Wednesday 5 November 1788,
at the Committee room, Spa Fields Chapel

Present - Messrs Weatherill, Langston, Astle, Hodson, Batley.

Read the Minutes of the General Meeting.

Resolved that notice be given next Lord's Day to the Subscribers to this Society that the second annual subscription had commenced and for them to pay their subscriptions to the trustees in the Committee room and the Minister or Clerk of the Chapel be desired to read the same.

[24]

Meeting of the Trustees,
Wednesday 3 December 1788,
at the Committee room, Spa Fields Chapel

Present - Messrs Hodson, Langston, Batley

Read the minutes of the last Meeting.

The Treasurer (Mr Hodson) reported to have received £51-9s. since the last report.

The Treasurer (Mr Hodson) also reported to have purchased £100 3 per cent Consols at 3¾ this day.

Resolved that a Person be appointed to collect the annual subscriptions.

[25]

Quarterly General Meeting
at the Committee room, Spa Fields Chapel,
Wednesday 7 January 1789

Present - Mr Hodson in the Chair. Mr Langston, Mr Butcher, Mr Weatherill, Mr Astle, Mr Tilney, Mr Batley.

Read and confirmed the Minutes of the last Meeting.

The Treasurer (Mr Hodson) reported to have received since the last General Meeting £53-11s.

The Treasurer (Mr Hodson) also reported to have purchased £100 3 per cent Consols and cost £73 17s. 6d.

Adjourned to the first Wednesday in April next to the same place.

[26]

Meeting of the Trustees,
Wednesday 4 February at the
Committee room, Spa Fields Chapel

Present - Mr Hodson, Mr Langston, Mr Weatherill, Mr Batley.

Read the Minutes of the last General meeting.

Mr William Parke, having been appointed collector agreeable to the resolution of the 3d December, paid this evening into the Treasurer's (Mr Hodson) hands £22-1s., being the amount of the subscriptions he hath hitherto collected.

The Treasurer (Mr Hodson) reported to have received £3 being half year's Dividend on £200 3 per cent Consols due at Midsummer last and £4-10s. for half year's dividend on £300 3 per cent Consols due at Christmas last.

[27]

Meeting of the Trustees,
Wednesday [4] March 1789,[10]
at the Committee room, Spa Fields Chapel

Present - Mr Langston, Mr Batley. No Business done.

Quarterly General Meeting
at the Committee room, Spa Fields Chapel,
Wednesday 1 April 1789

Present - Mr Hodson in the Chair. Mr Carr, Mr Langston, Mr Batley.

Read and confirmed the minutes of the last quarterly meeting.

Mr Hodson (as Treasurer) reported to have received since the last quarterly meeting £25-4s. for subscriptions and £7-10s. for dividends on stock; also that he had paid Mr William Parke £1-5s.

13

[28]

Meeting at the Committee room,
Spa Fields Chapel,
Wednesday May 6 1789

Present Mr Batley. No Business Done.

Meeting at the Committee room,
Spa Fields Chapel,
Wednesday 3 June 1789

Present - Messrs Hodson, Weatherill, Langston.

The Treasurer (Mr Hodson) reported he had received One Guinea since the last monthly meeting; also that he has purchased £75 3 per cent which cost £57-2s.

[29]

Committee Room, Spa Fields Chapel,
June 29 1791

Present - Mr Oldham, Mr Hodson, Mr Astle, Mr Langston, Mr Batley.

Resolved that in consequence of the Death of the Right Honourable The Countess Dowager of Huntingdon a General Meeting of the Apostolic Society be held at the Castle and Falcon, Aldersgate Street on Wednesday the 6th of July next precisely at Six o Clock in the Evening.

[30]

General Meeting at Mr Dupont's,
the Castle and Falcon, Aldersgate Street,
Wednesday 6 July 1791

Present - Mr Oldham in the Chair. Revd Dr Ford, Mr Lloyd, Mr Langston, Mr Towers, Mr Dupont, Revd Mr Jones, Mr Oldham, Mr Wilson senior, Mr Hodson, Mr Simpson, Mr H. Soames junior, Mr N. Soames, Mr Tilney, Mr Whittaker, Mr Fyffe, Mr Mason, Mr Astle, Mr Walsh, Mr Butcher, Mr Banks, Mr Bensley, Mr Chambers, Mr Hopper, Mr Weatherill, Mr Batley.

Read the Minute for calling the meeting.

Read the Plan for the Apostolic Society.

Resolved that the College be continued.

[31]

Resolved that for the present the College be continued in Wales where it now is, till a convenient place be found out nearer London.

Resolved that a Committee be appointed out of the Subscribers at large to look out for a place at the distance of from 10 to 50 miles from London and that the Committee be:

Mr Oldham	Mr Dupont
Mr Batley	Mr Banks
Mr Simpson	Mr Hodson

Resolved that the Trustees be a Committee to draw up a circular letter to be sent to such persons as may be supposed likely to give their support to the College.

Resolved that the next meeting be on Wednesday the 13th instant.

Resolved that notice be given from the pulpits of Spa Fields, Mulberry Gardens and Sion Chapels of the business and day of the next meeting.

Adjourned to 13 July 1791.

[33]

General Meeting, Mr Dupont's
the Castle and Falcon, Aldersgate Street,
Wednesday July 13 1791

Present - Mr Oldham in the Chair.
Mr Walsh, Mr Langston, Mr Hodson, Mr Weatherill, Mr Cooper, Mr Rusby, junior, Mr Millar, Mr Emerson, Mr Dupont, Mr Rowton, Mr Tutt, Mr Giles, Mr Simpson, senior, Mr Simpson, junior, Mr Gold, Mr Butcher, Mr Fyffe, Mr Best, Revd Mr Eyre, Revd Mr Wilks, Revd Mr McCall, Mr Owen, Mr B. Bryan, Mr Price, Mr Phillips, Mr Silver, Mr Wontner, Mr Wontner (sic), Mr Tilney, Mr Flower, Revd Mr Crowle, Mr King, Mr Ellis, Mr Batley.

[34]

Read and Confirmed the Minutes of the last Meeting.

Read and approved the Circular Letter drawn up by the Trustees.[11]

Resolved that 4000 of the same be printed.

Read an Extract from the Countess of Huntingdon's will bequeathing the Furniture, Library and Communion plate of her College to the Society.

Resolved that the Gentlemen composing the present meeting be a Committee to meet every evening at the Committee Room, Spa Fields Chapel, to commence on Saturday next for the purpose of circulating the printed Letter.

[35]

Resolved that the next General Meeting be, God Willing, on Monday the 25th instant at this place.

The Revd Mr Eyre concluded with prayer.

Adjourned to 25th July 1791.

Meeting of the Trustees,
Monday 3 August 1791

Present - Messrs Hodson, Weatherill, Langston, Astle, Dupont and Batley.

Read a Letter from Mr Thomas Davis of Wales desiring to be admitted to College. His letter sent, and application made to the Revd Mr Jones of Langan for enquiry.

Read a Letter from Mrs Powell, College, Trevecka, respecting the House-keeping.

Wrote to Mrs Powell desiring her to dismiss the Gardiner and to apply for money to Mr Evan Roberts.

Wrote to Mr Evan Roberts, Trevecka, requesting him to advance Mrs Roberts (*sic*) such money from time to time as may be necessary and to Draw on the Treasurer for the same.[12]

[36]

Wrote to the Revd Mr John Williams, Pantycelyn, near Llandovery, Carmarthenshire, intreating him to take the charge of the College during its continuance at Trevecka.

Meeting Trustees, Wednesday
14 August 1791

Present - Messrs Hodson, Weatherill, Astle, Bartley.

Read letters from Mr Best
John Barton to Mr Weatherill
Revd Mr Williams

Meeting Trustees,
24 August 1791

Present - Messrs Oldham, Hodson, Dupont, Astle, Langston, Weatherill, Batley.

Read and considered our letters in answer to the advertisement for a House.

Mr Dupont reported on a House he had seen at Endfield,[13] referred to Mr Fidler to enquire of Mr Bowles the Landlord.

[37]

General Meeting Mr Duponts,
Aldersgate Street, Monday
25 July 1791

Present - Revd Mr Platt in the Chair
Mr Hodson, Mr Astle, Mr Weatherill, Mr Simpson senior, Mr Bridgeman, Mr Butterworth, Mr Rusby senior, Mr Coxhead, Mr Butcher senior, Mr Robert Butcher, Mr Flower, Revd Mr James, Revd Mr Aldridge, Revd Mr Cottingham, Mr Dupont, Mr Giles, Mr Tilney, Mr Emerson, Mr B. Bryan, Revd Mr Charles, Mr Edward Jones, Mr Langston, Mr Cooper, Mr Strahan, Mr Oldham, Mr Andrews, Mr John Baker, Mr J. Jordan, Mr Longes, Mr Tilby, Mr James Cooper, Mr Dagleish, Mr Batley

The Minutes of the last Meeting were read and Confirmed.

Resolved 1st. To divide the Town and Contiguous Villages into several Districts.
[38]
2ndly. To make out a Book for each District containing the names of those Persons residing in the same who have or shall be wrote to.

3dly. To appoint a Deputation of two or more Members of the Society for each Distrct to wait on such Persons as have been or shall be wrote to.

4. To Continue the Open Committee at Spa Fields Chapel every evening this and next week for the purpose of entering Names, receiving subscriptions and sending out addresses.

5. To meet on Thursday Evening at Spa Fields Chapel to form the Districts and appoint the deputation.

6. The Deputies to pay in the Moneys they receive to the Treasurer or Sub Treasurer once a week or oftner.

[39]

7. A General meeting to be held at this House the first Monday in September for the Society to receive accounts of the Success the Deputation have met with.

Thanks of the Meeting were given to the Ministers present.

The Revd Mr Aldridge concluded with prayer.

Meeting Trustees,
September 7, 1791

Present - Messrs Hodson, Weatherill, Astle, Oldham, Batley.

Mr Best presented the Inventory of Books and Furniture.[14]

Mr Best informed us Mr Morgan of Glasberry near Hay would recommend a person to remove the furniture cheaper than any other.
[40]
Mr Hodson to answer Mr Williams' Letter of 13th last August.

Read a Letter from Mr Hughes[15] offering the House at Trevecka till Michaelmas and 2 or 3 Months afterwards if wanted.

Mr Batley to answer Mr Hughes' Letter.

Read an Answer from Mr Roberts complying with our request to advance Money to the Housekeeper as it may be wanted.

Read a Letter from Mr Olding offering Dr Addington House. [16]Messrs Hodson and Batley to see it.

Mr Hodson reported the House he and Mr Towers had seen at Woodford Mills[17] was too small.

Revd Mr Charles acquainted us Revd Mr Griffin had engaged on a Curacy but offered to take 2 or 3 Students for education.[18]

[41]
Castle and Falcon Aldersgate Street
September 5 1791

Present Mr Oldham in the Chair
Mr Weatherill, Revd Mr Charles, Mr Towers, Revd Mr Platt, Mr Bridgeman, Mr Butcher, Mr Wilkinson, Mr Tilney, Mr Robert Butcher, Mr Flower, Mr Emerson, Mr Burnell, Mr Cooper, Mr Walsh, Mr Newcombe, Mr Astle, Mr Dupont, Mr Ponton, Mr Burnett, Mr Andrew

The Minutes of the last General Meeting read and confirmed.

Mr Bridgman gave in the names of the Clerkenwell District Subscriptions amount £18. 1. 6.

Resolved that the House intended for the [42] College be within any distance of London not exceeding 50 miles.

Resolved that the Plan and Articles be read at the next General Meeting.

That the names of Persons eligible for an Assistant Committee be given in to the Trustee to be appointed at the next Meeting.

The Revd Mr Charles concluded with Prayer.

Adjourned to Wednesday 5 October 1791.

[43]

Quarterly General Meeting
Castle and Falcon Aldersgate Street
October 5. 1791

Present Mr Oldham in the Chair
Messrs Hodson, Langston, Cooper, Towers, R. Butcher, Bridgman, Hayter, Shadd, Astle, Burnell, Chambers, Thomas Hodson, Emerson, Revd Mr Platt, Francis, Bond, Revd Mr Kirkman, Elliott, Butcher Senior, Omer, Tilney, Weatherill, Wilkinson, W. Knight, Walsh, Dupont, Pontin, H. Batley.

Read and confirmed the Minutes of Last Meeting.

Read the Rules and Articles.

Proposed the following 14 persons as an assistant Committee to meet with and assist the Trustees [44] in conducting the business of the College in all matters which are not by the original Plan and Articles vested solely in the Trustees viz.

Mr Towers	Mr Cooper
Mr Butterworth	Mr Compigne
Mr Butcher Senior	Mr Simpson
Mr Bridgman	Mr Emerson
Mr Rowton	Mr Hicks
Mr Burnell	Mr Thomas Wontner
Mr Shadd	Mr Duthoit

The following Houses seen by the Trustees reported to the Meeting.

Dr Addington's at Mile-end,
a House at Woodford Mills,

Manor House at Cheshunt,
Mrs Shawe's House at Cheshunt.

The latter the best approved and recommended by them to the Society.

The Chairman reported the Amount of the Annual Subscriptions to be £252-5-0 and Stock in the 3 per Cents £785.

Adjourned.

[46]

Committee 14 September 1791
Trustees

Present Messrs Towers, Astle, Hodson, Weatherill, Batley.

Messrs Hodson, Towers and Batley reported they had seen Dr Addingtons House at Mile-end, the rent £30 per Annum Lease 23 Years Premium £200. [19]

Messrs Hodson and Batley had this day been to Cheshunt. Saw the Manor House, also the Vicarage House and a House belonging to Mrs Shawe which if rent suits appears to them the most eligible of any they had met with.

Mr Towers reported that he had seen a House at Kentish Town.[20]

[47]

Committee Trustees 21 September 1791

Present Messrs Weatherill, Hodson, Astle, Langston, Towers, Batley.

Read and Considered the Original Plan and Articles.

Resolved that as the Countess of Huntingdon died without building or endowing a College it devolves upon the Trustees to provide a suitable place as soon as possible.

Resolved 2dly that the Doctrinal Articles and Articles of Admission shall remain unalterable as the Basis of this Institution.

Resolved 3dly That the present Trustees will to the best of their Power conduct the College agreeably to the said Articles.
[48]
And whereas it hath been proposed to have a Committee to assist the Trustees in the Management of the external Concerns relative to the College it is resolved that the said Committee of Assistants shall consist of fourteen chosen from amongst the Subscribers at Large and to be approved of by the Trustees.

Meeting Trustees September 28 1791

Present Messrs Astle, Hodson, Weatherill, Towers, Oldham, (Emerson)[21], Batley.

Read the Minutes of last Meeting.

Mr Oldham acquainted us Mrs Shaw had agreed to let her House at Cheshunt to the Society at £50 per Year, but Mr Oldham was endeavouring to obtain it for less.
[49]
Mr Hodson said that Mr Dupont was disposed to part with his House at Endfield and offered it to the Trustees for the use of the Society at a Yearly rent.

Committee 12 October 1791

Mr Astle in the Chair.
Present: Messrs Weatherill, Towers, Astle, Cooper, Butcher, Bridgman, Batley, Hodson, Rowton, Oldham.

The Meeting began with prayer.

The Minutes of the Meeting 28 September read and confirmed.

Read a Letter from Mr Thomas Callaway of Guys Hospital offering a House at Endfield formerly Queen Elizabeth's to the Society - referred to a future consideration.
[50]
Mr Astle to see Mr Oldham to press him to finish the business of the House (Mrs Shawe's) and if not to be procured for less to close it on her own terms of £50 per Annum.

Mr Oldham coming into the room was acquainted with the above, he acquainted the Committee he had been on the business this day and expected shortly to finish it.

Committee 19 October 1791

Present Mr Hodson in the Chair.
Mr Hodson, Mr Towers, Mr Cooper, Mr Bridgman, Mr Butcher, H. Batley, Mr Langston, Mr Duthoit, Mr Rowton, Mr Weatherill, Mr Astle, Revd Dr Ford, Mr Oldham

The Chairman engaged in Prayer.

[51]

The Minutes of the last Meeting were read and Confirmed.

The Chairman acquainted the Committee from Mr Oldham the negociations respecting the House at Cheshunt was pending and expected to be more favorable.

H. Batley having seen Mr Hughes informed the Committee he expected £30 per Annum for the present College from Michaelmas last and wished to know how long it might be continued - it was resolved that six Months notice to quit from Christmas next be now given to Mr Hughes as under.

Mr Hughes
Sir, We hereby give you Notice that we shall quit the House and Premisses of the Late Countess Dowager of Huntingdon belonging to you at or near Trevecka in [52] South Wales at Midsummer next.
Signed by order of the Trustees appointed by the said Countess for carrying on the said College
Henry Batley, Secretary
London 19 October 1791

Letter sent with the above

Mr Hughes
Sir, At a Meeting of the Trustees and Committee for carrying on the late Countess of Huntingdons College held this Evening it was judged a matter of Propriety to give you legal notice of the time when we intend to quit your house, which I inclose you accordingly. At the same time I am directed to inform you that if it will be an acceptable accommodation to you we will quit it at Lady day instead of Midsummer and in case you wish it we shall be glad of timely Notice.

I am Sir
Your most humble Servant
William Hodson
Chairman of the Committee

London
19 October 1791

[53]

Dr Ford brought two donations of £20 each from Lady Caroline Harvey and Lady Amelia Harvey from Brighthelmstone.

Received from Mrs Powell the Housekeeper the following Bills

Her own Bill	£10	9	2
Mr Evan Roberts	16	3	11
Mr John Morgan	4	5	8
Mr William Davis	6	10	7
Mr Henry Howell	7	0	5
	44	9	9

Committee 26 October 1791

Present Mr Weatherill in the Chair.
Mr Langston, Mr Weatherill, Mr Butcher, Mr Towers, H. Batley, Mr Bridgman, Mr Emerson, Mr Hodson, Mr Rowton, Mr Oldham
[54]
The Chairman engaged in Prayer

The Minutes of the last Meeting read and Confirmed.

Read a Letter from Mr [and Mrs] [22] Hughes dated Pentonville Oct. 21. 1791 to H. Batley saying the longest term they could grant the College in Breconshire is to next Lady day and expect to be paid £15 for the half year.

Committee 2 November 1791

Present Mr Weatherill, Mr Rowton, Mr Butcher, Mr Duthoit.
No Business done.

Committee 9 November 1791

Present Mr Langston in the Chair.
Mr Weatherill, Mr Bridgman, Mr Hodson, Mr Butcher, Mr Duthoit, Mr Towers, [55]Mr Astle, H. Batley, Mr Rowton.

The Chairman engaged in Prayer.

The Minutes of the Meeting 26 October read and confirmed.

Read a Letter from Mr J. Jones Talgarth College October 29. Mr Hodson to answer it.

Read an extract of a Letter to Lady Anne Erskine from Mr Beasley dated College

November 2 1791 Recommending Mr Thomas Watkins to the College, also a Note from Lady Anne, desiring to know the Answer to be returned.

Lady Anne to be requested to write for Mr Watkins experience.

Read a Letter from Mr Cornelius Vanhorn, offering himself for the Ministry. H. Batley to desire his attendance next Wednesday.

[56]

Committee 16 November 1791

Present Mr Astle in the Chair
Mr Langston, Mr Towers, Mr Hodson, Mr Weatherill, Mr Butcher, Mr Cooper, H. Batley, Mr Rowton, Mr Duthoit, Mr Bridgman.

The Chairman began with Prayer.

The last Minutes read and Confirmed.

Mr Cornelius Vanhorn attended, desired to meet the Society on Monday evening to exercise his Gifts.

Mr Hodson reported for the Trustees that the whole of them (Mr Lloyd excepted) saw the House at Cheshunt on Friday last and unanimously approved of it - desired Mr Oldham to complete the Purchase.

[57]

Committee 23 November 1791

Present Mr Weatherill in the Chair.
Mr Astle, Mr Butcher, Mr Duthoit, Mr Bridgman, H. Batley, Mr Langston, Mr Oldham, Mr Rowton, Mr Simpson, Dr Ford.

The Chairman began with Prayer.

The Minutes of the last Meeting read and Confirmed.

The Oldham acquainted the Committee he had compleated the Purchase of the House at Cheshunt of Mrs Shawe for the sum of £950 beside the Gift of several fixtures for which they desire to return Mr Oldham their best thanks for his Great Pains and trouble in the business.

[58]

Committee 30 November 1791

Present Mr Oldham in the Chair
Mr Weatherill, Mr Hodson, Mr Bridgman, H. Batley, Mr Butcher, Mr Shadd, Mr Langston, Mr Duthoit.

The Chairman began with Prayer.

The Minutes of the last Meeting read and Confirmed.

Read a Letter from Mr Thomas Watkins, Brecon, November 20. 1791.

Read a Recomendatory Paper of the above Mr Thomas Watkins by Mr Beasley, Student, and signed by Messrs Walter Watkins, Charles Wild, Thomas Jones, Philip Phillips, Watkin Price Senior and Junior, Thomas Philips, Evan Edwards, many of them Ministers.

An Answer to be returned by Mr Hodson, referring him to the Revd Dr Ford and Mr Watkins at Hereford for examination - also to write to Mrs Powell, Housekeeper.
[59]
Resolved that an advertisement be drawn up by Mr Oldham and inserted in the Cambridge and Oxford and other papers he may think proper for a Clergyman of the Church of England as Tutor to the College.

Committee 7 December 1791

Present Mr Hodson in the Chair.
Messrs Weatherill, Butcher, Astle, Langston, Cooper, Hodson, Compigne, Oldham, Duthoit.

Mr Hodson brought and read a form of a Notice for the next Quarterly Meeting which was agreed to and ordered to be printed.
[60]
Resolved, That Mr Witham the Master of Spa Fields Chapel School be paid One Guinea for his Trouble in attending the Committee of the College and delivering their Circular Letters.

And that the Boys employed in the same business be rewarded with one shilling or sixpence according to the discretion of Mr Hodson.

Mr Oldham reported that he had since our last meeting had an interview with Dr Illingworth relative to the Tutorship and that the Doctor had promised him, that if at Lady Day we should not be provided with a proper Tutor, he will kindly undertake the Office till we are suited with one.

Mr Oldham brought a form of an advertisement which was agreed to and ordered to be inserted in the Whitehall Evening and one other evening paper, also in the Oxford, Cambridge, York and Leeds papers.

[61]

Committee December 14 1791

Present: Mr Langston in the Chair.
Mr Weatherill, John Astle, Mr Duthoit, Mr Best, Mr Cooper, Mr Butcher, H. Batley, Mr Compigni, Mr Oldham, Mr Rowton.

The Chairman engaged in Prayer.

Read a Letter from Revd F. Bowen and Mr Jones the Tutor recommending Mr James Parrott to the College, but he being a Baptist it could not be allowed to.

The Minutes of the 30th November read and Confirmed.

Resolved that an extract from the Plan necessary for the Use of persons applying to be received as Students [62] be made by Messrs Oldham, Hodson and Batley in order to its being printed and produced at the next meeting.

Mr Best be desired to write to Mr Morgan, Glassbury, to know on what terms the furniture (such of it as may be worth the removal) may be removed to Cheshunt.

Committee 21 December 1791

Present: Mr Weatherill in the Chair.
Mr Astle, Mr Langston, Mr Best, Mr Hodson, Mr Shadd, Mr Compigni, Mr Butcher, H. Batley, Mr Simpson, Mr Rowton.

Read and Confirmed the Minutes of Wednesday the 7th December 1791.
[63]
Read and Confirmed the Minutes of the last Meeting.

Mr Best brought the Extract referred to Messrs Oldham, Hodson and Batley which was read and the further consideration postponed to the next Meeting.

Mr Beasley attended, having a desire to return to the College to finish his studies, applied to be admitted, and was consented to by us on condition of his submitting to the intended examination by a Minister in the Connexion.

The business of the Society requiring a Secretary the same was proposed to Mr Best, her Ladyship's late Secretary, who on being asked, agreed to accept thereof.

Resolved Mr Best be allowed for the present Two pounds per Annum.

[64]

Committee 28 December 1791 [23]

Present Mr Astle in the chair.

Mr Weatherill, Mr Langston, Mr Duthoit, Mr Batley, Mr Hodson, Mr Cooper, Mr Bridgeman, Mr Shadd, Mr Oldham, Mr Butcher, Mr Rowton, Mr Simpson.

The minutes of the last meeting read and confirmed.

A Letter from the Revd Mr Young read Recommending his mother as housekeeper. No immediate answer can be given.

That Mr Batley be requested to write to the Revd Mr Haweis and Dr Ford to request them to head a subscription by way of donation towards discharging such part of the purchase money as may be wanted.

A Letter from the Revd Mr Gunn of Farnham to Mr Oldham read, declining the Tutorship, from his engagement to preach the Gospel.

[65]

Letters from the Revd Mr Kennedy No.19 Hanover Square; the Revd Mr Barton, Hampstead; Revd Mr Tyson, Thornhill near Wakefield; and Revd Mr Matthews, Cirencester, read. They are in answer to the advertisement for a Tutor; offering themselves as Tutors. Answers to be sent to them, that the religious character to be referred to, were such as the Revd Mr Romaine, etc.

Mr Batley requested to deliver the Plan of the College to Mr Cardale.

Letter from the Revd Mr Phillips (late Tutor of the College) to Mr Oldham read.

The rules and articles to be subscribed and observed by the young men who shall be admitted into the College to be printed. Mr Walsh to print 100.

[66]

Quarterly General Meeting
Castle and Falcon Aldersgate
4 January 1792

Present: Mr Burnhill, Revd Mr Platt, Messrs Francis, Astle, Langston, Hodson, Duthoit, Cooper, Batley, Revd Mr Irish, Messrs Weatherhall, Wontner, Tutt, Butcher, Rowton, Shadd, Robert Butcher, Tilney, Pullen, Bridgeman, Griffin, Revd Mr Meyers, Messrs Compigni, Emerson, Sergeant, Munn, Dupont, Oldham, Holmes and Walsh.

Mr Hodson in the chair.

Mr Platt opened the Meeting with prayers. The Minutes of the late General Meeting read.

The chairman informed the Meeting of the steps which the Trustees had taken to procure a suitable house and of their success in having absolutely purchased Mrs Shawes at Cheshunt; and that the Conveyance to the Trustees was [67] preparing by the advice of Counsel.

Also informed the Gentlemen that many applications had been made for a Tutor, that none had been yet obtained, but a Gentleman had offered himself to officiate, if one could not be provided before Lady day when the College is to be removed, and to act till a suitable person can be had.

The state of the Societies Fund to the 31st December 1791 (exclusive of 850 £3 per Cent Consols) reported by the Chairman as follows

Balance of cash in hand	24 2 3
Donations and subscription received in 1791	360 0 0
Dividends of stock	16 5 6
Total received in 1791	£376 5 6

Revd Mr Platt and Mr Welsh appointed auditors of the last years account who are to report their examination accordingly at the quarterly meeting next after it.

It was proposed that a Book for the [68] reception of free donations towards paying the purchase money for the House be opened. The title of one read, and several Gentlemen present gave in their names and donations.[24]

Revd Mr Meyers concluded with prayer.

Adjourned.

Committee, 11 January 1792

Present: Messrs Oldham, Weatherall, Astle, Batley, Langston, Duthoit, Hodson, Cooper, Bridgeman and Butcher.

Mr Oldham in the chair.

The last Minutes of the Committee read and confirmed.

Mr Batley reported that he had received an answer from the Revd Mr Haweis saying that he would give £11 towards paying the purchase money for the House.

[69]

Letter from Mr Thomas Davies at Redwich[25] offering himself as a Student - answered cannot at present be received.

Mr Mumford, Surveyor General, Gravel Street, Holborn, having made a Draft or ground plan of the premises at Cheshunt, and presented it to the Society as a gift, the Secretary was desired to send him a Letter of thanks for the same; and to inform him that it will be accepted as a donation.

Letters read from the Revd Mr Richard Evans of Hitchin, Herts. - Revd Mr Thomas Scott of Wrentham near Beccles - Revd Mr Edward Creswell of Lynby near Nottingham - Mr John Dawson Wrigglesworth, Catharine Hall, Cambridge - and the Revd Mr Lyne, Latton, near Cricklade, Wilts. offering themselves as Tutors - The same answer to be given as to the others.

Also a Letter from Mr Glazebrook read on the same subject. Mr Hodson requested to answer it.

Agreed that the house, Land and garden [70] at Cheshunt go together and the Tutor to have them for himself and the Students tax free worth £100 per Annum salary for himself and £20 per Annum for each Student. The Tutor to pay the Servants.

The people of Monmouth requesting the continuance of Mr Sutherland, it is agreed that Mr Bradley be permitted to go to College in his stead.

It is agreed that Messrs Dupont and King be allowed for the use of their room at the Castle and Falcon for the time past to Christmas 5 Guineas and in future 3 Guineas per Annum.

Adjourned.

Committee 18 January 1792

Present: Messrs Weatherall, Hodson, Batley*[26], Langston, Duthoit, Astle, Butcher, Wontner, Rowton, Sampson and Dupont.

[71]

The last Minutes read and confirmed.

Another Letter from Mr Wigglesworth received - the consideration of it to stand over till the next meeting.

Mr Batley reported the substance of a Letter received from Mr Morgan of Glassbury respecting the College furniture - Answer, that his proposal of 10s. per hundred for the Carriage is accepted, and desire him to direct the Books to be packed.

Letter from Mr Roberts to Mr Hodson read - Answered by Lady Huntingdon's Executors.

Read an additional Clause, proposed by Mr Batley to be incerted in the deed of Conveyance to the Trustees, how the house and Land shall be disposed of, in case it should be put out of the power of the Trustees to continue the College on the original plan, from default of subscriptions, legacies or donations, from popular commotions, insurrections or persecutions. Agreed that the [72] same be paid into the hands of Mr Casdale, to be incerted in the deed of Conveyance.

Committee 25 January 1792

Present: Messrs Langston*, Weatherall, Astle, S. Parke, Butcher, Cooper, Batley, Compigni, Hodson.

The last Minutes were read and confirmed.

The bills for the last Quarter to Christmas, amounting to £34 12s. 5d. sent up by Mrs Powell, the College housekeeper, to Mr Batley were laid before the Meeting - Mr Hodson requested to write to Mr Roberts to discharge them.

The Secretary to answer Mr Wrigglesworth that the Trustees wish a person of longer standing, etc.

Unanimously resolved that Mr Hodson be desired on any appearance of the Stocks being lower to sell the Societies 3 per Cents.

[73]

Committee 1st February 1792

Present: Messrs Astle, Langston, Weatherill, Hodson*, Butcher, Cooper, Batley, Duthoit, Rowton.

The last minutes read and confirmed.

Read a Letter from the Revd Mr Glasebrook to Mr Hodson declining the Tutorship; but recommending the Revd Mr Day or the Revd Mr Powley, Dewsbury near Wakefield, to whom Mr Hodson has written.

Read a letter from Mr Morgan of Glassbury respecting the goods at Trevecka. Answered by the Trustees present, Directing a sale by auction the first week in March, of such goods as are not worth to Carriage, or would be more for the Interest of the Trustees to be sold there than removed; and desiring that immediately after the sale, the remaining goods be packed and sent up.

[74]

Read a Letter from Mr Jones the Tutor respecting the inability of the Students to pay their expenses to Town. Resolved that each of them be allowed two Guineas from the old to the new College.

Resolved that the thanks of this Meeting be given to Mrs Cooper for her very kind and liberal donation to the Society towards the purchase money of the premises at Cheshunt.

Committee 8 February

Present

Messrs Weatherill*, Langston, Astle, Butcher, Bridgeman, Oldham, Hodson, Duthoit, Rowton.

Last minutes read and confirmed.

Read the deed of Bargain and sale of the Messuage and premises at Cheshunt from the [75] Revd Dr Herbert Mayo and Mrs Ann Shaw to Mr Sheen In trust for Mr Oldham.[27]

Read a Letter of thanks from Mr Lloyd of Swansea for the transmission of an Account of what has been done.

Proposed to write to the Revd Mr Robinson of Leicester and the Revd Mr Millner of Hull for the Recommendation of a Tutor in case Mr Day declines accepting the place.

That Mr Oldham be requested to [write] a Letter to Dr Hillingsworth and bring it with him next Wednesday Evening for the Trustees signature.

Committee 15 February 1792

Present

Messrs Cooper, Weatherill, Astle, Butcher, Cowper, Langston, Oldham*, Hodson, Batley, Duthoit.

Last minutes read and confirmed.

Mr Oldham brought a Letter to Dr Illingsworth, which was signed by the [76] Trustees present, and desired to be delivered by the Secretary.

Mr Oldham reported that application has been made to Mr Page to forward the business of the purchase; who had agreed that it should be completed, and possession given the first week in March.

31

Read a Letter from Mr Day, politely declining the Tutorship; and another from Mr Glazebrook to the same effect; also one from the Revd Mr Love to Lady Anne Erskine declining the offer of it.

Also one from Mr Jones the present Tutor, respecting the College Furniture.

The Secretary to write to Mr Robinson of Leicester, Mr Rose, Mr Cadogan, Mr Milner and any other Minister likely to recommend a Tutor.

Committee 22d February 1792

Present Messrs Weatherill, Langston*, Astle, Batley, Cooper, Butcher, Compigni, Hodson, Oldham.

[77]

The last Minutes read and confirmed.

Read a Letter from Mr Gardener of Temple Back, Bristol to Mr Batley, proposing a person as a Student, and offering his assistance to promote the institution.

Secretary reported that he had written to the Revd Mr Robinson, Leicester; Revd Mr Rose, ;[28] Honble and Revd Mr Cadogan, Reading; Revd Mr Milner, Hull; Revd Mr Charles, Bala; Revd Mr Griffiths, Llwyngwair; and Revd Mr [N] Rowland at Bristol to recommend a Tutor; and to Mr De-Courcy, Ditto.

Mr Shaws sale advertised for Saturday the 25 inst. at 11 at Cheshunt - agreed to send a person to buy in some of the things.

Resolved that £650 stock be sold out on Thursday next.

[78]

Committee 29 February 1792

Present

Messrs Langston, Hodson*, Weatherill, Butcher, Astle, Duthoit, Batley, Rowton, Oldham.

The last Minutes read and confirmed.

Read a Letter from Mr Jones, Tutor, respecting the Students and himself. Letter wrote to Mr Roberts to pay them 2 Guineas each and 12 Guineas to Mr Jones.

Read a Letter from Mr Burge at Bristol, begging to be admitted as a Student.

Mr Hodson reported that Mr Holmes, recommended by Mr Cooper, went down to Cheshunt on Saturday and bought most of the things desired, very much to the Committees satisfaction.

Also reported, that the £650 was sold this day at 95 and a ¼.

Also reported that Messrs Oldham, Langston and Hodson, had an interview with Dr Illingworth, who agrees to accept the office of Tutor; but cannot promise to continue on account of his advanced age, his precarious state of health, and his expectation of a living. As he declines to keep house Resolved that a suitable housekeeper be provided.

[79]

Read a Letter from Mr Cardale, agreed that the Secretary go to Cheshunt and examine whether the fixtures are left, and also the things bought in; and to ask the person who has the care of the House, whether she will continue till quarter day.

Committee 2d March 1792

Present
Messrs Batley, Dupont, Weatherill, Mr Astle, Duthoit, Butterworth.

The Secretary reported that he went to Cheshunt the 1st inst. and found all the things in the house, except a few which he had marked in the schedule and Catalogue; but there appeared to him (as per account thereof) several other articles left, not mentioned in the schedule of the fixtures, and [of] more value than the articles sold. Also reported that the woman in the house was willing to take charge of it till Lady day.

Resolved that Mrs Powell be wrote to, to come up, as housekeeper; and that the Secretary go to Cheshunt the 3d inst. to take possession of the house, land and fixtures etc.

[80]

Committee 7th March 1792

Present
Messrs Weatherill*, Langston, Astle, Butcher, Cooper, Oldham.

The Minutes of the 29 February and 2d March read and confirmed.

Mr Langston reported, that himself, Mr Hodson and Mr Oldham waited on Mr Thornton[29], had an hours conversation with him on the business of the Society; and he promised to take it into his consideration, and call on Mr Hodson.

The Secretary reported that he went to Cheshunt the 3d inst., and took posession of the House and premises; and drew the following Memorandum of it vizt.

Memorandum 3d March 1792 That Mary Greathead, and Edmund Blanks the persons in possession of the House and premises late of Mrs Ann Shaw at the Church Gate in Cheshunt and sold by her to James Oldham Oldham Esqr. did this day viz: the 3d March 1792 by the direction of Mrs Shaw in writing to them for that purpose [81] given, give up the possession of the same house and premises, with the fixtures and other articles, to the said James Oldham Oldham by giving up the Keys to George Best deputed by Mr Oldham to receive possession of the same on behalf of the Society for supporting and perpetuating the Countess of Huntingdons College removed from Talgarth in South Wales to Cheshunt.

Witness   William Bull
            John Ruskin Senior
            Robert Ruskin Junior

The Secretary also reported that he waited on the Earl of Dartmouth[30], who desired a few days to consider whether he should give any thing towards the purchase or not.

Read Mr Robinsons Letter with Mr Hodsons answer respecting Mr Rogers recommended by Mr Robinson as Tutor.

Read a Letter from Mr Milner of Hull mentioning that he could not recommend a Tutor.

[82]

Committee 14 March 1792

Present

Messrs Butcher, Duthoit, Compigni, Oldham, Weatherill, Astle, Langston, Dupont, Batley and the Revd Mr Rogers.

Read a Letter from Mr Morgan respecting the sale.

Ditto from Mrs Powell, who agreed to come up.

Adjourned.

Committee 21 March

Present

Messrs Astle, Hodson, Langston, Towers, Butcher, Oldham, Cooper, Rowton, Batley, Weatherill.

The Minutes of the 7 and 14 March read and confirmed.

Secretary reported That the Earl of Dartmouth declined doing any thing.

Read a Letter from the Revd Mr Griffiths.

The Trustees reported that last Wednesday Evening they met Mr Rogers at the Chapel House in [83] Lady Anne Erskines apartments, and that he seems very willing to accept the office of Tutor. That on Thursday he went to Cheshunt to see the place and very much approved of it. They met him again at the same place on Friday. But objecting to open the College by preaching in it to the neighbours, if he could not get into the Church; and wishing the Students not to preach during their stay at College except before the Tutor; the Trustees desired him to lay the matter before the Lord; and return them an answer.

Letter from the Revd Mr Haweis read, mentioning that he had received a donation of £10 and observing that as soon as he sees the College really going forward, he hopes from knowledge to speak of it in such a manner as may procure further assistance. That the thanks of this meeting be sent to him for his Letter.

Read an Estimate by Mr Richard Hilton of the work necessary to be done in the House at Cheshunt amounting to £ .[31] That the thanks of this Meeting be returned to him for his disinterested conduct in making the survey and estimate.
[84]
Read a Letter from Mr Rogers to Lady Anne Erskine accepting the office of Tutor. On the conditions stipulated by the Trustees. Mentioning, that if he should not be able to meet with a Church within the time mentioned (vizt a twelvemonth) he shall not hesitate a moment to open the College to the inhabitants of Cheshunt. And even if he should succeed in the Curacy, he observes, that he should still wish to pursue this plan, that the students might occasionally speak to a mixed Company in his presence. Mr Hodson requested to write to Dr Illingworth on the above occasion.

The four Students in Town, vizt. Bickerdike, William Jones, Bradley and Kemp to preach on next Monday Evening at 6 to the Trustees, Committee, etc. Mr Jones and Mr Platt to be informed of it, and their attendance requested that Evening; and Wednesday Evening to examine them.

[85]

Committee 2[8]³² March 1792

Present

Messrs Butcher, Bridgeman, Dupont, Batley, Oldham, Jones, Platt, Weatherill, Astle, Langston, Compigni, Hodson, Cooper, Duthoit.

The last Minutes read and confirmed.

Read Mr Rogers Letters to Lady Anne Erskine and Mr Hodson, declining the Tutorship, from his affairs at his present place of abode, having taken so singular and sudden a turn as to render his removal to Cheshunt impracticable.

> Mr Bradley examined.
> Mr Bickerdike Ditto.
> Mr Kemp Ditto.
> Mr W. Jones Ditto.

Read a Letter from Mr Morgans shopman, informing the Trustees that the goods would arrive at Cheshunt the 31 inst.

[86]

Quarterly General Meeting at the Castle and Falcon, Wednesday 4 April 1792³³

Present Mr Oldham in the Chair.

Messrs Weatherill, Langston, Dupont, Batley, Hodson, Astle, Revd Mr Platt, Messrs Bell, Burnell, Holmes, Shadd, Tilney, Bridgman, Flower, Cooper, Duthoit, Hodson, Revd Mr Crole, Revd Mr Simpson, Revd Mr Kirkman, Revd S. Underwood, Messrs Francis, Butcher, Hayter, Walsh, Tutt, Emerson.

Revd Mr Simpson began with Prayer.

Read the Minutes of the last Meeting.

The Chairman acquainted the Gentlemen that the Estate at Cheshunt is paid for by the Sale of £650 3 per Cents and £344-11-6 [87] received in Donations and that possession was given the 3d of March to Mr Best the Secretary. That we have quitted the College in Wales, and that the Library, and such part of the furniture as was not sold are arrived at Cheshunt. That some Repairs are judged immediately necessary, and some Windows to be stopped,³⁴ which will take up three or four Weeks; and that Mr Weatherill is kind enough to go down and superintend the same.

Read the Auditors Report of the State of the Society's Fund at the end of the Year 1791 as follows, viz.

Cash in hand 31 December 1790	2	8	11
Received in 1791	360	10	6
Dividends on 3 per Cents	16	5	6
	379	4	11
Paid for £350 3 per Cent Consols	302	14	1
Sundry Expenses	104	7	1
Deduct	379	4	11
Due to Treasurer	27	16	3

Against which there was £850 3 per Cent Consols.[35]

[88]

The Chairman further acquainted the Meeting that notwithstanding all our enquiries, writing to Ministers and advertising we are yet without a Tutor. The Revd Mr Rogers of Ravenstone in Leicestershire had been at Cheshunt, had three conferences with the Trustees, and had consented to accept the Office, but afterwards wrote them a Refusal.

Mr Batley (the Secretary being at Cheshunt) read several Letters which had been received on the subject of the Tutorship from the Revd Messrs Milner, Robinson, Glazebrook, Day, Griffiths, Love and Rogers.

Mr Platt recommended it to the Trustees to write to the Revd Mr Richardson of York. Mr Coulthurst of Halifax was also mentioned as likely to know some suitable Person.

Mr Kirkman concluded with Prayer.

[89]

Committee 11 April 1792[36]

Present

Messrs Towers, Hodson*, Butcher, Bridgeman, Oldham, Batley, Duthoit, Astle, Rowton, Cooper.

The Minutes of the 28 ult. confirmed.

Mr Hodson reported that he had paid Mrs Greetwood for a months care of the House etc. at Cheshunt.

Also reported that he had written to the Revd Mr Nicholson, recommended by the Revd Mr De Courcy as Tutor.

The Secretary desired to write to the Revd Mr Simeon, Cambridge;[37] the Revd Mr Richardson, York; the Revd Mr Coulthurst, Halifax; and the Revd Mr Pentycross of Wallingford, to recommend a Tutor.

[90]

Committee 18 April 1792

Present
Messrs Cooper, Hodson, Butcher, Towers, Batley, Bridgeman, Astle*, Platt, Oldham, Rowton, Dupont.

The last Minutes read and confirmed.

The Secretary reported that he had written to the Revd Mr Simeon, Richardson, Coulthurst and Pentycross.

Revd Mr Simeons answer - Has it not in his power to recommend a Tutor.

Read a Letter from Mr Charles to the same effect.

A Letter to be wrote to Mrs Powell to get the Linen mended, etc.

Committee 25 April 1792

Present
Messrs Oldham*, Batley, Astle, Hodson, Butcher, Towers, Rowton, Duthoit.

Read and confirmed the Minutes of the last Meeting.

Read a Letter from the Revd Mr Rogers [91] in answer to one wrote to Mr Robinson by Mr Hodson, desiring an explanation of his reasons for withdrawing his consent after he had given it to accept the office of Tutor. His principal reason he says was, that the Trustees did not give security for the permanency of the Salary, house etc.

Read again a part of Mr De Courcy's Letter wherein he recommends the Revd Mr Nicholson. Read also a letter received from Mr Nicholson[38] informing us that he found himself inclined to accept our call and that he would be in Town on Friday Evening.

Committee 2d May 1792

Present

Messrs Batley, Butcher, Bridgeman, Astle, Towers, Compigni, Hodson*, Cooper, Rowton, Oldham.

The last Minutes read and confirmed.

Mr Nicholsons Letter read again.

Mr Hodson reported that Mr Nicholson had been with the Trustees, who very much approve of him; that they had taken him to Cheshunt, and asked him for his determination before he left Town. But as he had [92] promised his wife not to make an absolute engagement till his return, he said he would send a definitive answer in a week.

Read an extract of a Letter from Mr Jones the late Tutor requesting £10 to be sent to him. The Secretary to write to desire him to send a receipt in full, and that on receiving it he would have the balance of 9-18-0 sent to him.

Committee 9 May 1792

Present

Messrs Hodson, Butcher, Batley, Astle*, Bridgeman, Towers, Rowton.

The last Minutes read and confirmed.

Read a Letter from Mr Oldham informing the Committee that he had received no information from Chester.

Mr Hodson reported that he had paid the Gardener for work done and [93] seed sown in the Garden at Cheshunt.

Read a Letter from Henry Thornton Esqr. to Mr Hodson declining his assistance towards the support of the College, from prior engagement, and other opportunities of the same kind opening to him.

Committee 16 May 1792

Present

Messrs Astle, Batley, Langston*, Hodson, Butcher, Rowton.

The last Minutes read and confirmed.

Read a Letter from the Revd Mr I. Nicholson to Mr Oldham Wherein he observes that the call (to be the Tutor) appears to him to be the voice of God in his providence, and that answers in the affirmative to the three following questions, principally for the satisfaction of Mrs Nicholsons friends, will remove every objection on [94] their part, and at once fix him resolve to come up Vizt. Is it not intended to allow him £100 per annum, with the house, offices, Garden and Meadow clear of rent, repairs or taxes? Is it not the design that his continuance in the said office of Tutor in the College shall be permanent? Is it not proposed that he should be allowed (as he understood Mr Hodsons Letter) £20 per Annum for the Board of each student, exclusive of washing?

Committee
23 May 1792

Present Messrs Cooper, Bridgeman, Butcher, Langston, Batley*, Astle, Compigni, Rowton, Oldham.

The last Minutes read and confirmed.

Read a Letter from Mr Morgan of Glasbury - to be referred to Mr Hodson. [95]
Read a Letter from Mr Thomas Davies school master, who applied before to be admitted as a Student. The Secretary to answer him that he cannot be received.

Mr Oldham reported that he immediately answered Mr Nicholsons Letter in the affirmative, except as to the washing, which he observed should make no difference between them.

Committee 30 May 1792

Present
Messrs Duthoit, Hodson*, Butcher, Cooper, Rowton, Batley, Astle, Langston, Dupont, Oldham.

The last Minutes read and confirmed.

The Secretary to write to Mr Morgan in answer to his Letter read at the last meeting to pay Mr Hughes £15 and to desire Mr Roberts to send up his bill.

Read a Letter from Mr Nicholson to Mr [96] Oldham Wherein he observes that Mr Oldham's Letter was God's answer to his prayer. Therefore in the fullest confidence that God's will and the Trustees are the same in this instance, he is bound in conscience to obey the call; and that he may be expected at Cheshunt the last week in June or the first in July.

Read a Draft of an address to the public - a copy to be sent to Mr Nicholson with a Copy of the Catalogue of the books.

Mr Oldham requested to write a Letter of thanks to Mr De Courcy for recommending Mr Nicholson.

Committee 6 June 1792

Present

Messrs Weatherill, Hodson, Oldham*, Butcher, Astle, Towers, Langston, Batley, Cooper, Duthoit, Rowton, Emerson.

The last Minutes read and confirmed.

Mr Blanks to be wrote to, to remove the Hay from the Barn.

[97]

Mrs Powell and the maid to have notice to leave the College the latter end of June or the beginning of July.

Agreed that the deed of Trust contain the most material parts and not the whole of the Plan; and that the Trustees appoint a time with Mr Cardale to meet on the business.[39]

Also agreed that the House and premises at Cheshunt be licenced.[40]

Committee 13th June 1792

Present

Messrs Weatherill, Hodson, Butcher, Dupont*, Batley, Astle, Langston, Emerson.

The last Minutes read and confirmed.

Read another Letter from Mr Thomas Davies schoolmaster. The Secretary to write to him, That his Letter was laid before the meeting this Evening; and they desired he might be informed that for the reasons before given, as to their apprehension, from inquiry, of his not being capable of attaining the english language, he cannot be admitted, and that he must have recourse to Books for the knowledge which he requests the Trustees to communicate.

[98]

Committee 20 June 1792

Present

Messrs Weatherill*, Langston, Hodson, Cooper, Batley, Butcher, Astle, Rowton, Duthoit, Oldham.

Read a Letter from Mrs Graham respecting the Revd Mr Wests expences - To be answered, That had the Trustees sent for Mr West, they would have considered themselves bound in honour to pay his expenses; but as his coming was altogether without their knowledge, as Trustees for the public assisting them, they do not think it would be justifiable in them to pay his expences.

Mr Hodson reported That Messrs Langston, Batley, Emerson, Weatherill and himself went to the College on Saturday last in order to see the state of the place, and what would be necessary to be provided previous to Mr Nicholson's arrival. When [99] it appeared to them, that for the present the large parlour may be made use of as a Chapel, if accommodated with benches, and a desk for the Minister. Also found that some bedsteads, chairs, tables, looking glasses, sundry kitchen furniture, and other necessaries, will be immediately wanted - the procuring of which was referred to different Gentlemen at this meeting.

Mr Hodson brought a notice of the next general meeting, and of the opening of the College, which was read and approved of.

Mr Batley moved, and it was agreed that Mrs Powell be permitted to stay a week at the College, after the arrival of Mr Nicholson.

Committee 27th June 1792
Present
Messrs Weatherill, Bridgeman, Butcher, [100]Astle*, Batley, Hodson, Rowton.

The last Minutes read and confirmed.

Read a Letter from Mr Evan Roberts inclosing his bill to Lady day last, and for binding and repairing some of the Books, amounting to £29 16s. 10d. The Secretary to write to Mr Morgan to pay the above, and Mr Hughes £15 for rent.

Read a Letter from Mr Nicholson which mentions that he cannot be at Cheshunt before the 2d week in July.

Quarterly general Meeting
At the Castle and Falcon
Wednesday 4 July 1792
Present
Messrs Langston, Oldham, Towers, Weatherill, Fife, Walsh, Hodson, Astle, Rowton, Pontin, Butcher Junior, Chambers, Batley, Tilney, Holmes, Emerson, Dupont, Bell, Burnell, Serjeant, Silver, Bridgeman, Butcher senior, [101]Goldsmith, Compigne, John Cooper, Flint, King, French, Tutt, Jones, Andrew, Wontner.

Mr Oldham in the chair opened the meeting with prayer.

Read the Minutes of the last general Meeting.

Mr Oldham mentioned the reasons which Mr Rogers gave for declining the Tutorship, and how unwilling the Trustees were to be disappointed of him. Read his Letter on the occasion. The chairman informed the meeting that many applications had been made to several Gospel Ministers in the establishment, to recommend a master. That the Revd Mr De Courcy had recommended the Revd Mr Nicholson of Coddington near Chester.

[102]

Read the correspondence in consequence of the above recommendation.

The chairman stated that Mr Nicholson came to Town, went to the College, approved of the place and was satisfied with what was proposed; and left Town with a determination to accept the office, if his wife agreed to come up. That on his return home a Letter came from him agreeing to accept the Tutorship if certain questions which he asked were answered in the affirmative. This having been done, he proposed coming up to Town the latter end of June, or the first week in this month, but some unforeseen circumstances having prevented his coming up as proposed, he defers it till the 2d week in this month.

[103]

That he appears in every respect qualified for the office - a gracious and judicious man.

That the College will be opened for the reception of the Students, as soon as Mr Nicholson is a little settled in the House and ready to receive them.

That a considerable part of the furniture in Wales was sold, and sundry articles brought here.

That it is in contemplation to make a chapel of the Coach house and Stable; if the number of people attending to hear should make it necessary. But for the present, the great parlour is intended to be fitted up for that purpose.

That the Book of Donations (which some Gentlemen perhaps have not heard of) continues open. The donations received amount to 431-18-6.

[104]

That the 24th of August being the birth day of the late Countess of Huntingdon; and the day on which the old College was opened; and also Bartholomew day, on which upwards of 2,000 ministers in the reign of Charles the 2d were ejected from the church, and many thousands of Protestants massacred in the dominions of france on Bartholomew day, in a former period; it is proposed, the Lord willing, to have a formal opening of the new College on that day. In the mean time a general invitation to the subscribers etc. will be given to attend it.[41]

Messrs Oldham, Hodson, Dupont, Weatherill, Langston, Batley, Astle, Bridgeman, Emerson, Cooper, Wontner, and Serjeant appointed Stewards for the day.

Mr Langston concluded with prayer.

[105]
Committee 11 July 1792

Present

Messrs Astle, Hodson, Weatherill, Cooper, Bridgeman, Langston*, Batley, Towers, Duthoit, Rowton, Dupont, Emerson, Wontner.

The last Minutes of the Committee read and confirmed.

Mr Langston reported that he had applied to the Revd Mr Eyre to preach the sermon at the opening of the College the 24 August which he most readily agreed to.

Mr Weatherill to request Mr Nicholson (if arrived at the College) to come to Town, in order to meet the Committee next Wednesday.

Committee 18 July 1792

Present

Messrs Towers, Batley*, Butcher, Cooper, Rowton, Langston, Astle, Platt, Hodson, Dupont, Oldham, [106]Compigni, Duthoit, Emerson, Serjeant, Weatherill, Nicholson.

The last Minutes read and confirmed.

The chairman reported that the Revd Mr Nicholson was arrived. Resolved that a person or two be employed at the Expence of the Trust to clear the garden and Court yard of the weeds under the direction of Mr Nicholson.

Resolved that for want of room at the College to accomodate the company expected to dine at the opening of it, a Letter be sent to the subscribers to inform them that the Dinner will be prepared at the 4 Swans Waltham Cross.

Mr Nicholson informed the meeting that he should be ready next week to receive the 2 Students who are in Town.
[106]
All having withdrawn except the Trustees, [42]Mr Oldham moved that the Revd Isaac Nicholson late of Coddington near Chester be elected President and Tutor;

which was seconded by Mr Hodson; and the Revd Isaac Nicholson was accordingly elected President and Tutor of the College: having been previously examined by the Reverend Thomas Haweis and approved of by him.

Committee 25 July 1792

Present

Messrs Hodson*, Weatherill, Towers, Langston, Astle, Batley, Rowton, Compigni, Bridgeman, Emerson, Butcher.

The last Minutes read and confirmed.

[108]

One of Mr Nicholson's Family having a putrid sore throat, it is judged prudent to detain the 2 Students in Town a little longer.

Mr Hodson requested that a large handsome book be provided to keep the Accounts of the Society, [43]and that another be provided in order to record the most material occurrences relative to the College;[44] and also other necessary Books for the use of the Society.

Mr Astle moved that they be accordingly provided, which was unanimously agreed to; and Mr Hodson requested to procure them.

Received a Letter from Lady Ann Erskine respecting Mr William Robertson, and Mr Hutchings of Portsmouth, the former requesting to be readmitted as a Student and the latter to be admitted into the College as such.

Read 2 Letters from Mr Robertson and Mr [109] Hutchings to Lady Anne on the occasion.

Agreed that Lady Anne be requested to write to the Revd Mr Dunn of Portsmouth, inquiring Mr Hutchins character etc.

Also agreed that Monday Evening at 7 to be appointed for Mr Robertson to preach in Spa Fields Chapel, before the Trustees and Committee.

Read a Letter from the Revd Mr De Courcy respecting a Mr Rawlins who had been under Mr Nicholsons tuition for the ministry, while at Coddington, and requesting his admission to the College, either as a pupil of Mr Nicholson's or as a Student - Mr Hodson requested to answer Mr De Courcy.

Some of the Furniture at the old College bequeathed by the Countess of Huntingdon, having been sold on account of the distance, Mr Batley moved, that a parlour and bed-chamber be furnished [110] for the use of the President and that a Committee be appointed to procure the furniture, which was seconded by Mr Towers, and unanimously agreed to.

That Messrs Hodson, Astle, and Batley be the Committee.

That a notice in large Letters on a board be placed in some conspicuous part of the College, prohibiting smoking of Tobacco by any of the Students as an idle custom tending to promote indolency in many, by an almost continual use of it when masters of their own time.[45]

Resolved that Mr Hodson be requested to wait on the Revd Mr Crowle to assist at the opening of the College.

Committee 1st August 1792

Present Messrs Dupont*, Hodson, Astle, Oldham, Emerson, Cooper, [111] Haweis, Charles, Bridgeman, Batley, Butcher, Langston.

Read and confirmed the last Minutes.

Read Testimonials approving the character of Mr Robertson.

Mr Hodson reported his satisfaction of Mr Robertson's probationary sermon preached on Monday Evening, as did several other Gentlemen.

William Jones and William Kemp entered the College this day as Probationers.

Read a Letter from Mr Hodson to Mr De Courcy, respecting Mr Rawlings.

Mr Hodson reported that he waited on Mr Crowle agreeably to the resolution of the last meeting, which he agreed to very cordially.

Mr Langston requested to purchase 10 Students gowns of different sizes.

Messrs Haweis and Charles Examined Mr Robertson in the presence of the Trustees and Committee and his Examination[46] appeared satisfactory.
[112]
Resolved that Mr Robertson be admitted a probationer for 3 months.

Read the Revd Mr Dunns Letter to Lady Ann Erskine recommending Mr Thomas Hutchings as a Student.

Resolved that Mr Thomas Hutchings be wrote to, to attend the next Wednesday meeting.

Committee 8 August 1792

Present
Messrs Weatherill*, Hodson, Langston, Butcher, Batley, Towers, Astle, Oldham, Compigne, Emerson, Rowton, Duthoit.

The last Minutes read and confirmed.

Mr Weatherill reported that Mr Robertson went down to the College on Monday the 6 inst.

Mr Hodson reported that Mrs Powell (now Hornby) had made a demand of 20 or £15 per Annum for her wages, which was thought too much. But as she left it to the meeting when she attended, it was agreed to give her after the rate of 10 Guineas per Annum, the whole amounting to 11:16:0 from [113] the 24th June to the 6th inst. which Mr Hodson accordingly paid her And also 3:11:7¼ for her Expenses from Wales and back and 9:12:4¾ for House Expenses amounting to £25 in all.

Mr Wilson (who had served in Lady Huntingdons Connection at Chatteris) attended to obtain leave to be admitted to the college, But having candidly confessed, that he could not hold infant baptism, he was informed, that he could not be admitted; such sentiment being contrary to one of the articles.

Mr Hutchings attended. The meeting very much approved of him, from conversation. Agreed that Mr Charles and Caldwell be requested to examine him tomorrow morning. Also, that Mr Weatherill, Astle, and Batley, be a Committee to receive the examination of Mr Hutchings from the ministers; and if approved of, an order to be given by them for his admission into the College.

Mr Langston moved that each Student be allowed two clean shirts, 2 cravats or stocks, one pair of stockings, one pocket Handkerchief and one night cap every week, which was unanimously agreed to.
[114]
Mr Hodson moved that Mr Nicholson be allowed One pound ten shillings per annum for washing and mending, for each Student, which was unanimmously agreed to.

Mr Hodson moved, and it was agreed that 4 Guineas be allowed by the College to the Chapel Fund for the support of Mr Jones the Student near 13 weeks, and other Students occasionally for attending at Spa Fields Chapel House for examination.

Committee 15 August 1792

Present
Messrs Weatherill, Langston*, Cooper, Oldham, Batley, Astle, Compigni, Emerson, Butcher, Duthoit, Dupont, Hodson, Burnell.

Mr Batley reported, that Mr Hutchings being examined and very much approved of by Messrs Charles and Caldwell, he and Mr Weatherill gave an order for his admission into the College, and he went on Friday.

Mr Thomas Winter, who attended this Evening, having been examined by Messrs Charles and Caldwell, and approved of by them, and also approved [115] of by this meeting, Messrs Oldham and Langston gave an order for his admission, and also the admission of John Bickerdike, who was examined and approved of the 28 of March last, as probationers in the college for 3 months.

As Mr Hodson is going to Cheshunt, Mr Oldham moved, that he be requested to consult Mr Nicholson concerning the alteration of the rules respecting the time of the Students rising, breakfast, and dinner.

Mr Batley moved, that the ministers report of the examination of those applying to be admitted into the College be in future given in writing, and entered in the Minute book, which was unanimously agreed to.[47]

Committee 22d August 1792

Present

Messrs Langston, Weatherill, Batley*, Butcher, Cooper, Compigne, Bridgeman, Astle, Rowton, Burnell, Emerson, Duthoit, Dupont.

The last Minutes read and confirmed.

[116]

Mr Weatherill reported that Mr Robert Bradley being arrived in Town, and having been examined the 28 of March last, and approved of; he and Mr Hodson gave an order for his admission into the College; and he went on Sunday the 18th instant.

Mr Langston reported that Mr John Davies being arrived from Wales, spoke at the Chapel at the prayer meeting on Sunday morning the 19 inst. and related his experience to the Trustees the afternoon of the same day. His narrative was plain and simple. But a difficulty arising about his being found in cloaths, he was desired to consult friends on that head - It was resolved that Mr Charles and Mr Caldwell should examine him; which they accordingly did; and made and signed the following report of his examination vizt.

'To the Trustees of the College

Gentlemen
    We have examined Mr John Davies, and are satisfied as to a work of God upon his heart, and think him a proper person to be admitted into the College as a Probationer if the Trustees approve of him - Thomas Charles[.] Robert Caldwell - Spa Fields, August 22d 1792.'

Read a Letter from Mr De Courcy withdrawing his request for Mr Rawlins admission into the College.

[117]
Committee 29 August 1792

Present Messrs Oldham, Weatherill, Batley, Cooper, Astle*, Butcher, Rowton, Compigne, Emerson, Duthoit, Langston, Hodson.

The last Minutes read and confirmed.

Mr Henry Atley attended to request admission into the College.

Resolved that Mr Atley have leave given to go to the College as a Probationer for 3 months and if then approved of, and he finds he shall be able to make progress, he is to stay 12 months at least before he leaves the College - to go down the latter end of September or beginning of October next.

Mr Hodson having reported that Mrs Nicholson could not undertake the mending It was agreed that Mr Nicholson be allowed 26s. a year for washing each Stu[118]dent [sic] and a woman two pence each for mending.

Also reported that Mr Hutchings abruptly left the College on Tuesday the 21st instant under a pretence of going to see his friends But the true reason was, his want of a disposition to submit to the rules.

Resolved that the Secretary write to the Revd Mr Dunn of Portsmouth, who gave Mr Hutchings a character, and report his conduct to him.

Committee 5 Sep. 1792

Present
Messrs Weatherill, Towers, Langston, Oldham*, Hodson, Batley, Butcher, Astle, Burnell, Compigni, Duthoit.

The last Minutes read and confirmed.

The Secretary reported that he had written to the Revd Mr Dunn - read a copy of the Letter: [119] the conclusion of the business deferred to the next meeting.

Resolved that a 1000 copies of the proceedings of the day, at the opening of the College the 24 August and the charge and sermon be printed at the expence of the Trustees.[48]

The President requesting to be allowed candles for study, it was proposed to beg Mr Dupont to call on him, and settle what will be a proper allowance.

Adjourned to the 26 September.

49

Tuesday 18 Sep. 1792

A special meeting of the Trustees was held in consequence of intelligence from Mr Nicholson, sent by Mr Robertson, that an intimation had been given him of some design against the College to set it on fire.

Present Messrs Weatherill, Langston, Batley, Astle, Hodson.

Resolved to add £ 49 to the Insurance [120] Resolved that a bedstead be brought downstairs, and two of the Students sleep below in rotation, for a few weeks or months, with a large bell in the room where they sleep to be rung in case of alarm and a Lamp to be burnt in that room every night.

Committee 26 Sep. 1792

Present
Messrs Weatherill, Oldham*, Butcher, Hodson, Bridgeman, Cooper, Burnell, Astle, Batley, Langston, Duthoit, Compigne, Rowton.

The last Minutes read and confirmed.

Read the Letter from Mr Nicholson, and the Anonymous Letter, alluded to in the last minutes.

Resolved that the House, Barn, Books and Furniture, with the Communion plate be insured in the Names of all the Trustees, as in the possession of Mr Nicholson.
[121]
Read a Letter from John Rogers desiring to be admitted into the College as a Student - deferred for further consideration.

Mr Hodson reported, that Mr Haweis recommends a young man of the name of Thompson in the neighbourhood of Brighthelmstone as a Student – To be further considered when Mr Haweis arrives in Town.

Read a Letter from Mr Thomas Hutchings to Lady Anne Erskine, which is considered as impertinent.

The conduct of Mr Hutchings in his manner of leaving the College was taken into consideration, and it was resolved unanimously, That the disingenuity and duplicity which Mr Hutchings was guilty of, were such as are diametrically opposite to that uprightness of character a Professor of Christianity, and a candidate for the ministry ought ever to sustain.

That the Trustees and Committee conceive, that it merits their decided disapprobation and censure, to express which, it is resolved, [122] That the said Mr

South (East View) of the Countess of Huntingdon's College,
at Cheshunt in Hertfordshire.

Plate 1: The College Buildings in 1792. Taken from *The Order Observed at the Opening of the Countess of Huntingdon's College....*
(Cheshunt archives, 64/1)

Hutchings shall not at any future time be admitted either into the College, or into that Connection where humility and sincerity must be always expected in the servants of the Lord.

Mr Oldham reported that Mr Crole wished to recommend a French Usher of his as a student - Left for further consideration.

Read a Letter from Miss Hill[50] to Lady Anne Erskine, inclosing a £10 Note as a donation to the College from Miss Hillier.

Mr Hodson reported, that he had received a Letter from Mr Morgan of Glazebury inclosing the balance for the furniture.

Quarterly General Meeting
At the Castle and Falcon,
Wednesday the 3d of October
1792

Present

Messrs Oldham*, Batley, Langston, Weatherill, Towers, Flower, Tilney, Cole, P. Duthoit, [123] J. Duthoit, Franklin, Dornford, Hayter, Emerson, Holmes, Tutt, Hodson, Walsh, Walsh Junior, Capel, Butcher Junior, Bell, Astle, John Cooper, Parke, Burnell, Rowton, Compigne, Harris, Fyffe, Butcher Senior, S: Bridgeman, Pontin, William Knight, Earle, Carpenter.

The last Minutes of the general Meeting were read.

The chairman informed the Gentlemen, that very soon after the last Meeting, Vizt., on the 13th of July, the Revd Mr Nicholson with his family arrived at Cheshunt, but some part of his family being ill with what was thought to be a putrid sore throat, it was judged prudent to delay sending any Students for a week or two - That the following have been sent vizt.

August1 William Jones and William Kemp
      6 William Robertson
     10 Thomas Hutchings
     16 John Bickerdike and Thomas Bevan Winter
     18 Robert Bradley
     23 John Davies

[124]

The chairman acquainted the Gentlemen that Thomas Hutchings had left the College and of the manner of his leaving it and read the vote of Censure passed upon him in the Minutes of the 26th of September.

That the College was opened the 24th of August last, as no doubt most of the Gentlemen present knew, from the pleasure they received in attending the opening of it.

Read Mr Nicholson[s] Letter to Mr Hodson containing the present state of the College By which it appears

1st 'That harmony, concord and peace prevail amongst the Students.

2dly All due deference and respect are paid by them to their President; and proper attention is given to his various mandates.

3dly They are, in general, very diligent; and in some, there appears a more than ordinary thirst for literature. This is [125] manifest from close application to study.

4thly Three or 4 are possessed of good natural parts. One of the seven has given satisfactory proof of his being endowed with great abilities. The Student alluded to is Jones. The rapidity of his progress incontestably proves the strength of his mental powers. His application is also equal to his capacity. In consequence of which Mr Nicholson cannot doubt of his doing honour to the seminary, provided he be kept humble and lowly. Robertson improves considerably. His brogue, Mr Nicholson hopes, will in time be laid aside; but observed that a consummate victory over evil habits, to which we have been long enured, is not easily gained. Mr Bradleys mode of speaking was extremely disgusting at first; but it is much better than it was. There is reason to believe that he will be a useful preacher of the glorious Gospel of the blessed God. Mr Kemp has tolerable natural parts, and his call to the ministry seems clear. Mr Winter is dull. In consequence of full conviction that he would never make any considerable progress in learning, Mr Nicholson exam[126]ined him very closely Respecting the motives by which he was influenced to come forward as a candidate for the ministry, he is constrained to add, in justice to the young man, as well as for the information and satisfaction of those, by whose bounty he is supported, that notwithstanding his former prejudice conceived against him on account of his want of aptness to learn, his doubts respecting his call were totally removed - he must say also that he does improve - Bickerdike is a young man of good abilities; but not the scholar that he expected from his character. However Mr Nicholson thinks he may venture to predict, that he will come forth an able minister of the new Testament. After all, he must confess, that he entertains the most sanguine expectations of great emince [sic] and usefulness from the poor Welshman Davies.'

The chairman reported, that Mr Nicholson was exceedingly well attended as a preacher of the Gospel at the College; and that the Parlour was not large enough to receive the people attending.

The Revd Mr Haweis moved, Whether it is not necessary as well as desirable [127] to have a proper place fitted up as a Chapel and public place for examination of the Students.

Should it be agreed to, Mr Hodson moved, that a specific book be kept for public subscriptions for fitting up a chapel, and the fund to be separate from that for the support of the College.

Resolved unanimously that a subscription be entered into, and a separate Book kept as above.[51]

Mr Dornford moved, That Mr Haweis be requested to reduce to writing, and lay before the Trustees, the sentiments which he delivered this Evening * concerning this Institution in general, which were introduced by a conversation repecting the propriety of having a Chapel to *[52] the neighbouring people of the College; which in effect were, That in this case in particular, as well as it respects the Connexion in general, it was not from any opposition to other places opened for the Gospel, either by the Church method[128]ists or dissenters, but from a desire to give a more universal spread to the Gospel, by steering clear of the rocks of Bigotry on either hand, the Church on the one, and the stiff Dissenters on the other - Mr Batley seconded this motion, and it was unanimously agreed to.

Read Mr De Courcys Letter recommending Mr Rawlins, and the correspondence in consequence of it.

The chairman having reported, that there were three vacancies in the assistant Committee Messrs Fyffe, Tilney and Holmes were unanimously chosen.

The chairman also reported the present state of the donations received this year towards paying for the estate, and that the Trustees have been enabled to replace £200 3 per Cent consols of the £600 sold out. The said £200 were purchased the 1st inst. at 90⅜.

He further reported, that all matters [129] were settled in Wales, the balance for the furniture sold there received, and everything owing paid.

He also mentioned that the order observed at the opening of the College, and the charge and sermon on the occasion, were printed at the price of 1s. the profits arising from the sale to be applied for the use of the College.

Mr Haweis mentioned that he had applied to Mr Brewer of Stepney, and Mr Hodgkinson to give their assistance towards the support of the College. Also that Lady Caroline and Lady Emilia [Hervey] had sent £20 a piece by him as Donations. And promised to exert himself at Bath in favour of the Institution. He mentioned also a young man living in the neighbourhood of Brighthelmstone whom he wishes to recommend. He is of godly parents, and he thinks he is gracious. He has some knowledge of the french; understands something of the [130] mathematics, and writes a fine hand; and is capable of instructing the Students in writing, and in arithmetic, which he perfectly understands.

Mr Oldham also informed the Meeting that Mr Crole likewise wished to recommend a young man, a frenchman, who he thinks has some awakenings of conscience.

Mr Bridgeman moved, That the thanks of this Meeting be returned to Mr Haweis, for his zealous exertions in support of the Institute which was unanimously agreed to.

Mr Oldham having quitted the chair, and Mr Haweis taken it, Mr Langston moved, and it was unanimously agreed, that thanks of the Meeting be transmitted by the Secretary to the Ministers officiating at the opening of the College, For their readiness in anticipating [131] the wishes of the Trustees, and the kind part which they took on the occasion.

Mr Tilney also moved, and it was unanimously carried, that thanks be returned to the Stewards for their attention at the opening of the College, preparing the Dinner etc. Also that thanks be given to Mr Oldham for his faithful and disinterested conduct as chairman.

Committee 7 Nov. 1792

Present

Messrs Langston, Weatherill, Holmes, Compigne, Park, Cooper, Butcher, Bridgeman, Towers, Tilney, Fyffe, Burnel, Platt, Oldham, Dupont, Duthoit.

Mr Hodson in the chair.

The last minutes read and confirmed.
[132]

Mr Langston moved, and it was unanimously resolved, That the resolution in the Minutes of the 29th August 1792 respecting Mr Atleys admission into the College be rescinded.

Mr Jedediah Thompson attended and was examined. Having withdrawn, the question was put, whether he was a proper person to be admitted by the Trustees into the College? It appeared to the meeting and it was unanimously agreed, That he was too young in the knowledge of divine things, for the Trustees to think themselves justifiable in his admission.

The Memorandum alluded to in the Minutes of the Quarterly Meeting having been drawn up by Mr Haweis and presented to this Meeting by Mr Hodson; It was unanimously agreed, That as the sentiments therein contained have in effect been conveyed [133] to the public before, the printing of it is at present unnecessary.

Resolved, That the last Wednesday in this month to be fixed on for the Examination of the young men, in the Committee room at Spa Fields, previous to their admission as Students: of which the President of the College, with the Ministers subscribing to the instution [sic] and the rest of the Trustees and Committee to have notice.

Committee 28 Nov. 1792

Present

Messrs Towers, Weatherill, Langston, Griffiths, Oldham*, Burnel, Tilney, Astle, Batley, Compigne, Cowper, Holmes, Rowton, Butcher, Bridgeman, Nicholson, Platt, Hodson, Duthoit, Emmerson, Kirkman, Dupont, Fyffe, Crowle, Underwood.

[134]

William Jones, William Kemp, William Robertson, Thomas Bevan Winter, John Bickerdike, Robert Bradley, and John Davies attended and were examined.

The President gave them all a general good character for application and orderly behaviour in the College Except Mr Robertson, who had in some instances shewn an unbecoming spirit, and had particularly offended Mrs Nicholson.

Messrs Jones, Kemp, Winter, Bickerdike, Bradley and Davies were accordingly admitted as Students on the Foundation.

But Mr Robertsons admission was suspended till the Meeting of the Committee the first Wednesday in February, to be determined according to the report to be received from the President.

[135]

Committee 5 December 1792

Present

Messrs Towers, Weatherill*, Langston, Parke, Burnell, Astle, Butcher, Hodson, Oldham, Tilney, Rowton.

The Minutes of the 7th and those of the 28th of November read and confirmed.

The Trustees having encouraged Mr Thompson to come up, they thought it just to allow him his expences.

It is agreed that Mr Parke the Collector shall have one shilling in the pound for all subscriptions not exceeding two Guineas; and that for subscriptions exceeding two Guineas be the amount what it may, he [136] shall receive two shillings each.

Resolved that blank Receipts be printed.

Quarterly General Meeting
29 January 1793
Present
Messrs Weatherill, Langston, Astle, Jones, Parke, Francis, Glascot, N: Rowland, Holmes, Burnell, Chambers, Dornford, Cooper, Emerson, Broady, Hodson*, Walsh, Bridgeman, Dupont, King, Butcher, Butcher Junior, J. Long, Tutt, Platt, Hodgkinson, Berridge, Fyffe, Tilney.

Mr Glascot went to prayer.

The last Minutes of the quarterly Meeting read and confirmed.

The chairman reported that the time of probation having expired in [137] November last the seven Probationers came to Town, and were examined by three ministers (the Trustees and Committee present) six of whom were accordingly admitted as Students But Mr Robertsons admission was suspended as in the Minutes of the 7th Nov. which was read.

The chairman reported that he had seen Mr Nicholson, the President, who informed him, that the reproof given to Mr Robertson had a very salutary effect, and he has since behaved very well, as had all the rest of the Students.

The chairman was in expectation of being furnished with other matter from the President, to communicate to the Meeting respecting the state of the College and improvement of the young men But apprehends that there was some mistake in putting the Letter into the post, as Mr Nicholson informed Mr Dupont a few days since that he would send a Letter. [138] Mr Dupont mentioned, that he had heard most of the young men, that he believed they were called to the work of the ministry, and that they promised usefulness.

The chairman also reported, that the admission of the young man recommended by Mr Haweis was suspended for the present and also of the other person named by Mr Crole.

In answer to that part of the minutes respecting Mr Dornford's motion, the chairman read the first circular Letter observing that as that contained the substance of Mr Haweis sentiments delivered at the last general meeting, the Trustees were of opinion, that the publication of these sentiments might at [139] present be dispensed with Particularly as the Society had invariably discovered a firm attachment to the Church, and shewn that they were not inimical to the dissenters.

Resolved unanimously, that Messrs Platt and Dornford be appointed auditors of the accounts of the year 1792 and report the state thereof at the next Meeting.

The chairman reported that the amount of the subscriptions, donations etc. was as follows

Received in subscriptions	320	15	0
In Donations	587	10	0
Collection at Spa Fields	54	5	6
Dividends	15	15	0
	978	5	6

Read two Letters from Messrs Tissier [140] and Cureton late Students at Trevecka, shewing the pleasure which it gave them in hearing of the opening of the College at Cheshunt, and praying for its success.

The chairman informed the meeting, that the Book was opened for the subscriptions at the chapel, and that it would lay at the Committee room Spa Fields.

Mr Platt concluded with prayer.

Committee 6 February 1793

Present

Messrs Weatherill, Langston*, Tilney, Holmes, Cooper, Butcher, Astle, Burnell, Fyffe, Hodson, Duthoit, Dupont.

[141]

The last Minutes read and confirmed.

Read two Letters from Mr Nicholson The first dated 1 January, the other 15 January respecting the good behaviour of the Students.

Ditto another from him reporting the good behaviour of Mr Robertson On which Mr Batley moved that he be admitted as a student which was unanimously agreed to.

The Surcharge respecting the windows of the College was read. Given to Mr Robertson to take back to Cheshunt for an explanation.

Mr Nicholsons bill to Christmas last amounting to 72:7:8½ presented by Mr Hodson as paid. And the following bills were ordered to be paid Viz. Mr Weatherill 5:5:9 Mr [142] Penn Glazier 3:11:10 Webb 3s. 6d. Knightley Bricklay[er] 1:4:1 Leighton Plomber 16:16:11 Mr Camp, Carpenter 26:17:7 and Mr Oldham 35:1:2.

Read a Note from Lady Anne Erskine mentioning two young men who had applied as students, Mr Burge at Mr Stockdales, Bristol, and Mr Watts, Glocester. The Secretary to write to Mr Caldwell respecting Mr Watts, and to Mr Gardener respecting Mr Burge.

Her Ladyships note also contained a recommendation from Mr Jones of Langan of a young man in Wales who wishes to be admitted as a Student. Lady Anne [143] to be desired to write, that if he is a converted young man and called to the work of the Ministry, he will be received as a Probationer, on the same footing as others.

Resolved that a Schedule or Inventory of the furniture, Books, etc. at the College belonging to the Trustees, be taken the first convenient opportunity.

Resolved that Mr Carr be requested to be Surveyor of the intended chapel at the College and Wednesday the 20th inst. be fixed for the Trustees to meet him at the College to make a survey.

[144]

Committee March 6th: 1793[53]

Present

Messrs Towers, Holmes, Batley, Weatherill, Dupont, Cooper, Astle, Hodson, Bridgman, Langston, Fyffe, Butcher, Duthoit, Burnell, Compigne, Rowton.

Mr J.O. Oldham in the Chair.

Read and confirmed the Minutes of the last Meeting.

Mr Langston reported that six of the Trustees and three of the Committee met Mr Carr, at Cheshunt Wednesday the 20th of Feb: last to take a Plan of the intended Chapel.

Read a Letter from Mr Caldwell referring [145] Mr Watts to Mr Hawes [sic] and by[54] Mr Hawes to the Trustees.

Read a Letter from Mr Burge, declining his entering the College, on account of bad health.

Read a Letter from Mr Gardiner in favor of Mr Burge.

Read a Letter of grateful acknowledgements from Mr Best, in consequence of his removal to the Country.

Read a Letter from Mr Nicholson, of sundry wants, and an enquiry if the Students are to serve at Waltham.

Resolved that Leave be given for Students to serve at Waltham and that Mr Nicholson be acquainted therewith.

Resolved that 500 Receipts be printed.

Messrs Hughes and Walshs Bill for Stationery [146] and Books, amounting to £15:6:8 be directed for Payment.

Mr Carr, attended and produced Plans of the intended Chapel; The Plan, and Estimate, to be brought forward the next General meeting.

Resolved that 500 Copies of the State of the Society, with Lists of the Subscribers, be printed against the next General Meeting.[55]

Mr Briskell applied for admission to the College, but objected to, he being a married man.

Resolved that Thomas Witham be Secretary and allowed one guinea per quarter; for the Services of the Society.

[147]
Ap:3
1793

Quarterly General Meeting

Present

Revd Dr Ford, Mr Platt, Mr Underwood, Messrs Butterworth, Jones, Burnell, King, Butcher, J: Long, Oldham*, Cooper, Rowton, Weatherill, R. Duthoit, Shadd, Hodson, Dornford, Tilney, Langston, Fyffe, Walsh, Batley, Flower, Senior, Astle, Francis, Holmes.

The Revd Mr Platt began with Prayer.

Read and confirm'd the Minutes of the last Meeting.

Read the Presidents Report of the State of the College: which came to [sic] late to be Read at the last Meeting, And also his Report for the last [148] Quarter; both which were very satisfactory.

Read the Auditors Report of the State of the Society, which is as follows

Viz

State of the College at Lady Day 1793

Students admitted on the Foundation

Robert Bradley	William Kemp
John Bickerdike	William Robertson
John Davis	Thomas Bevan Winter
	William Jones

[149]

Receipts and Disbursements A.D. 1792

Dr	£	s	d
To Annual Subscriptions	322	17	0
To Donations	587	10	0
To Collections at Spa-fields Chapel	54	5	6
To Dividends on 3 per Cent Consols	15	15	0
To the Sale of £650 ditto	619	2	6
To Balance due to the Treasurer	58	17	9
	£1658	7	9

To £500 Three per Cent Consols standing in the Names of Four of the Trustees

Cr	£	s	d
By Balance of last years Account due to the Treasurer	27	16	3
By the Purchase of the Estate at Cheshunt	950	0	0
By Sundry repairs done	48	10	3
By Furniture Bought	87	0	10
By the Purchase of £300 3 per Cent Consols	260	5	0
By the President's Salary, Board of Students, Books, Printing, Secretary, Collector, and all other Expenses	284	15	5
	£1658	7	9
By Balance due to the Treasurer	58	17	9

[150]

Read sundry Letters received by the Trustees since the last Meeting.

The Chairman reported that the Trustees had heard of two or three Candidates for the College, and one had made a personal Application: but it appearing that he was a married Man and did not intend to enter the College so as to reside in it in common with the other Students, he was not admitted.

Printed Plans of the College with the Subscribers Names being produced at this Meeting, it was resolved that one or more be sent to each Subscriber not present.

The Chairman reported that six of the Trustees and three of the Committee had been to Cheshunt and met Mr Carr there Their Surveyor, in order to fix on the [151] Place and Dimensions of the Chapel, which it is in Contemplation to build there. Mr Carr attended this Meeting this Evening and produced Plans and Elevations with an Estimate of the Expence. This Design was very much approved, but the Estimate being £1011 deducting £150 for old Materials, The further Consideration about erecting the said Chapel was postponed.

The Chairman informed the Gentlemen present that the Trust Deed is in great forwardness, and as he believes is just Finish'd.

The Revd Dr Ford concluded with Prayer.

[152]

Committee, May 1st 1793

Present

Messrs Weatherill*, Butcher, Cooper, Batley, Bridgman, Compigne, Hodson, Burnell.

Read and confirm'd the Minutes of the last Meeting.

Mr Rogers having some months since wrote to the Trustees of the College for his Admission therein[56] having lately signified to Mr Weatherill that it is still his desire. It was proposed that he attend the next Monthly Meeting.
[153]
Read Mr Hodsons Letter to Mr Cardale, pressing the Completion of the Deed; and Mr Cardale's Answer: requesting longer time.

Read the Revd Mr Nicholsons Quarterly Bill and Receipt; the same being discharged.

Read the Bill of Sheeting, bought for the College, and the Receipt; the same being discharg'd.

Mr Hodson produced an Extract from the Will of Mrs Betty Newborn of Watchett Somersetshire, lately deceased; who has left £400 3 per Cent Consols: The Interest to be paid to her Husband James Newborn, during his Life and after his decease it is to be paid to the Treasurer of the Apostolic Society [154] For Supporting the Countess of Huntingdon's College in Wales; on Condition that the Society sends a Minister or Student, to preach in the Meeting at Watchett, and its Neighbourhood; If the College ceases, or the Society neglects to send a Minister, The Interest goes to Mr Evans' Academy etc., And at last, in the case of a failure of performing Conditions, It goes together with the Principal to Mr Simon Day, one of Mr Wesley's Preachers, and to his Heirs for ever.

CHESHUNT COLLEGE

[155]

Committee June 5th: 1793

Present,

Messrs Dupont, Butcher, Weatherill, Burnell, Hodson, Compigne, Langston, Fyffe, Batley, Rowton, Astle, Towers

Mr William Astle in the Chair.

Read the Minutes of the last Meeting.

The Revd Mr Roby and the Revd Mr Lewis Jones having recommended Mr John Parry, to be received as a Probationer in the College, He attended and was Examined.

Read the Revd Thomas Haweis and Dr Fords Account of the Examination of the Students by them the 14th of last Month, in the Presence of Messrs Oldham, and Hodson, at the College.

[156]

Read the Copy of Mr Hodsons Letter to Mr Cardale, pressing the immediate Completion of the Deed, And Mr Cardale's Answer to Mr Hodson, that the Deed should be finish'd out of Hand.

Read the Copy of a Letter, of Mr Hodson to the Revd Mr Nicholson, on the important matter of a Student going to Sierra Leone in Africa. [57]

Resolved that the Coach-house, Stabling etc, at the College be converted into a Chapel, the Expense not to exceed the Sum of £300 And that Mr Carr be applied to by Mr Burnell, for the undertaking of the same but should Mr Carr not be able to undertake it [157] It was requested that Mr Batley be pleas'd to make it known to Mr Hilton, and that a Plan of the intended Chapel be ready, for the ensuing General Meeting.

Read Mr Clement Barkers proposals, for repairing the Paling round the Field at the College at Cheshunt, for the Sum of £15:10 or less. The same agreed to and referred to Mr Hodson to forward the same.

Mr John Parry Aged 32, being approv'd as a Probationer, an Order was made out and sign'd for his Admission.

Mr John Rogers Aged 22, was examined; but not judged proper for Admission in the College at present.

[158]
July 3rd   ***Quarterly General Meeting***
1793

Present

Messrs Dupont, Butterworth, Carr, Weatherill, Burnell, Duthoit P., Hodson, Butcher Senior, Flower, Langston*, Butcher, Fyffe, Astle, Bridgman, Jones, Curtis, King, Cooper John, Rowton, Shadd.

The Chairman began with Prayer.

Read, and confirmed the Minutes of the last General Meeting.

The Chairman inform'd the Gentlemen present, That the Trust Deed is finish'd: and is gone to be enroll'd in the Court of Chancery. [58]

Read the Revd Thomas Haweis and Dr Fords Account of the Examination of the Students [159] The 14th of May last, which was very satisfactory.

Read the Revd Mr Nicholsons Quarterly Report, which was also very satisfactory.

Mr Carr produced a Plan of a Chapel to be built in the Place of the Coach-house and Stable at the College: for the Sum of £300 exclusive of the old Materials, left for further consideration.

The following Gentlemen were Elected Stewards for the Dinner, on the Anniversary on Monday the 26th of August.

Messrs Silver	Fyffe	Butterworth
Burnell	King	Butcher Senior
Bridgman	Hodson	Dupont

Mr Hodson concluded with Prayer.

[160]
July 29th   ***Committee***
1793

Present

Messrs Oldham, Butcher Senior, Dupont, Burnell, Weatherill, Cooper[59], Hodson, Holmes, Langston, Rowton, Batley, Towers, Astle

The Revd Mr Charles in the Chair.

Read a Letter from the Revd David Jones relating to Mr David Morgan, Aged 24 years, who offers himself a Candidate for the College.

Mr Charles interrogated him at considerable length, respecting his Experience of a Work of Grace on his Heart, and also his knowledge of Gospel Doctrines.
[161]

His Answer as far as we could understand (for he speaks but little English) were simple, and in a good measure satisfactory. He was also ask'd if he came with the consent of his Friends - Answered in the Affirmative. With respect to his Call to the Ministry: he said he did believe, it was the Will of God he should speak for him, and his Views in this matter appeared quite simple, and his Motives disinterested.

After his Examination it was unanimously resolved, to admit him as a Probationer for 3 months, and an Order was given accordingly.

Mr Oldham laid before the Meeting a Letter he received from Dr Hillingworth, complaining that he had been ill-treated, in not being appointed Tutor to the College.

Resolved that an Answer to the same in Vindication of the Trustees, and of Mr Oldham in particular, be wrote, and signed by all the Trustees.

[162]
Committee 7 Aug: 1793

Present

Messrs Weatherill*, Butcher, Hodson, Burnell, Langston, P. Duthoit, Batley, Holmes, Astle.

Read and confirmed the Minutes of the last Meeting, the Quarterly Meeting; and that of the 29th ultimo.

Mr Phillips master of an Academy at Blackheath presented Charles Beaching (aged only 14 years) for admission into the College, but he was unanimously judged too young.
[163]

Read two Letters from Mr Slew of Rochdale, and a Recommendation from Dr Drake, Vicar of that Place. Mr Hodson was desired to write him an Answer, referring him for Examination to the Revd Mr Robey of Wigan.

Read a Letter from John Jones of the Parish of Lampeter Velfry Pembrokeshire South Wales, to Lady Anne Erskine, expressing his desire of being admitted into the College; Resolved that Lady Anne be requested to write to the Revd Mr Rowland, and Mr Griffiths Junior whom he mentions in his Letter, to enquire what they know concerning him.

Read Mr Hodsons Letter in Answer to the Revd Dr Illingworth which was approv'd of and the Secretary ordered to copy the same sign it officially and deliver it.

[164]

Mr Hodson produced a Plan he had drawn up for conducting the Anniversary on the 26th instant at the College - The same was read, and approved, and the Secretary ordered to write three, or four Copies thereof.

Committee 4th Sept: 1793

Present

Messrs Dupont, Butcher, Weatherill, Bridgman, Hodson,* Cooper, Langston, Holmes, Batley, Rowton, Astle, Towers.

[165]

Mr John Parry from the College began with Prayer.

Read and Confirm'd the Minutes of the last Meeting.

Read the Revd Mr Nicholson's Report concerning Mr Parry whose time as a Probationer is expired. He attended, and was examined, and his full Admittance unanimously agreed to. He requested to go for a few days to settle some Matters at Worcester, which was granted.

Read a Letter from the Revd Mr Roby concerning Mr Thomas Slew, acquainting the Trustees, that Mr Slew had been to Wigan as was desired but that Mr Roby being that day out of Town, he had not seen him. [166] The Letter mentioning that Mr Slew had been a Student in the Academy at Northowram[60] Mr Hodson was desired to write to him, to enquire how long he had been in that Seminary and why he quitted it. Also what were his Intentions if he should be admitted into the College, as Mr Roby intimated he did not mean to continue in the Connection.

Paid the Secretary 2 guineas for half a years Salary, due September.

Special - Meeting 11 Sept. 1793

Present - Messrs Weatherill, Hodson, Langston, Batley, Astle, Towers.

[167]

Lady Anne Erskine sent in a Letter which she received from Mr John Clark and Mr William Claridge of Banbury; inclosing a very long one from Mr Thomas Isham, a young man of Buckingham; who is desirous of Admission into the College. The Letter contained a sort of Confession, or Declaration of his Faith, and Principles; wherein there appears so much of Arminianism, that it was unanimously resolved he could not be admitted at present; and Mr Hodson was desired to write to him accordingly.

CHESHUNT COLLEGE

Sept. 25th 1793
Special - Meeting of the Trustees
and (168) Committee for Reading
of the Trust Deed to which the
whole of them were summoned

Present

Trustees	Committee
Messrs Weatherill	Messrs Butcher
Hodson	Bridgman
Batley	Cooper
Astle	Compigne
	P:Duthoit
	Rowton
	Shadd*

Mr Shadd Read the Trust Deed.

Quarterly General Meeting
Oct: 2nd 1793

Present

[169]   The Revd Mr Platt, Messrs Oldham, Butcher Senior, Jones, Dupont, Butcher Junior, William Knight, Weatherill, Burnell, John Long, Hodson,* Bridgman, Shadd, Langston, Cooper, Towers, Batley, Dornford, Tutt, Astle, Flower, Walsh Senior, Francis, Enoch Hodgkinson Esq.

Read the Minutes of the last Meeting.

Read the Presidents report, which contained a satisfactory Account of the progress of the Students; in their Studies.

Read several Letters received since [170]the last Meeting, particularly from Mr Thomas Slew and Mr Thomas Isham, who had solicited, to be admitted into the College. read also a Letter from the Revd Mr Robey, relative to the former; and Copies of Letters written by Mr Hodson, concerning each of them. Mr Slew not approving of our Plan and Mr Isham being of Arminian Principles they were neither of them received.

The Chairman produced Mr Cardale's Bill for the Deed of Purchase, and the Trust Deed, and enrolling the same in the Court of Chancery: the whole amounting to £35:2:11. Mr Cardale having charged nothing for his own great Trouble, and Attention in the whole of the Business it was [171] Resolved that the Thanks of this

Society be presented to Mr Cardale, for this his extraordinary Kindness and Liberality.

On this Occasion Mr Walsh Senior moved that the Thanks of the Society [61] be presented to Mr Oldham, for his excellent Conduct, in managing, and concluding the purchase of the Estate which passed unanimously.

The Chairman reported that he had received by the hands of the Revd Mr Haweis from the Ladies Emily and Caroline Hervey Twenty Pounds each, on Account of the College.

Messrs Emerson, Shadd and Simpson being those three of the Committee who have attended the Monthly Meetings, the fewest times; of course go out; and Messrs Everard, Francis and Silver were chosen in their Room.

The Revd Mr Platt concluded with Prayer.

[172]
Monthly Meeting, Wednesday November 6th 1793

Present

Messrs Weatherill, Burnell, Langston*, Butcher, Hodson, Bridgman, Batley, Cooper, Astle, Towers.

The Chairman began with Prayer.

Read and confirmed the Minutes of the last Monthly Meeting, and read the Minutes of the last general Meeting.

Mr Astle reported that he had desired a Bill of the Pails and washing Tubs etc. supplied by Mr Parry of Grays Inn Lane for the use of the College, and that he desired the same might be accepted as [173] a Present to the College. Resolved that the Secretary transmit to him the Thanks of the Society.

Mr David Morgan having compleated his three Months Probation, attended with a Letter from the President approving of his Conduct, and commending his Abilities. He was re-examined concerning his desire to the work of the Ministry, which he expressed in the most satisfactory terms, as likewise his Adherence to the 15 Articles; and was thereupon fully Admitted as a Student.

Two new Candidates for the College attended, Viz·

Mr John Chamberlain, aged 29, and
Mr William Macdonald, aged 28.

the former recommended by Mr Cureton, and a Certificate of his moral [174] Conduct etc. signed by the Revd Mr Cannon. The latter recommended by the Revd Mr Piercy[62], and various Persons referred to, for his Character. They were both examined, desired to attend on Monday Evenings to give a Specimen of their Abilities and were referred for further Examination, the former to the Revd Mr Platt, and the latter to the Revd Mr Crole.

Read a Letter from the Revd Mr Rowlands relative to Mr John James, a Candidate for the College, which being very satisfactory; it was resolved, that Mr James be wrote to, that he may come up, and attend at the next Monthly Meeting.

Mr Hodson brought Mr Clement Barkers Bill for repairing the Fence of the Field and Garden, at Cheshunt: and fitting up a Place for the Students to wash themselves in, and making way for them to come [175][63] down from their Apartments into the Yard, without passing through the Kitchen. The amount of the Bill is £30:5:2. Order'd to be paid.

Mr Nicholson requested a Supply of Sheets and Towels Those brought from Wales being grown very old and bad. Mr Hodson was desired to buy Sheets, and it was thought Towels might be made out of the old Sheets.

The Students having renewed their Request for an Alarm-Clock, to call them up in the Morning, Mr Towers kindly offered to make a Present of one, which was thankfully accepted.

A new Minute-Book being wanted Mr Hodson was desired to order one of Mr Walsh.

FOOTNOTES

Minutes 1

1 Page ii is blank. This folio was not included in the contemporary pagination

2 This is the *Plan* printed below

3 This is now in the College archives - C5/ 1

4 For this circular letter see the *Records* printed below pp 173 ff

5 Corrected to '1788' in pencil subsequently

6 Messrs Galpin, Best, Eyre and Bennett did not sign the Plan

7 The day of the month was omitted by accident

8 Dr Lyon resigned because Lady Huntingdon had dismissed Rev. Thomas Wills from the Connexion. See E. Welch (ed.), *Two Calvinistic Methodist Chapels* (London Rec. Soc., 1975), p. 76 and *A Farewell Address from the Rev. Mr Wills to the Various Congregations and Societies* (London, 1788)

9 The day is left blank in the original

10 The day is left blank in the original

11 This letter is printed below in the *Records* pp 173 ff

12 Evan Roberts was one of the leaders of the Trevecka Family *(Y Teulu)* after Howell Harris's death

13 Enfield was then a growing country retreat two miles north-east of London. The Earl and Countess of Huntingdon had lived in the Chase for a few years. A Connexion chapel was opened there by 1793 and served by the Cheshunt students

14 This inventory is no longer to be found in the College archives

15 This was Samuel Hughes who married the daughter of Joseph Harris (Howell's elder brother) and inherited the family property

16 This was the house at Mile End - where Sion chapel was established in 1790

17 Woodford Mills in Essex, then eight miles from London

18 For Rev. Edward Griffins' letter see D.E. Jenkins, *Thomas Charles* (Denbigh, 1910), pp. 84-85

19 The premium was usually called a fine and was paid when the lessee took possession of the property

20 Kentish Town was then a pleasant village three miles north of London

21 This name appears in brackets in the original

22 'and Mrs' added later

23 From this point the minutes are written by Mr Best. His accounts as secretary are printed below

24 These entries appear in the College archives, C9/ 5/ 2 and are printed below pp 219 ff

25 This word, which is difficult to read, is probaboly intended for Redditch

26 From this point the entries for the appointment of a chairman and the note of adjournment are omitted from this transcript. An asterisk in the list of those present shows who presided at the meeting

27 The original deed is in the College Archives - C21/ 4

28 This was left blank in the original

29 This was Henry Thornton, a member of the Clapham evangelicals and a friend of Lady Huntingdon

30 The Earl of Dartmouth was another supporter of the Methodist movement and a friend of Lady Huntingdon

31 This was left blank in the original

32 This was left blank in the original

33   The minutes of this meeting are not in George Best's handwriting. They were probably written by Batley

34   Windows were often bricked up at this period to reduce the amount of window tax paid

35   See the accounts in College archives, C5/ 1

36   George Best's handwriting reappears

37   This name was added later

38   The first half of this sentence was added later

39   A pencil mark has been made against this entry by a later reader of the minutes

40   The College chapel was licensed for religious worship under the Toleration Act (1 Wm & Mary 1, c. 18)

41   The accounts for the anniversary dinner are printed below

42   This phrase has been underlined in pencil at a later date

43   This volume is now in the College archives - C 5/1. Bound in rough calf with a red leather label on the spine it is indeed large and handsome

44   This is printed below

45   A pencil mark has been made against this entry at a later date

46   'his Examination' is written over an erasure

47   See the College archives, C 9/ 9/ 1, for these entries

48   A copy of this book is in the College archives - C 4/ 1/ A second printing was required

49   This is blank in the original

50   Miss Hill was a sister of the Rev. Rowland Hill and a friend of Lady Huntingdon

51   Donations from Spa Fields chapel were entered in their account book (College archives, D 1/ 4, ff. 7-9)

52   The words between the asterisks are written over an erasure

53   All future minutes were written by Thomas Witham

54   This phrase was added later

55   This is printed below

56   These two words were added later

57   The Connexion still has a mission in Sierra Leone

58   The trust deed was enrolled in Chancery under provisions of the Mortmain Act (9 Geo. II c. 36)

59   Cooper's name was added later

60   The dissenting academy at Northowram near Halifax (Yorks) was dissolved in 1795

61   'Society' is altered from 'Meeting'

62   Rev. William Piercy had been Lady Huntingdon's choice as president of Bethesda (near Savannah in Georgia), but a subsequent quarrel over its operation led to his exclusion from all her chapels. At this time he was the minister of a chapel at Woolwich.

63   These entries were made on the endpaper of the volume

II

APOSTOLIC COLLEGE

GOVERNORS'

MINUTES

COLLEGE MINUTE BOOK B [1]

[2r]

Copy of a Letter from the Trustees of the College to the Revd Mr Nicholson

London 17th November 1793

Reverend and dear Sir,

A Report was brought to the Trustees of the College on Sunday last, That all the Students are disaffected to the present Government, and wish Success to the French Revolution. Such a Report, however ill founded, will materially injure the College, as far as it spreads; and if true will bring such an Odium on the Institution, as cannot be wiped off but by the explusion of the guilty. God forbid that a Seminary instituted for Piety and Learning should ever [2v] become a Seminary of Disloyalty and Sedition!

It requires no great depth of penetration to discover, that while we are at War with France, we cannot wish Success to the sanguinary, unjust and tyrannical Faction that now rules the unhappy and distracted Country, but we must in the same proportion wish our own Government to be defeated and vanquished. A Crime involving in it a degree of Treason and Rebellion! And if Those who are to be Teachers of others, are Themselves tainted with this Crime, who knows how far the Mischief may spread?

They who read and study the sacred Scriptures, ought to know that our Lord and his Apostles, both by Precept and Example, taught Obedience and Submission to the higher Powers - that is - to the Governments under [3r] which Christians live: and as it is the duty of Christians in general to pray for, wish well to, and support that Government under which they enjoy Liberty and Protection, so it is the particular duty of the Ministers of the Gospel to teach Men so.

Whatsoever divine Purposes the blessed God intends to bring about by permitting the Potsherds of the Earth to dash one another to pieces, are profound secrets to us: but whatever his sovereign and wise designs may be, we are by no means warranted to approve that which is evil in itself, under the Idea that God will bring Good out of it.

We hope, Sir, you coincide with us in these Sentiments and beg you will impress them in the most forcible manner on the Minds of your Pupils: and if any of them should not acknowledge and receive [3v] Them we desire you will inform us thereof, that we may act as in such a case it will become our duty to do so.

The College, no doubt, has already many Enemies. It is our earnest Prayer to God that they may have nothing whereof to accuse us: and that we shall be very happy to hear that the Stigma of Disloyalty and Disaffection does not belong to us.

We are,
Reverend and dear Sir
Your affectionate Brethren in Christ,
James Oldham Oldham
Thomas Weatherill
William Hodson
William Langston
Henry Batley
William Astle
Matthias Dupont

[4r]

Monthly Meeting Wednesday 4 December 1793

Present: Messrs Dupont, Hodson*, Batley, Cooper, Francis, Langston, Holmes, Butcher, Astle, Burnell, Duthoit, Revd Mr Platt, Mr Bridgman, Messrs Weatherill, Fyffe and Rowton

The Chairman began with Prayer.[2]

Read and confirmed the Minutes of the last Meeting.

The Chairman reported that he had sent the Alarm Clock presented by Mr Towers to the College. For which the Secretary was ordered to write him a Letter of Thanks.

Resolved that a Vacation for three Weeks be [4v] allowed at the College, to commence on Saturday the 21st instant and expire on Monday the 13th of January. Mr Hodson was desired to inform the President thereof by Letter.

Mr John James from Wales, being come to Town, attended this Meeting, and was very particularly examined as to his Conversion and Call to the Ministry, when it appearing to the satisfaction of every one present that he is a truly gracious and humble Man, and his Call to the Work of the Ministry such as he cannot in Conscience resist, being determined to speak for the Lord whether admitted into the College or not, being also well recommended by the Revd Mr Rowland the the Revd Mr Griffiths, he was unanimously admitted a Probationer and having no Friends in [5r] Town his Order was made out for him to go Tomorrow. His age 24.

Mr John Chamberlain having been refer'd for Examination to the Revd Mr Platt, who being present, testified his Approbation of him, Mr Chamberlain was called in and particularly interrogated as to his Views and Motives and his Adherence to the Doctrines contain'd in the 15 Articles. His Answers being satisfactory he was Admitted a Probationer, to go the 13th January after the Recess provided his Character, for which he gaves References is irreproachable.

The Secretary brought a Letter he had received from the Revd Mr Crole, to whom Mr William Macdonald had been referred for Examination. The Letter being satisfactory and the Deputation appointed to enquire into his Character reporting that it was highly in his favor [5v] Mr Macdonald was called in and after a little further Examination was admitted as A Probationer, to go the 13th of January.

Richard Proudfoot, aged 24, recommended by the Revd Messrs Munn, Freer and Underwood, having been Servant in a Shop or Warehouse and four Months out of Place was very fully examined: but as his Call to the Ministry did not appear evident, he was not received into the College, but inform'd he might be at some future time if it should then be made apparent that his Call was clear.

Three other Candidates for the College attended viz. Mr John Ellis, Aged 26 years, bred a Farmer, has been Shopman to a Cheesemonger and now out of Place, Mr John Cooper, aged 21 years, late Servant to Samuel Thornton Esqr and now out of Employment, and [6r] Mr Andrew Horn, aged 26 years, Cabinet Maker, but it growing late their further Examination was postponed to Wednesday the 18th instant to which time the Meeting was adjourned and the Secretary ordered to give Notice thereof to such of the Trustees and Committee as were not present.

Adjourn'd Meeting of Trustees and Committee Wednesday 18th Dec: 1793

Present: Messrs Langston, Holmes, Compigne, Weatherill, Cooper, Bridgman, Astle, Burnell, Hodson, Revd Mr Platt, Messrs Dupont*, Francis, Batley, Fyffe, Rowton, Oldham, Butcher.

The Revd Mr Platt began with Prayer.
[6v]

Mr John Ellis was examined slightly for it appeared that his character was not that which is necessary for any young Man who offers himself as a Candidate for the College - He was unanimously rejected on that Account.

The Secretary produced a Letter which he had receiv'd from the Revd Mr Crole, in favor of Mr Andrew Horn who was examined respecting his Conversion and Call to the Ministry which was very satisfactory but his Father being a godly Man residing in Edinburgh and not at all acquainted with his Intention it was thought expedient that he should be consulted respecting his Admission into the College. He was therefore advised to write to his Father and get his Answer against the ensuing

Quarterly Meeting. The Trustees to meet at half past five to see the same and Admit Mr Horne if they approved. [7r] The Increase of Students requiring some additional Rooms to be contrived as Students Apartments, Mr Dupont, Mr Burnell and Mr Francis were desired to go to the College on Monday the 28th instant, to see what Accommodation they could make and to give Orders that the same might be carried into effect immediately.

1794 Wednesdaay 1st January

The Trustees met at the Castle and Falcon Aldersgate street half an hour before the General Meeting and admitted Mr Andrew Horn as a Probationer, he having received an Answer from his Father, who though greatly surprized at his Sons Intention did not object to it.

Quarterly General Meeting 1st January 1794

Present: Messrs Hodson, Langston, Dupont, Cooper, Francis, Burnell, Revd Mr Platt, [7v] Messrs Astle, Dornford, Fyffe, Revd Mr Nicholson, Messrs Oldham*, Weatherill, Curtis, Mr Butcher Senior, Messrs Pontin, Butterworth, Jones, King, Mr Thomas Wontner, Mr Butcher Junior.

The Revd Mr Nicholson began with Prayer.

Read and confirm'd the Minutes of the last Meeting. The Chairman inform'd the Meeting that himself and Mr Hodson had waited upon Mr Cardale paid his Bill and presented the Thanks of the Society agreeably to the Resolution of the last Meeting.

Read the Presidents Quarterly Report of the Students which was very satisfactory.

Read the Presidents Report of Mr Parry also a few necessaries mentioned as Sheets etc. which were sent.

Mr Langston reported that Mr Thomas Hodgson [8r] had left a Legacy of £20 to the College.

Mr Hodson reported that the Revd Mr Cureton of Newcastle lately deceas'd had left his Library of Books to the College.

The Chairman moved and it was resolved that a Board be put up at the College whereupon all Donations by Will should be recorded.

The two Auditors elected for Auditing the Accompts of the Year 1793 were Mr Henry Fyffe and Mr Thomas Wontner.

The Chairman inform'd the Meeting that a Report having been rais'd of the Students being disaffected to Government the Trustees had wrote a Letter to the President on the Subject and had received an Answer thereto which was now read and the Revd Mr Nicholson in Person declared the Charge was groundless whereupon Mr Pontin moved and it was resolved, That the Author of the said Report (Mr Williams, Cutler, in Smithfield) [8v] be prohibited all Access to the College and the Students to Him.

The Revd Mr Platt concluded with Prayer.

Monthly Meeting, Wednesday Feb 5th

Present: Messrs Weatherill, Parke, Hodson, Batley, Compigne, Towers, Holmes, Cooper, Astle, Langston*, Burnell, Butcher.

Read, and confirmed the Minutes of the last Monthly Meeting Dec: 4th: 1793, and the Adjourn'd Meeting of the 18th: ditto.

Read the Minutes of the last Quarterly Meeting.

The Chairman read the Copy of the Bond [9r] given by Mr Parke, Collector for the College who petitions for some Augmentation of his Allowance, Viz: That instead of one Shilling in the Pound on all Subscriptions not exceeding Two Guineas per Annum, and two Shillings for every Subscription above Two Guineas; it may be one Shilling in the Pound for all Subscriptions not exceeding Five Guineas, and Sixpence in the Pound for all Subscriptions above Five Guineas. This Request was granted in consideration of Mr Parke's Diligence and Assiduity; The Bond being in some Respects improper, Mr Hodson was desired to prepare a new one.

The Chairman read two Letters from the President of the College, informing that a Gun had been Fired on the 1st and 4th of January, into the front Parlour of the College.

Read Mr Hodson's Letter in Answer to the above, also one of the Printed Bills, of which an 100 were [9v] sent to be posted up, offering a Reward of £20 for apprehending, and bringing to Justice, the Offender, or Offenders.

Read a Letter from the Revd Mr Nicholson informing that the increase of Students, required more Tables, Looking Glasses and Candlesticks: also stating that the Washing could not now conveniently be done at home, and requesting it might be put out. Mrs Cole who does the Mending, will take the Washing at Nine pence per Week for each Student which was agreed to.

Read the following Bills received from Mr Nicholson, Viz.

	£	s	d
Thomas Knightly, Bricklayer	8	15	0
Thomas Woollard, Smith	3	16	7
Stephen Leighton, Plumber & Glazier	6	1	7

They were ordered to be paid, but as several of the [10r] Matters charged, had been done without the knowledge of the Trustees, Mr Hodson was desired to write to Mr Nicholson, to acquaint the Trustees and Committee at their monthly Meetings; of whatever might be wanted in future.

Read a Bill for Quilt and Blankets, and a Bill for six Students Gowns, which have been paid.

Read a Letter to Lady Anne Erskine from Henley on Thames; giving a satisfactory Account of Mr Jones, a Student, preaching there with Acceptance, during the late Vacation.

Read a Letter to the same from Knaresborough, Yorkshire, of a Person being a Candidate for the College: it was thought necessary that my Lady be pleased to answer the same, and enquire into the young Mans principles etc. against the ensuing monthly Meeting.
[10v]

Mr Hodson inform'd the Meeting of Joseph Lancaster, a young Man aged only 15, or 16 years, whom Mr Pontin recommended to the College, The same was called in, and examined respecting his conversion and Call to the Ministry; A Letter was read which intimated a well wish to him, if accepted: but there appearing no sufficient evidence of his Call; he was unanimously rejected for the present.

Mr Hodson was desired (previous to the next monthly Meeting) to write a Title for the intended Board of Legacies; to be put up at the College, and Mr Batley was desired, to enquire of a Frame-maker, what is the proportional Size, and the Expence.

Monthly Meeting March 5th 1794

[11r]
Present: Messrs Burnell, Holmes, Langston, Hodson, Butcher, Bridgman, Cooper, Campigne, Astle*, Oldham.

Read, and confirmed the Minutes of the last Meeting.

Read the Benefactions left to the College: intended to be inscribed on a Board to place in the College.

Read a copy of the Letter, Mr Hodson wrote to Mr Nicholson, agreeable to the last monthly Meeting.

Tuesday the 25th instant was fixed for the public Examination of the Students at the College, and the Ministers to be invited were agreed to be the Revd Mr Eyre, the Revd Dr Ford, and the Revd Mr Caldwell, and in the case of either of those Gentlemen not going, the Revd Mr Crole and the Revd Mr Platt were to be invited.

[11v]

Read, and approved the Form of the Notices, for the said public Examination, and the ensuing Quarterly Meeting. Also read, and approved the State of the Society and College 500 of which were ordered to be printed, and one, or more sent to each Subscriber.

Mr Hodson produced Messrs Hughes and Walsh Bill [3] for Books, Printing and Paper to the Amount of £8-15-6 which he had paid; the same being right.

Mr Hodson reported; that the President humbly requests an Assistant for the younger students: Resolved that Mr Bickerdike be granted him for the purpose, and that £10 per Annum be allowed him as a Salary.

Resolved further: That whenever the Number of Students exceed Twelve, the President be allowed an Assistant; the Head Scholar for the Time being to be always elected to that Office, if he chooses to accept it, and there is no reasonable objection to him.

[12r]

Mr Hodson informed the Meeting that half a Years Salary was due to the Secretary, when the same passed with leave to be paid.

Public Examination of the Students
at the College at Cheshunt on
Tuesday March 25th 1794

Revd Mr Crole and Revd Mr Platt, Examiners together with the President.

The Students being all in their Gowns, were ranged along the great Room on the left hand side from the lower to the upper end in the following Order, which was according to their degress in Learning Viz: Mr Macdonald, Horn, Parry, James, Chamberlain, Morgan, Winter, Bradley, Jones, Robertson, Kemp, Davies, Bickerdike. The President in his Robes was seated in the Centre, opposite the Students, with Mr Crole on his right hand and Mr Platt on his left; and the six Trustees [12v] who were present, Viz: Messrs Oldham, Weatherill, Hodson, Langston, Batley and Astle were seated three to the right of Mr Crole, and three to the left of Mr Platt. the rest of the Company sat immediately behind them and consisted of the following, Viz:

Mr S. Bridgman)
Mr Burnell)
Mr Butcher, Senior)
Mr Compigni) Members of the Assistant
Mr Cooper) Committee
Mr Fyffe)
Mr Rowton)

Mr Batley Junior
Mr Baxter and Mrs Baxter
Mr Blundell
Mr R. Butcher Junior
Mr Carpenter and Mrs Carpenter
Mr Emerson
Mr Hall
Mr Rooke, Mr Rowton's Friend
Mr Thomas Wontner

[13r]

Soon after 10 we began with singing Hymn 81st Page 126th Love divine all Loves excelling.[4]

And Mr Crole pray'd fervently, for the Institution and all concern'd in it.

The first six Students then read each a little English and were examined in the English Grammar.

The next three read and construed Latin, and were examined in the Latin Grammar.

The next three, read the Greek Testament and gave the English and Mr Bickerdike read Greek and translated it into Latin. He also read a little in Horace.

Sung Captain of thine enlisted Host, and Mr Platt concluded with Prayer, about one o'Clock or a little after.

Quarterly General-Meeting
April 2 1794

Present: Messrs Holmes, Weatherill, Cooper, Oldham*, Langston, King, Astle, Francis, The Revd Mr Platt, [13v] Messrs Butterworth, Hodson, Fyffe, Burrell, Flower, Compigne, Butcher Senior, Guriller, Emerson, Cole, Jones, Dornford, Dupont, Mr William Knight, Newcombe [5]

The Revd Mr Platt began with Prayer.

Read and confirmed the Minutes of the last General Meeting.

Mr Fyffe, one of the Auditors, made his Report that Mr Thomas Wontner and himself had examined the Treasurers Account for the year 1793, and found the same right, by which it appears that there is a Balance in hand of £31-4-5 besides £500 3 Per Cent Consols.

Read two Letters from the Revd Mr Nicholson, informing of a Gun twice fired into the Parlour of the College the 1st and 4th of January.

Read the posting Bill which the Trustees order'd to be printed on that occasion offering a Reward of Twenty Pounds, on Conviction of the Offender. [14r] No discovery has been made, nor any further violence committed.

Read a Letter from a Mr Hewitt of Henley on Thames, to Lady Anne Erskine, in favour of Mr Jones the Student, who preached there during the Christmas Vacation. Mr Hodson reported that Mr Bradley also had preached at Halesworth, and Mr Bickerdike at Sheerness, with much acceptance.

Read a Letter from Mr Nicholson expressing sundry Wants, and requesting that the Washing might be put out, as it is now inconvenient to have it done at home; all which has been complied with.

Mr Hodson reported that Mr Nicholson had by reason of the increase of Students requested an Assistant, and that the same had been granted: That Mr Bickerdike was elected to that Office: with a Salary of Ten Pounds per Annum.
[14v]
The Chairman read the Presidents Quarterly Report, which was much in favor of the Students, and the Revd Mr Platt reported the satisfaction the Revd Mr Crole and himself received at the public Examination of the Students on Tuesday the 25th of March, wherein their own diligence, and the great Attention of their Tutor appeared very conspicuous. Mr Hodson moved that the Thanks of this Meeting be given to the Revd Mr Crole and the Revd Mr Platt, for their kind Attendance on that occasion; as the examining Ministers, which was unanimously agreed to.

Resolved, that the Society dine at the Kings-head at Enfield, at the next Anniversary in August, there being no Room large enough at the Swan, at Waltham Cross.

The following Gentlemen were so kind as to accept of the office of Steward for this Year [15r] Viz: Messrs Francis, Holmes, Cooper, Compigne, Butcher Junior.

The Revd Mr Platt concluded with Prayer.

CHESHUNT COLLEGE

Monthly Meeting, 7 May 1794

Present: Messrs Weatherill, Cooper, Hodson*, Holmes, Butcher Senior, Rowton, Batley, Burnell, The Revd Mr Platt, Messrs Astle, Towers, [6] The Revd Mr David Jones, Messrs Fyffe, Dupont, Silver.

The Revd Mr Jones began with Prayer.

Read a Letter from the Revd Mr Nicholson being a Report of the Probationers, whose time of Probation is expired viz Messrs James, Macdonald, Chamberlain and Horn. The Report was much in favor of James, Horn, and Chamberlain, who are possessed of better natural Abilities than Mr Macdonald, of whom [15v] Mr Nicholson stood in some doubt at first, but since Mr Bickerdike's being appointed Assistant, Mr Nicholson has taken peculiar pains with Mr Macdonald, which have been rewarded with an Improvement beyond his Expectation. They were called in separately, and interrogated by the Chairman assisted by the two Ministers present. They appeared in general to have been exercised with doubts respecting their Call to the Ministry, which nevertheless they cannot give up, being all determined by the Grace of God to persevere; Mr James particularly seem'd to question whether he ought to spend his time in the Acquisition of Learning: and whether he ought not rather to be immediately employed in the Work of the Ministry. Mr Jones offered him suitable Encouragements to persevere in the line the providence of God had brought him in, assuring him he would reap the Benefit of it, when called out to public Work.

[16r]

After they had been all examined respecting their Call to the Ministry, and their Approbation of the 15 doctrinal Articles; they were all called in together; and informed: that they were unanimously admitted as Students. And they were allowed 6 shillings each for their Coach-hire from, and to the College.

Lady Anne Erskine sent in Extracts of Letters, from the Revd Mr Teissier [7] Revd Mr Waring and Mrs Oldfield respecting a Mr William Mather of Newcastle upon Tyne, a Candidate for the College. Mr Hodson was desired to write to Mr Teissier for some further Information concerning him, and to request that He would hear him pray, and speak in the Company of a few Friends and give his Opinion of his Abilities.

Mr Dupont produced the dimensions of the Piers at the College where the Inscription Boards are to be placed. Agreed to get an Estimate of the Expence against the next Monthly Meeting. Mr Dupont also reported the want of Steps to the Pulpit at Cheshunt and a Seat for the Minister; to rest on after preaching [16v] both which Mr Dupont was desired to order.

Monthly Meeting 4 June 1794

Present: Messrs Lanston, Burnell, Holmes, Weatherill*, Batley, Compigne, Hodson, Butcher, Cooper, Astle, Dupont, Rowton, Francis.

Read and confirm'd the Minutes of the last Monthly Meeting.

The Chairman read the dimensions of the Boards for the inscriptions of the Benefactors at the College. Mr Hodson was desired to see Mr Patterson of Bishopsgate Street, concerning the Painting and Writing of it.

Resolved that the Vacation at the College begin on Monday [17r] the 13th of July.

Read the Copy of Mr Hodson's Letter to the Revd Mr Teissier at Newcastle concerning Mr William Mather to which no Answer has been received.

Resolved that a Letter Book be provided for such Letters, as may thought fit to be inscribed therein [sic], and that the Letters already received, be selected for insertion.[8]

Thursday 19 June. A Special Meeting of the Trustees was held in consequence of a Complaint, exhibited by the President, against William Jones one of the Students, whose Conduct has been very inconsistent with his Character and Profession.

All the Trustees were present: Mr Dupont went to Prayer.

Read the Revd Mr Nicholson's Letter, giving an Account of the Matter complained of: after considering the same it was resolved [17v] That Mr Dupont and Mr Astle be desired to go to the College Tomorrow Morning, and there make particular Enquiry of Mr Nicholson, and of the Servants into the whole of Mr Jones's improper Conduct, and report, at a future Meeting to be held, the result of their Investigation.

Monday the 30th of June, The Trustees met again - all present except Mr Dupont who is out of Town.

Read Messrs Dupont and Astle's Report, which confirms the Account already given by Mr Nicholson in its fullest Extent. Mr Jones was called in and addressed by Mr Oldham with Christian Tenderness, and withal with much Plainness and

Faithfulness. Mr Jones did not in the least extenuate his fault, but appeared much humbled and broken down under a sense of it.

[18r]

We had the satisfaction however to find that Mr Jones's Misconduct had been confined to the College alone, and that he has not been permitted to fall so as to commit the gross Act of Sin. It was proposed by Mr Oldham and agreed to by all, that Mr Jones should be desired to write the present feelings of his Heart in a Letter address'd to the Trustees, and another to the President, and send them under Cover to Mr Hodson on Wednesday, and appear before the Trustees again, on Thursday Evening, at 7 o'Clock.

Thursday the 3rd of July - The Trustees met again. Present Messrs Oldham, Hodson, Langston, Batley and Astle.

Mr Hodson brought the two Letters Mr Jones had written to the Trustees and President, which were read and appeared to be the genuine language of a true Penitent.

The whole of the Case was considered and it was thought that absolute Expulsion was a Punishment too severe for the Crime, [18v] and yet it was necessary a proper Censure should be passed by way of Example to the other Students; as well as to express the Trustees Disapprobation of his Conduct to himself: It was therefore resolved

1st   That Mr Jones be suspended from the College for six weeks, during which time he shall not go out any where to preach, nor ever go to the College, but that he spend the time in Retirement, in studying the Scripture and Prayer.

2nd   That his two Letters should be sent to the President inclosed in one which Mr Oldham will write, to be publickly read by him to all the Students.

3rd   That on Friday the 22nd of August Mr Jones may come to the Trustees and give an Account of his Conduct during the time of his Suspension, which if satisfactory, they will readmit him, that he may not suffer the disgrace of being absent at the Anniversary.

[19r]

Mr Jones was impressed with gratitude on receiving this Sentence, but at the same time declared he did not know what to do for a Subsistence during the Suspension, as his Father is a very poor Man, and he has no friends to go to. In consideration of his Circumstances the Trustees agreed to allow him one shilling a week for a Lodging, and seven shillings a week for Subsistence, which was a favor, he very thankfully acknowledged.

Quarterly General-Meeting, 2 July

Present: Messrs Batley, Cooper, Andrews, Mr Peter Duthoit, Messrs Franklin, Weatherill, Langston*, Holmes, Ravenshear, Burnell, Jones, Burridge, King, Francis, The Revd Mr Platt, Messrs Hodson, Walsh Senior, Astle, Butcher Senior, Rowton, Fyffe, Butcher Junior, Mr William Hall, Mr Parker.

The Revd Mr Platt began with Prayer.

[19v]

Read and confirm'd the Minutes of the last General Meeting.

Read the Revd Mr Nicholson's Quarterly Report.

Read a Letter from the same, in favor of the Probationers, lately admitted fully as Students.

Read Extracts from three Letters respecting Mr William Mather, of Newcastle upon Tyne, a Candidate for the College; also Mr Mather's own Letter to Lady Anne Erskine, and a Copy of Mr Hodson's to the Revd Mr Teissier concerning him.

The following Gentlemen were so kind as to accept of the Office of Stewards for this Year, in addition to the five chosen at the last Meeting: Viz: Mr P. Duthoit, Mr William Hall, Mr John King, Mr George Burridge, Mr Walsh Senior and to these ten are to be added Mr John Wontner and Mr Emerson if they will accept the Office.

[20r]

The Chairman acquainted the Meeting: that the Anniversary is to be this Year, on Wednesday the 27th of August, and that the Revd Mr Haweis is to preach on that Occasion.[9]

The Revd Mr Platt concluded with Prayer.

Monthly Meeting 6th August 1794

Present: Messrs Langston*, Burnell, Batley, Cooper, Holmes, Butcher, Oldham, The Revd Mr Platt, Messrs Dupont, Hodson, Astle, Weatherill, Compigne, Burridge.

The Revd Mr Platt began with Prayer.

Read and confirm'd the Minutes of the last Monthly Meeting.

Read the Minutes of three Meetings of the Trustees, on the 19th and 30th of June and 3rd of July [20v] respecting William Jones one of the Students, who has been guilty of improper Conduct and is in consequence therof, suspended from College for six weeks.

Read also the Minutes of the last Quarterly Meeting.

The Chairman reported that it was agreed by the Trustees; to have two Sermons preached at Spa fields Chapel, on Sunday the 24th instant, for the Benefit of the College: that in the Morning by the Revd Mr Platt, and that in the Evening by the Revd Mr Crole; as they were the two Ministers, who were so kind to attend the public Examination.

Mr Hodson produced the Revd Mr Nicholson's Quarterly Account to Midsummer, which with Taxes paid and Mrs Cole's Washing Bill, amounts to £108-3-5. He also brought Clement Barker's Bill for Carpenter's Work done at the College [21r] in fitting up the additional Rooms for the Students and other Things; amounting to £34-2-5. It was thought a fair bill and ordered to be paid.

Mr William Mather's Letter to Lady Anne Erskine dated the 7th of May was again read, and as no Answer has been received by Mr Hodson to the Letter he wrote to Mr Teissier, concerning Mr Mather: Mr Hodson was desired to write to Mr Mather himself.

The Chairman reported; that a Trespass had been committed by Mr Josiah Eburne, on the Premises of the College, by breaking open a Door way through the Wall, near the River, and also by erecting a Cowhouse, partly upon the said Wall.

Read a Copy of the Notice sent to Mr Eburne by the Trustees.

Mr Hodson reported that he had seen Mr Eburne; who said that what he had done was by Mr Nicholson's Consent, and for his Accommodation. [21v] Resolved to let the matter rest 'till the Trustees have seen the Premises, and have conversed with Mr Nicholson respecting what is done.

The Revd Mr Platt reported, that contrary to the Resolution of the Quarterly Meeting of the 1st of January last: the Students still frequent the House of Mr Williams, for that Three of them had been there the first week in July.

Resolved that Mr Hodson be desired to write to Mr Nicholson sending him a Copy of the said Resolution and requesting him, to enforce it, and to inform the Students, that whoever disobeyed it, would be dealt with in a proper manner.

Thursday 21 August 1794
At a special Meeting of the Trustees
Present all; but Mr Langston

[22r]

The six weeks of William Jones's Suspension being expired; he attended this Evening, and being interrogated by Mr Oldham, how he found the present frame of his Mind, and where he had been, and how employed himself - answer'd that he had been greatly distress'd in mind, and very ill in body, part of the time, but had been much relieved since his two letters, had been sent to Mr Nicholson, who had thereupon wrote a few lines to him: That he had the same Views of his Sin, as when he met us last, and hoped he should be kept from relapsing into it: That he had been kindly received by Mr John Bryan of Newgate Street, at whose house he had resided, that he had attended preaching and had employed a good deal of his time in reading and Prayer.

Mr Bryan himself attended, confirmed Jones's Account and said moreover that his Compunction had been very great, but that he had been comfortably liberated under a Sermon of Mr Davis [22v] in Bartholomew Close. That he had generally led the Worship of his Family, and that his Conduct had been consistent, and becoming his Profession.

Mr Jones was admonished and exhorted to much Watchfulness and Prayer and unanimously readmitted.

Monthly Meeting 3 Sep: 1794

Present: Messrs Holmes, Weatherill, Cooper, Butcher, Compigne, Astle*, Hodson.

Read and confirm'd the Minutes of the last monthly Meeting.

Read also the Minutes of the Special Meeting of Trustees the 21st of August respecting the readmission of William Jones.
[23r]
Mr Hodson reported that the Revd Mr Platt and the Revd Mr Crole Preached two Sermons for the Benefit of the College at Spa Fields Chapel the 24th of August and the Collection amounted to the Sum of £60^{10}. Also that the Anniversary was held on the 27th Ultimo at the College when the Revd Mr Haweis preached. Two of the Students Bickerdike and Davis delivered each an Oration in English and Kemp one in Latin which after he delivered in English. The Anniversary was well attended.

Mr Hodson produc'd a Catalogue of the Books left by the Revd Mr Cureton which are as follows
>Henry on the Bible, 2 Vols Folio
>Cruden's Concordance, 1 Vol Quarto
>Cocordance to the Apocrypha, in Marble Cover
>Brooke's Gazetteer 1 Vol Octavo
>Claudes Essay on the Composition of a Sermon
>2 Vol: Octavo
>Legh's Critica Sacra 1 Vol: Octavo [23v]

Part of Hebrew Bible 1 Vol: Octavo
History of the Churches 3 Ditto Ditto
Prideaux's Connection 4 Ditto Ditto
Grant's Sermons 1 Ditto Ditto small
Fulfilling of Scripture 1 Ditto Ditto Ditto
Hervey's Meditations 1 Ditto Duodecimo
Young's Night Thoughts 1 Ditto Ditto
Social Religion 1 Ditto Ditto
Testament Greek and Latin 1 Ditto Ditto
Marshall on Sanctification 1 Ditto Ditto
Aldridge's Hymns
Addington's Tunes
Principles of the Christian Religion
Perry's English Dictionary
Scriptures Sufficiency
Rowe's Devout Exercises very small 24mo

Read a Copy of Mr Hodsons letter to Mr William Mather of Newcastle upon Tyne, to which no Answer has been received.
[24r]
Mr Hodson informed the Meeting that half a Years Salary was due to the Secretary, which was ordered to be paid.

Quarterly General-Meeting
1st Oct: 1794

Present: Mr Cooper, Mr P. Duthoit, Messrs Butcher Junior, Burridge, Hall, King, Hodson, Mousley, Mr Edward Cooper, Messrs Langston, Batley*, Compigne, Brown, The Revd Mr Platt, Messrs Weatherill, Rowton, Walsh Senior, Burnell, Mr William Jones, Messrs Gaveller, Butcher Senior, Enoch Hodgkinson Esqr, Mr Joseph Wilson, Mr Shadd.

The Revd Mr Platt began with Prayer.
[24v]
Read and confirm'd the Minutes of the last General Meeting.

The Chairman inform'd the Meeting that no Quarterly Report had been sent by Mr Nicholson, and that two Sermons had been preach'd for the benefit of the College on the 24th of August, by the Revd Mr Platt and the Revd Mr Crole, and that the Collection amounted to the Sum of £60. Also that the Anniversary was held on the 27th of August and the Revd Mr Haweis preaching on that Occasion; The Chairman moved that the Thanks of this Meeting be given to the three Ministers which was unanimously agreed to.

Thanks were also voted to the Stewards for their Assiduity and Attention in providing an excellent dinner on that day.

[25r]

Two of the Assistant Committee Viz: Messrs Everard and Tilney having never attended were of course out of Office at this Meeting. Mr Duthoit and Mr Silver had each attended only once and it being represented by Mr Hodson that Mr Silver is generally out of Town on a Wednesday Evening, and consequently that there is more probability of Mr Duthoit attending in future, Mr Silver was accordingly fixed on to go out and Mr Duthoit to remain in. The three new Members chosen were Mr William Bell of Spa Fields Chapel, Mr Henry Munn of Sion and Mr John Dudman of Mulberry Gardens.

The Revd Mr Platt concluded with Prayer.

[25v]

Monthly Meeting 5th Nov: 1794

Present: Messrs Weatherill*, Bell, Astle, Langston, Burnell, Hodson.

Read and confirmed the Minutes of the last Monthly Meeting; also the Minutes of the last Quarterly Meeting.

Read the Revd Mr Nicholson's Quarterly Report which was very satisfactory.

Read the Quarterly Bill and Receipt for the same Amounting to the Sum of £101-4-11.

Monthly Meeting 3 December 1794

Present: Messrs Cooper, Bridgman, Langston, Hodson*, Burnell, Holmes, [26r] Weatherill, Astle, Butcher.

Mr Hodson reported, that as the Revd Mr Nicholson had inadvertently given his consent to the Door way broke through the Garden Wall by Mr Eburne; the Trustees had desired him to get the same brick'd up again: and that they would pay for it.

The Chairman reported that John Lloyd Esqr[11] of Bath whas [sic] nominated in the Countess of Huntingdon's Will to be a Trustee for the College, departed this life [blank] of last month; That his Death occasions no Vacancy in the Trust, because the original number of Seven is still compleat, and Mr Lloyds Nomination has been always considered: either as arising from Lady Huntingdon's not recollecting [26v] that the Vacancy occasioned by Dr Lyon's Resignation was filled up by her Appointment of Mr Astle; or at most: it was a Mark of Respect from her Ladyship to Mr Lloyd for his life only.

The Chairman reported that a Donation of Ten pounds had been paid into the hands of the Collector, for the use of the College by Mr Chapman Junior.

Read Mr Wightman's Bill, for the Inscription Boards: and ordered the same to be paid.

The Chairman reported: that he had received £20 each, from the Lady's Emily and Caroline Hervey.

Resolved that the Christmas Vacaction at the [27r] College; commence on Friday the 19th instant and continue 'till Monday the 12th of January.

The Chairman read a Letter address'd to him from Mr Hutchins, relative to the manner of his leaving the College in August 1792: on which reference was had to the Minutes, and to former Letters on that subject; Mr Hutchins wish'd the Vote of Censure passed on him on that occasion to be rescinded: but it was resolved that the present Letter contains only some Extenuation, but not a Justification of his Conduct: and therefore to rescind the Vote would be improper.

Quarterly General Meeting
7th Jan: 1795

[27v]
Present: Messrs Batley, Langston, Holmes, Astle, Flower, Burnell, Oldham*, Jones, Hodson, The Revd Mr Platt, Messrs Cooper, Burridge, Bridgman, Butcher Junior, Dupont, King, Hall, Francis, The Revd Mr Nicholson.

The Revd Mr Platt began with Prayer.

The Chairman read the Revd Mr Nicholson's two Quarterly Reports; as that for the last Meeting, did not come to hand in time to be then read.

The Chairman inform'd the Meeting; that five of the Students have been sent out this Vacation by Lady Anne Erskine, Viz: Mr Bickerdike to Derby, Mr Bradley to Woodbridge, Mr Jones to Arundel, Mr Davies to Goring, and [28r] Mr Winter to Henley.

The Chairman read a Letter from Mr John Carnson, a Candidate for the College, and Mr Hodson's Answer to the same.

The Chairman read a Letter from Mr Parke to Mr Hodson: informing of some Subscriptions not paid, and some Subscribers deceas'd.

Mr Jasper Thomas Holmes and Mr William Hall were chosen Auditors for this Year.

The Revd Mr Nicholson being present the Chairman desired to know; if all the Students paid due Attention to their Studies, and made a suitable Improvement. By Mr Nicholson's Answers, which were corroborated by the Testimony of Mr Dupont, it appeared Mr Bradley does not improve as might be expected from his standing either in point of Learning, or Preaching, and it appeared to them both; that his continuance in College [28v] was not likely to be of any great Use to him, or Credit to the Institution; at the same time they both bore Testimony to his excellent moral Character, and suitable Demeanor at College. It was left to the Trustees, to consider of what was proper to be done in this Case.

The Revd Mr Nicholson concluded with Prayer.

Monthly Meeting 4th Feb: 1795

Present: Messrs Langston*, Holmes, Astle, Bell, Hodson, Batley, Burnell, Butcher, Oldham, Bridgman, Dupont, Duthoit, Compigne.

Read and confirm'd the Minutes of the [29r] last Monthly Meeting, and read the Minutes of the last General Quarterly Meeting.

The Chairman reported; that Mr Bickerdike had preached at Derby, during the late Vacation: with much acceptance and approbation.

The Chairman reported that Mr George Towers was dead; but had remembered the Institution with a Legacy of £100.

Read a Letter from Lady Anne Erskine to the Trustees; thanking them for all their assistance; and praying their further help: if any of the Students could be spared: to supply Churches wanting Ministers.

The Chairman reported that Mr Bradley had been granted to her Ladyship: and was sent out.

Read a Letter from Lady Anne, containing Extracts of Letters from Derby, Arundel [29v] and Goring expressing satisfaction with the Students, who were sent to those Places in the late Vacation.

Read a Letter from Lady Anne Erskine, containing a Copy of a Letter from Mr Carnson who wishes to be admitted into the College.

Read a Letter from Mr William Mather, desiring to know the Times of Meeting; and Mr Hodson's answer thereto.

Read a Letter from Mr Nicholson: respecting the allowance for Boarding Students: being at present £20 each; which he says is inadequate and requests it may be augmented to £25 each: which was agreed to; and is to commence, from Christmas last.

Read the Quarterly Bill from Mr Nicholson, amounting to the sum of £102-1-11 1/2 and the Washing Bill £7-0-10 which the Treasurer has paid.[12]

Read Mr Patterson's Bill for Painting and Writing the Inscription Boards: which was ordered to be paid Amount £9-2-0.

Read Mr Stephen Leighton's Bill, Plumber and Glazier: which was ordered to be paid: amounting to £6-15-5 but his allowance of 16s. per C: for old Lead; was thought to be too little.

Read Mr Barker the Carpenters Bill: Amount £2-8-6, and Hughes and Walsh's bill £6-7-6 both ordered to be paid.

Mr Oldham reported that Mr Chapman Junior's Donation of £10 lately received: had been apply'd for by his Parents to be returned: alledging that the young Man is not Compos-Mentis, which evidently appear'd on Monday Evening, when he was before the School Committee, and had £20 return'd, which he had sent in a [30v] Letter to that Institution - Resolved therefore; that the said £10 be return'd.

Monthly Meeting 4th Mar: 1795

Present: Messrs Langston, Burnell, Weatherill, Hodson, Butcher, Cooper, Batley*, Astle, Francis.

Read, and confirm'd the Minutes of the last Monthly Meeting.

Read Mr Hodson's Letter to Mr Nicholson; acquainting him that his Request, for an augmentation of allowance for the Board of Students was complied with - Read also Mr Nicholson's Letter of Thanks for the same.
[31r]

Read Lady Anne's Letter, on Mr Morgan's leaving the College; and Mr Morgan's Letter to that Lady with his Apology for so doing.

Mr Langston mov'd; and it was resolv'd; that a Letter of Censure pass on Mr Morgan's manner of leaving the College; and Mr Hodson was desired to write to him.

Read a Letter from Mr Tessier respecting Mr William Mather, and Mr John Carnson; the former of whom he strongly recommends but is not satisfied that the latter has ever experienced a work of Grace on his Heart - Resolved therefore, that as Lady Anne is about to write to Carnson's Father, she be requested to prevent the Son's coming up to Town.

Read a Letter from a Mr James Hill, of Newcastle to Lady Anne, and a Recommendation of him, as a Candidate for the College by Mrs Oldfield; but it not appearing from Mr Hill's own Letter [31v] that he is a proper Subject for the College; Mr Hodson was requested to write him very concisely to that purport.

Read a Letter from Mr William Jones a Student; for leave to Preach for the Revd Mr Boddily of Wallingford a few weeks - It was considered that granting this; might be attended with disagreeable Consequences, as it might prove a Precedent for other Applications; would be a great Interruption to Study: and break in, upon the Order of the College - So Mr Hodson was desired to write him: that it could not be complied with.

Resolved that on the Revd Mr Haweis coming to Town: he be requested to Preach a Sermon at Bath; for the benefit of the College.

Mr Hodson reported that half a year's salary was due to the Secretary; which was ordered to be paid.

[32r]

Quarterly General-Meeting
April 1st 1795

Present: Messrs Langston, Hodson*, Cooper, Holmes, Andrew, John Bryan, The Revd Mr Platt, Messrs Astle, Fyffe, Batley, Dornford, Butcher Junior, King, William Hall, Bell, Newcombe, Dupont.

The Revd Mr Platt began with Prayer.

Read and confirm'd, the Minutes of the last Quarterly General-Meeting.

The Auditors reported that they had examined the Treasurers Accounts for the last Year, and found a Balance agreeable to the printed Statement of £19-1-4½.

The Chairman informed the Meeting that Mr William Bradley had been sent to Newark by Lady Anne Erskine, where he meets with Acceptance.
[32v]
Read a Letter from Mr Nicholson to Mr Hodson on the Allowance for the Board of Students, requesting an Augmentation of Five pounds per Annum for each Student. On Account of the Dearness of Provisions etc. - also Mr Hodson's Answer thereto and Mr Nicholson's thankful acknowledgement for his Request being complied with.

Read Mr Nicholson's Quarterly Report, which is in commendation of the Application, Diligence and Improvement of the Students.

The Chairman reported; that the public Examination of the Students this Year, is intended to be in May; of which Notice will be given to the Subscribers.

93

The Chairman read Mr Morgan's Letter of apology to Lady Anne Erskine, for his abrupt manner of leaving the College (which he did without leave) at the last Christmas Vacation.

[33r]

Read a Letter from Mr James Hill of Newcastle, to Lady Anne Erskine, as a Candidate for the College. And Mr Hodson's answer thereto, not encouraging him to come.

Read a Letter from Mr Tessier, respecting Mr William Mather, and Mr John Carnson, the former of whom he recommends as a lively experimental Christian; but doubts whether the Latter has experienced any Change of Heart!

Read a Letter from Lady Anne Erskine to Mr Hodson, informing of Mr William Mather being in Town. The Chairman reported he had seen him this day, and it was agreed that the Trustees and Committee meet 'tomorrow Evening for his Examination.

Mr Batley informed the Meeting: that Mr George Towers deceased had left a Legacy of one hundred pounds to the College.

Read a Letter from Mr William Jones a Student, requesting leave to go for 3 or 4 weeks, to preach for the Revd Mr [33v] Boddily, of Wallingford, and Mr Hodson's answer thereto - It was thought by the Trustees and Committee, that such as Absence between the Vacations was improper.

Mr Langston mov'd; that it might be taken into consideration for two General Meetings in the Year, instead of four: as they are in general so thinly attended and there is so little Business to be done.

Mr Dupont reported: that it is the Wish of the Students; that they, or some of them: may be taught French; as they hope there will be a great Opening in France, for the preaching of the Gospel. Referr'd to the Trustees and Committee.

The Revd Mr Platt concluded with Prayer.

[34r]

Special Meeting of the Trustees and Committee
Thursday 2nd of April 1795

Present: Mr Oldham in the Chair. The Revd Mr Platt, Messrs Astle, Batley, Weatherill, Hodson, Butcher, Langston, Cooper, Francis, Burridge.

Mr Platt began with Prayer.

Mr William Mather, from Newcastle, attended this Meeting; and was very particularly examined respecting his Experience of a work of Grace on his Heart, and his Call to the Ministry: when it appeared to the satisfaction of all present; that he is a truly converted Man, and though naturally of a very bashful turn of mind, as to praying, or speaking in public, yet his Impulse of the Work of the Ministry is irresistable; He was therefore unanimously admitted as a Probationer, and went to College, on Monday the 6th instant, being Easter Monday. His Age 25.

Special Meeting of the Trustees
Thursday 21st of April 1795

[34v]

Present: Revd Mr Caldwell in the Chair, Messrs Weatherill, Langston, Batley, Hodson, Butcher, Bell.

Mr John Carnson, from Annan in Dumfries-shire, aged 19, or 20, he cannot tell which; was born in Ireland, his Father was called about 7 years ago: to be the Minister of Annan.

This young Man heard a Mr Steele, in Ireland: under whom he received about 5 years ago, his first serious Impressions.

After a long Examination, the Trustees could not obtain a full Conviction, of his being called to the Ministry, nor could they totally reject him. It was therefore - Resolved, that he be sent to the College 'till the public Examination, which is to be in May - By which time it is hoped: the Lord will make it apparent, whether he is a proper [35r] Subject for the College or not. Mr Hodson was desired to write a suitable Letter, to Mr Nicholson for him, to take with him tomorrow.

Monthly Meeting 6th May 1795

Present: Messrs Holmes, Weatherill*, Batley, Burnell, Cooper, Butcher, Astle, Duthoit, Hodson, Bridgman.

Read and confirm'd the Minutes of the last monthly meeting; read also the Minutes of the last Quarterly General Meeting: and read and confirmed the Minutes of the Special Meetings of the 2nd and 21st of April.

Read Mr Nicholson's quarterly Bill and Receipt, including Ann Coles: for Washing etc. [35v] Amount £107-19-4.

Mr Hodson reported that the New River Company had ask'd leave to take down the Fishing House on the Bank of the River in the College Garden, which had been done by leave of the Trustees.[13]

Read a Letter from Mr James Brotherton Aged 21 of Arundell to Lady Anne Erskine; from her Ladyships Knowledge of him, it was thought proper: that he may be desired to attend the next monthly meeting.

Read Knightley the Bricklayer's Bill Amount £17-17-8. Woollard the Smiths Bill Amount £1-10-6 and Webb the Cabinet-maker's bill Amount £6-1-0 which were ordered to be paid.

The public Examination of the Students at the College; was fix'd for the 20th or 27th Instant as is [36r] most convenient to the Revd Mr Haweis, to whom Lady Anne will write.

Monthly Meeting 3 June 1795

Present: Messrs Hodson, Langston*, Astle, Batley, Cooper, Butcher, Burnell, Bell, Oldham.

Read and confirm'd the Minutes of the last Meeting.

Mr Hodson reported that the publick Examination of the Students was on Wednesday the 27th of last Month by the Revd Mr Haweis:

Present: The Revd Mr Platt

Messrs Oldham	)	
Weatherill	)	
Hodson	)	
Langston	)	Trustees
Batley	)	
Astle	)	
[36v]		
Messrs Butcher	)	
Burnell	)	
Bridgman	)	
Cooper	)	Assistant Committee
Fyffe	)	
Rowton	)	

Messrs John Bryan
Butcher Senior
Baxter
George
And Mr Ritchie, a Friend of Mr Fyffe's

The Examination began soon after eleven and continued 'till near two - The Result was: that Mr Haweis was of opinion, the Students had made as great a progress as might be expected: and that it appear'd to him, as it did also to Mr Nicholson and Mr Platt; that Mr Bickerdike and Mr Robertson might now be sent out, and Mr Davies might go in a few Months: if there should be an opening for him.

Read Mr Nicholson's Account of Mr John Carnson, together with the joint opinion's of the Revd Mr Haweis [37r] and Mr Platt, Read also that part of the Minutes of the Special Meeting on his account which relates to his conversion and call to the Ministry; which being still doubtful, the Trustees and Committee present were ask'd severally. He was also examined himself, but no further Evidence appearing, it was resolved he could not be admitted: which he was informed of, and acquiesced: but beg'd permission to return to the College a week or so, 'till he receiv'd a Letter from his Father.

Resolved that the Midsummer Vacation commence Friday the 26th instant, and expires Monday July 19th.

Mr Brotherton was expected this Evening: but not being come to Town, his examination is deferred 'till August Meeting.

Mr Hodson reported, that he had paid Mr Bickerdike a Year and a Quarters salary, up to the 1st instant: and informed Mr Nicholson, that another Assistant would not be elected, until 13 Students were on the Foundation.

Read a Draft of a Testimonial for Mr Bickerdike [37v] which was approved, and ordered to be written handsomely on Vellum. Testimonials also are to be prepared for Mr Robertson, and Mr Bradley.

Mr Nicholson requested by the humble desire of the Students leaving College; that they may have Books. When it was agreed; that those who leave the College with approbation, might receive a Bible, a Concordance, and Hymn Book.

The Chairman reported that some necessary Repairs of Paper etc. are wanting at the College: Ordered the same be done against the ensuing Anniversary.

Agreed on Mrs Coles, requesting an advance in the price allowed for washing etc: that Mr Hodson pay her an Advance not exceeding 2d. per Week for each Student.

[38r]

Quarterly General-Meeting, 1 July 1795

Present: Messrs Langston, Batley, Cooper, Holmes, Stickland, Hodson*, King, Burnell, Compigne, Rowton, Dornford, Mousley, The Revd Mr Platt, Messrs Walsh Senior, William Hall, Jones, Dupont.

The Revd Mr Platt began with Prayer.

Read and confirm'd the Minutes of the last General Meeting.

The Chairman reported that the Examination of the Students at the College, was on the 27th of May last, and that the opinion of the Revd Mr Haweis, and Mr Platt, was that the Students had made as considerable a progress as could be expected, and that Messrs Bickerdike, Davies, and Robertson, were adjudged fit to be sent out, the former of whom is gone to Brighton, for a few weeks, and then is design'd for Derby.

[38v]

Read a Testimonial of Mr Bickerdike, which was as follows

To all to whom these Presents shall come. These are to certify, that Mr John Bickerdike, born in London Anno Domini 1774, was admitted into the Countess of Huntingdon's College, at Cheshunt in Hertfordshire, in August 1792, being the first Opening of the same; and continued there 'till June 1795, when it was judged by the Revd Thomas Haweis, Rector of Aldwinkle, in Northamptonshire, and the Revd William Francis Platt, Minister of Holywell Mount Chapel, in London, and by Us, whose Names are hereunto subscribed that He had acquired a competent and sufficient share of Learning, for the purpose for which the said College was instituted; and that his Knowledge and Experience of divine Truth are such, that He is properly qualified to go out as a Minister of the Gospel of our Lord Jesus Christ [39r] And We bear our united Testimony, that his Diligence and Attention to Study have been constant and close, and his Attainments considerable: insomuch that on the 1st of March 1794 He was appointed Assistant Tutor. And we further testify that his Conduct and Deportment during the whole of his Residence in College, was orderly, regular, and becoming his Christian Profession. Given under our hands this 20 day of June 1795

President of the College
Trustees

Read Mr Nicholson's Quarterly Report, which was very satisfactory.

The Chairman reported that Mr John Carnson not giving perfect satisfaction to the Trustees and Committee, had been admitted to the College, only for a few weeks, 'till the public Examination, and was dismissed [39v] from the same. Mr Nicholson's account of him was read, by which it appears; that neither himself nor Mr Haweis, nor Mr Platt, were satisfied of his Conversion or Call to the Ministry.

Mr Langston reported that Mr Bickerdike met with acceptance at Brighthelmstone.

The proposition of having only two General Meetings in the Year, instead of Four: was taken into Consideration; and in discussing that Matter it was thrown out that the General-Meetings might be held in the Committee Room of Spa-Fields-Chapel, and in that Case, they might continue to be Quarterly; which was unanimously agreed to.

The Anniversary this Year was fix'd for Monday the 24th of August, and the Secretary to give Notice thereof to the Stewards.

The Revd Mr Platt concluded with Prayer.

[40r]

Monthly Meeting, 5th August 1795

Present: Messrs Cooper, Holmes, Hodson, Astle, Weatherill*, Burnell, Batley, Butcher, Langston, Dupont, Rowton.

Read, and confirm'd the Minutes of the last Monthly Meeting: read also the Minutes of the last General Meeting.

Mr Hodson reported that Messrs Weatherill and Cooper waited on the Revd Mr Brewer to ask him to preach at the ensuing Anniversary; but that he declined on account of his Age (being 73) and also because if he complied he would be ask'd to preach for other Society's or Institutions - That in consequence of Mr Brewer's Non-compliance they had waited on the Revd Mr Crole, who kindly consented.
[40v]
Also that the Revd Mr Eyre would preach the Collection Sermon, on Sunday the 16th instant; and the Revd Mr Kirby in the Evening.

Mr Hodson reported that Mr Brotherton, who was expected this evening is rendered an improper Subject for the College, by a Complaint of the Rupture kind: which is likely to incapacitate him for preaching.

Read Mr Nicholsons Quarterly Bill, amounting with Mrs Coles bill for washing etc. to £119-9-7.

Read the Form of the Notice for the ensuing Anniversary.

Mr William Mathers time of probation being expired he came to Town, with a Letter from Mr Nicholson highly in his favor: was re-examined, and fully admitted as a Student.

Read a Copy of a Letter, found in the Room of Mr John Carnson, left at the College; wherein are some things which shew it was a kind Providence [41r] we did not admit him.

Mr Hodson reported concerning the Students having Books on leaving the College - That a Concordance, Bible and Hymn Book were not such Books as Mr Nicholson and the Students meant; but some useful Books of Learning, which they might have occasion for at times, to keep in Memory what they had learnt. Resolved that when a Student quits the College with approbation The President be desired to make out a List of such Books as he thinks needful, not exceeding forty shillings in Value; and they may be granted.

CHESHUNT COLLEGE

Monthly Meeting 2nd September 1795

Present: Messrs Cooper, Astle, Batley, Compigne, Langston*, Butcher, Holmes, Hodson, Bell, Rowton.

[41v]

Read, and confirm'd the Minutes of the last Monthly Meeting.

Read a Letter from Lady Anne Erskine to the Trustees recommending Mr John Meffen, Aged 19, a Member of the Congregation at Ipswich; for his Admission to the College. Also a suitable Letter from his Parents shewing their willingness either to part with him for the work of the Ministry, or to receive him again. He attended, was interrogated respecting his conversion, and call to the Ministry; which was satisfactory: but was referred to the Revd Mr Charles for further Examination: whose Report is to be received on Friday evening.

The Chairman reported that two Sermons had been preach'd for the benefit of the College at Spa Fields Chapel the 16th of August; that in the Morning by the Revd Mr Eyre, and that in the Evening by the Revd Mr Kirby; and that the [42r] Collection amounted to £62-14-6.[14] Also that the Anniversary was held at the College, on Monday August 24th and was well attended. When the Revd Mr Eyre began with Prayer; Three of the Students read the Psalms and Lessons for the day, Chamberlain and Jones delivered each an English Oration, and Kemp a Latin one, afterward in English. The Revd Mr Crole preach'd an excellent Sermon from Acts 11th and 26th.

Mr Hodson reported that the Legacy of £100 left by the late Mr George Towers was received.

At the Anniversary the Trustees saw Mr Josiah Eburne, and desired him to remove the Cow-House which he had erected on, and against the Wall of the Premises and part of the Freehold which he promised (but unpleasingly) to remove.

Resolved to prevent the like imposition or Trespass, that a Stone be placed within the Wall [42v] with this Inscription: The Boundary of the College Estate extends 4 Feet, 8 Inches in Breadth from this Wall, the whole Length of the Wall.

The Garden at the College being much neglected; it was Resolved that a Man be employed to put the same in Order against the next Anniversary: And it was thought he should be employed a Month to get it in compleat Order.

Adjourn'd Meeting Friday 4th Sep: 1795

Present: Messrs Hodson, Batley, Astle, Langston, Cooper, Weatherill, Butcher, The Revd Mr Charles, and the Revd Mr Jones.

The Revd Mr Charles delivered his opinion of Mr Meffen, after Examining him very [43r] fully which being satisfactory, he was unanimously admitted.

Mr Hodson reported that Mr Wright of Norwich had sent a Donation of £5-5-0.

Quarterly General Meeting
7 October 1795

Present: Messrs Hodson, Langston, Cooper, Weatherill, William Jones, Astle, Oldham*, Butcher, Butcher Junior, Walsh Senior, The Revd Mr Platt, Messrs Berridge, Compigne, Cole, Phillips, Brown, Bell, The Revd Mr Haweis, Messrs Rowton, Knight, Batley, Fyffe, Duthoit James, Duthoit Peter.

The Revd Mr Haweis began with Prayer.

Read and confirm'd the Minutes of the last General Meeting.
[43v]
The Revd Mr Haweis reported that very agreeable accounts have been received concerning those Students who have lately gone from College, and particularly concerning Mr Bradley's Acceptableness at Newark; where they are very unwilling to part with him.

Read a Letter from the Parents of Mr John Meffen, now a Probationer in the College, and a Letter from Lady Anne Erskine introducing the same.

Read a Letter from Mr Nicholson respecting Mr William Mather, on the expiration of his time of Probation: which was much in his favor, and Mr Hodson reported that he was fully admitted as a Student.

Read a Letter from Mr Josiah Eburne giving us Notice to repair our Fence.[15]

Read the Account of the Trustees visiting the College, on Wednesday Sept: 30th which is as follows [44r]

Wednesday Sep: 30th 1795

The following Trustees of the College went to Cheshunt Viz. Weatherill, Batley, Hodson, Astle, Langston.

Mr Carr was so obliging as to come to them.

Mr Drummond, a Nursery Man at Enfield, met them by appointment about converting a considerable part of the Garden-Ground into an Orchard: when it was agreed to fell 18 useless Trees, Fir, Ash and Maple, and to plant 50, or more good Fruit Trees. The sorts of which were all specified, chiefly keeping Apples, some Pears, Plumbs and Cherries, and one Mulberry. The Shrubs to be collected from the different parts where they are now dispersed and planted in 6 Clumps. Viz. one just at the Entrance into the Garden on the right hand, one at each Corner of the Kitchen Garden, and one at the extremity of the Ground near the Summer house. [44v] The Pond to be filled up, And a strait Gravel Walk made 6 feet wide, 6 feet from the River all along the River side, and to join the other Gravel Walk at the Summer house.

Clement Barker, the Carpenter was sent for, who agreed to grub up the 18 Trees at his own Expence: and pay the Trustees 5 Guineas for them.

The Windows of the Summer house being sadly broke: it was agreed to have outside Shutters to the same, which Barker was ordered to make according to Mr Carr's direction.

The Fence between the College Yard and Mr Eburne's Field, being much out of Repair, and Mr Eburne having sent Mr Oldham a written Notice to repair it; the same was survey'd, and instead of the present Palisado Fence it was agreed that a Brick-Wall about 6 feet high, a brick and half thick, would be best, and cheapest in the end. Mr Knightley, the Bricklayer, was sent for, [45r] and made an Estimate. Mr Carr also made an Estimate, and it was agreed that Knightley build the said Wall in April next for 17 Guineas; he being allow'd the Bricks of the Wall surrounding the Melon Ground, and all the loose Bricks upon the Premises - Barker in the mean while to mend the Fence, by nailing up a few Boards where needful.

The Watercourse mention'd in an old Paper amongst the Writings of the Estate, as being on the outside of the Wall, and within the Close, or Field, now in the occupation of Mr Eburne, was look'd at, and was found to be an open Ditch, which it behoves all present, and succeeding Trustees of the College to keep clear.

The Cowhouse, which Mr Eburne had erected against the said Wall, and which he had Notice to remove, is removed.
[45v]

A Chapel, where the Coach-house and Stable now stand, seems very desirable, and especially on the Anniversaries; and Mr Langston suggested that if ever we are enabled to build a Chapel it might be advisable to have a pair of folding Doors, next the Yard, to be thrown open on all public Days, when the Chapel will not contain the People assembled.

Dined at the Green Dragon, and invited Mr and Mrs Nicholson.

Read a Letter from Mr Nicholson about some old Timber, for which two Guineas was offered and accepted.

Read Mr Nicholson's Quarterly report, which was very satisfactory.

The Chairman read the attendance, and non-attendance of the Committee; when it appeared that [46r] the three following Viz. Messrs Fyffe, Dudman and Munn had never attended, and Mr George Towers being deceased; four new Members were to be elected, which were Messrs Gaviller, Walsh Senior, Pontin and Newcombe.

Mr Fyffe moved that the Assistant Committee might have Notices sent them, previous to each Monthly Meeting, which was agreed to.

Monthly Meeting 4th Nov. 1795

Present: Messrs Cooper, Langston, Peter Duthoit, Weatherill, Hodson, Burnell, Bell, Batley*, Butcher, Compigne, Francis, Gaviller.

Read and confirm'd the Minutes of the last Monthly Meeting, Read also the Minutes of [46v] the Adjourn'd Meeting of the 4th of September and the Minutes of the last Quarterly General Meeting.

Read a Letter from Mr Nicholson of Treating with a French Tutor; and Mr Hodsons Answer thereto: That the Introduction of French into the College would impede the other necessary Studies and might prove entirely useless: but that if any of the Students should after leaving the College with Approbation; have a clear and promising Call to preach the Gospel in France: he, or They should be instructed in the French Tongue, at the Expence of the Society.

Mr Langston mov'd: and it was resolv'd that in order to make the College more known to the Religious World, The Revd Mr Haweis be [47r] requested to publish the same in the Evangelical Magazine.

Mr Hodson reported that he had a Surplus of Cash in hand, more than would be wanted for the remaining Expences of the Year. Resolved that the same be laid out in the Purchase of 3 per Cent Bank Annuities.

Monthly Meeting, 2 Dec: 1795

Present: Messrs Hodson, Batley, Oldham*, Cooper, Burnell, Weatherill, Bell, Newcomb, Langston, Holmes, Astle, Walsh, Dupont, Butcher
[47v]
Read, and confirm'd the Minutes of the last Monthly Meeting.

The Chairman mov'd that the Thanks of this Meeting be given to Mr Walsh, Junior for his trouble in purchasing £200 Bank Annuities and not accepting Brokerage.

Read a Letter from the Church of Newark to Lady Anne Erskine, setting forth the usefulness of Mr Bradley's Ministry among them and requesting his continuance.

Mr Hodson reported, that Mr Davies is useful at Ashbourne, and Mr Robertson at York.

Read a Letter from Mr Pritchard of Derby to Lady Anne Erskine in approbation of Mr Bickerdike, and requesting his Ordination and Settlement among them.

Read a Letter from Mr Bickerdike to Ditto on the same subject.

Resolved, That it would be most proper, and generally acceptable that the Ordination of Mr Bickerdike, Mr Davies, etc. [48r] should be at Spa Fields Chapel. Notices thereof to be sent to every Subscriber.

Read a Letter from Mr Thomas Williams to Lady Anne Erskine, expressing a desire of admission to the College. Mr Williams not being present, Lady Anne was requested to write to him, to attend next Lords-day after morning Service: when the Trustees and Committee might have an opportunity of asking him some Questions.

Resolved That the Christmas Vacation commence on Friday the 18th inst. and end on Monday the 10th of January.

Read a Letter from Mr Nicholson, brought by Mr John Meffen, whose time of Probation is expired. He attended, was examined and was unanimously admitted a Student. Mr Nicholson's Report being very satisfactory.

[48v]

Sunday 6th December

Most of the Trustees and some of the Committee had an interview with Mr Thomas Williams, who is about 19 Years of Age, a native of Wales, has had a good Education, but is very young in Grace and divine knowledge: having been awakened but about six months, under a Funeral Sermon preached by the Revd Mr Wills [16], at Silver Street. His desire for the Ministry according to his own Account arises from the consideration of the state poor Sinners are in (as was lately his case) and an earnest desire to be made instrumental in bringing them to the Knowledge of the Saviour.

It was recommended to him to attend Mr Weatherill's Prayer Meeting on Sunday Mornings, to continue his attendance on Mr Wills's preaching, and to come again at the [49r] Monthly Meeting in February.

Quarterly General Meeting
6 January 1796

Present: Messrs Weatherill, Compigne, Bell, Long, Holmes, Langston, Cooper, Hodson*, The Revd Mr Haweis, Messrs Walsh Senior, Astle, Fyffe, King, Butcher Senior, The Revd Mr Platt, Messrs Cole, William Hall, Frances, Berridge, P.Duthoit, Edmund Gouldsmith.

The Revd Mr Haweis began with Prayer.

Read and confirm'd the Minutes of the last Quarterly General Meeting.

Read a Letter from Mr Nicholson respecting Mr John Meffen at the expiration of his three months of Probation which having been very satisfactory to the Trustees and Committee was fully [49v] admitted as a Student.

Read Mr Nicholson's Quarterly Report which was very satisfactory.

Read Mr Nicholson's Quarterly Bill and Receipt including Mrs Coles Bill for Washing, amount £105-19-4½.

Read a Letter from some of the Congregation at York requesting the Ordination of Mr Robertson, but saying they were not in Circumstances to pay for his Journey to London.

Resolved that if Congregations will bear the expence of their young Ministers to Town, they may be ordain'd here: otherwise it is best to be done in the Country, at or near the Place where they are.

Mr Langston moved that the Minutes of December be read, so far as relates to the Revd Mr Haweis being requested to publish some Account of the College in the Evangelical [50r] Magazine. Mr Haweis being present, acquainted the Meeting that he had anticipated their wishes, having already drawn up something for that purpose; which being desired, he went for the Paper and read it: The same met with the Approbation of the Meeting, and Mr Haweis was thanked for it.

Mr King and Mr Burridge were chosen Auditors for the Examination of the Treasurer's Accounts for the last Year.

The Chairman reported, the Lord had been pleas'd in this least year to take away by Death several Subscribers, But others were raised up in their stead, and that by the assistance of Mr Towers's Legacy £200 had been purchas'd in the 3 per Cent Consols besides paying for the Current Expences of the Year.

The Revd Mr Platt concluded with Prayer.

[50v]

Monthly Meeting 3 February 1796

Present: Messrs Langston, Weatherill*, Burnell, Cooper, Hodson, Bell, Newcomb, Compigne, Holmes, Butcher, Bridgman, The Revd Mr Platt, Messrs Francis, Astle, Gavillier, The Revd Mr Haweis, Mr P. Duthoit.

Read and Confirm'd the Minutes of the last Monthly Meeting: Read also the Minutes of the last Quarterly Meeting.

Mr Hodson reported that Mr Drummond had called on him to know if Fruit Trees were to be planted against the Walls. Resolved that as they were expensive and detrimental to the Walls there should not be any.

Read Mr Webbs bill and receipt for Looking glasses, Papering etc. Amount 19/9.

Read Mr Parke's Receipt for Collecting from last Year Amount £19-16-6.

[51r]

Mr John Williams (referred for a farther examination to this Meeting) attended and was interrogated respecting his conversion and call to the Ministry. Resolved that in consideration of Mr Williams's youth and inexperience in the Christian Life He does not appear to be a proper Person to be proposed to the Trustees as a Probationer at present. He was therefore encouraged to attend upon the Means of Grace for six months, and if his Views should then be the same To come again at the expiration of that Time.

Read a Letter from Mr John Brich, Aged 26 years to the Revd Mr Crole on his motive for desiring to be admitted into the College.

Read a recommendation of him from the Revd Mr Whitaker of Cheshire.

Read also the Revd Mr Crole's recommendation of him. Likewise his own Letter to a Friend in answer to certain necessary questions which had been proposed to him.

He attended [51v] was examined, gave good Evidence of a work of Grace on his Heart, and his Call to the Ministry, and the Testimonials in his favour being quite satisfactory, it was unanimously agreed that he be proposed to the Trustees to be admitted a Probationer.

But being a Servant, and necessarily obliged to give a proper warning to leave his place: it was recommended to him to give his Masters immediate Notice of his Intention to quit their Service, and to attend the next monthly Meeting for Admission.

The Chairman mov'd, and it was resolved that the Names of those who bequeath Legacies to the College shall be either written on a Board and hung up in the Committee Room, or else on the Pannels of the Wainscot.

The Revd Mr Haweis concluded with Prayer.

[52r]

Monthly Meeting, 2 Mar: 1796

Present: Messrs Langston*, Hodson, Cooper, Burnell, Butcher, Astle, Bell, Holmes, Bridgman, Weatherill.

Read and confirm'd the Minutes of the last monthly meeting.

Resolved that Canvas be put on Frames for the purpose of Inscribing the Benefactions to the School and College.

Read a Petition from the Students in College for an allowance of Pens and Paper to write their Execises [sic] etc. thereon - Resolved for the present that a Quire of Paper and 100 Pens be sent them, with an admonition for their carefulness in the use of such Articles.

Read and abridg'd what Mr Haweis has written for publication this Year, with the State of the College and List of Subscribers.

Resolved that 500 of the same be printed.

[52v]

Mr Brich attended and said he was not yet at liberty from his Masters; on which account he was told that when he was at liberty he might attend in the Committee Room on Lords day after Service and receive the Order for Admission.

The Chairman reported that half a Years Salary was due to the Secretary: the same was ordered to be paid.

Sunday the 13th of March

Mr Brich attended in the Committee Room and said he hoped he should be at liberty to go down to College on Tuesday next, whereupon an order for his Admission was given to him.

At the same time Mr Bickerdike who is come from Derby on Account of his ill Health and had requested of the Trustees permission to spend a few weeks at College for the Restoration of the same, had leave given him in consideration of the high situation in which he stood at College; the Esteem he has [53r] gained as a Minister of the Gospel, and the want of Friends to afford him the means of Country Air and Exercise while incapacitated from preaching.

CHESHUNT COLLEGE

This Indulgence not to be established as a Precedent for the present, or any future Trustees to be bound by, in case of any other Application of this nature: but They remaining at perfect liberty to act according to their own Judgement and the nature of the Case.

Quarterly General Meeting
6 April 1796

Present: Messrs Cooper, Cole, King, Burnell, Langston, Andrew, Bell, Dupont*, Bridgman, William Knight, Butcher, Astle, Hodson, Newcomb, Curtis, Walsh Senior, Gavillier, Weatherall, John Phillips, Long, The Revd Mr Platt, Messrs Butcher Junior, Francis

[53v]

Read and confirm'd the Minutes of the last Quarterly General Meeting.

Read the Auditors Examination of last Years Accompts, whereby it appears that there is a Balance of £16-13-7 in the Treasurers hands.

Read Mr Nicholson's Quarterly Report, which was very satisfactory; in which was mentioned Mr James' ill state of health and the necessity of some Cessation from Study: on which Account Lady Anne is going to send him, by consent of the Trustees, to Hereford for a time.

Read Mr Nicholson's Quarterly Bill and Receipt including Mrs Cole's for Washing etc. Amount £104-5. Also Mr Patterson's Bill for writing Mr Towers's Legacy on the Inscription Board at Cheshunt Amount £1-11-6.

Read Mr Bickerdike's Petition to the Trustees for leave to abide at Cheshunt College for a few weeks, thinking the same (by Gods blessing) might [54r] be a means for the recovery of his health. The Trustees granted his Request in Consideration of his not having Friends to render him the Assistance he needs at this time; but do not mean to establish it as a Precedent.

Mr Hodson reported that Mr John Brich was admitted a Probationer, and the Revd Mr Platt being present affirm'd his being very promising.

Mr Hodson reported that William Jones and William Kemp had lately preached at Spa Fields Chapel, and Mr Gavillier reported that Mr Chamberlain had preached at Sion Chapel, all with great acceptance.

Mr Langston reported that several Subscribers having expressed a wish to have the Anniversary earlier in the Year, when the days are longer than in August The Trustees have fix'd it for this Year to be held on Wednesday the 29th of June, being a Holiday and the days almost at their greatest length, and that the Vacation is to take

108

place immediately after, when those Students will leave the College who shall at the public Examination in May be thought fit to send out.

[54v]

The Chairman inform'd the Meeting that William Jones had express'd a Concern to him that when he should quit the College he could not be employ'd in the Connection. Mr Hodson said he was persuaded that not only Mr Jones but all who should quit College this Year might have immediate Employment, but that Mr Jones had express'd to Lady Anne his Aversion to the plan of itinerating, and wish'd rather to be settled over a Congregation, on which terms Lady Anne could not engage to provide for him. The Revd Mr Platt observed that neither the Trustees nor this Society at large had stipulated with the young Men who entered the College for anything more than Board and Education, That therefore no blame would attach to them if any or all the Students should be totally unprovided for at the Expiration of their appointed time for Residence in the College. Mr Platt desired that this might be remembered by the present and succeeding Trustees, and it was resolved that Mr Jones had not any right to complain.

[55r]

Mr Platt further observed that although this Society is not, or ought to be under any obligation to provide for the Students when their Education is compleated, Yet by reason of its friendly Union with Lady Huntingdon's Connection the Students in this College have an Advantage beyond those in other Seminaries, inasmuch as there is almost a Certainty of young Men of Gifts and Abilities being provided for in that Connection, if they will conform to the Rules of it, namely the plan of itinerating at least for a time. On the whole it was resolved that Mr Jones be desired to attend the next Meeting of the Trustees and Committee.

Monthly Meeting 4th May 1796

Present: Messrs Cooper, Bell, Burnell, Astle, Dupont*, Gavillier, Walsh, Bridgman, Weatherill, The Revd Mr Platt, Messrs Compigne, Butcher, Holmes, Hodson.

[55v]

Read and confirm'd the Minutes of the last Monthly Meeting. Read also the Minutes of the last Quarterly Meeting wherein that part of the Minutes relative to Mr Jones was considered but Mr Jones not attending this Meeting as was desired a farther Examination of the matter rests 'till he shall attend

The Chairman inform'd the Revd Mr Platt that it was the desire of the Trustees that he should preach on the Anniversary of 29th of June. Mr Platt express'd a diffidence of his Ability, but being inform'd the Trustees had resolved that every

Minister of the Gospel who subscribes to the College should be invited to preach in his Turn and that it came to him by Rotation consented.

Mr Hodson reported that the public Examination is fix'd for Wednesday the 25th inst. if Mr Haweis is at liberty to attend that day.
[56r]
The Revd Mr Platt concluded with Prayer.

The Meeting then broke up, but the four Trustees that were present together with Messrs Compigne and Holmes stayed to see if Jones would come and in a short time he came when a long conversation took place.

Being desired to relate what pass'd between him and Mr Dupont, he said he told him it was a pity some thing was not done to keep the Students in the Connection. This he explained to mean that there was many disagreeable things in the Connection which occasioned every one to leave it as soon as he had an Opportunity of settling himself out of it. Being press'd to declare what those disagreeable things were, we found they were principally the small Emoluments that Ministers have in many Country places. He was told that if the Lord bless'd his Ministry he would open the Hearts of the People to supply his temporal Wants.

In relating what pass'd between him and Lady Anne, we all understood him as Mr Dupont had [56v] done before, namely, that her Ladyship had said she could not provide for him in the Connection but this he explain'd by saying she could not then nominally employ him: that is she had no place by name that she could then have sent him to: but no doubt was either express'd or implied of her sending him to some place when the time came that he was to leave the College.

Mr Jones said his objections to itinerating arose partly from the fear of losing his Learning, not being able to carry his Books with him from place to place and partly from the disagreeables before mention'd, but that he had settled it with Lady Anne that she was to send him out [,] only if he should have a Call over a People he was to be at Liberty to accept it. He was told that all have that Liberty and that none are bound to the Connection by any other Tie than that of Gratitude.

On the whole there appeared in Mr Jones a great deal of carnal Reason and Self-seeking [57r] not that simple Dependence upon God and Devotedness to Him which we should have been happy to have seen. And it also appear'd that the prejudices he has imbibed against the Connection have not been concealed from his fellow Students, whose minds there is reason to fear may have been rendered evil affected towards it by his insinuations. He censured the Management and Managers of the Connection, said there ought to be an Inspector to look into Things etc. by which he meant the Congregations ought to be made to support their Ministers better than many of them do. He was told that the Trustees of the College had no share in the Management of the Connection. That he ought to inform Lady Anne of every thing that he know to be essentially and materially wrong in it, and that it was very improper for him to be Employed in a Connection which he so much disapproved of.

As his coming to Town was by Order of the Trustees, it was resolved that six shillings be given him for his Coach-hire.

[57v]

At a Special Meeting of the Trustees of the College, held on Friday Evening May 20th 1796

Present: All the Trustees except Mr Batley, Also of the Assistant Committee Messrs Cooper, Compigne and Holmes.

Resolved, That some Disorders having crept into the College, it becomes the duty of the Trustees as far as in them lies to apply Remedies thereto: knowing that under God the prosperity of the Institution depends on the Administration of proper Discipline on the one hand and the Exercise of due Subordination on the other.

The Disorders complained of are these, Viz:

1. A worldly minded Spirit in some of the Students

2. A contempt of Lady Huntingdon's Connection

3. A despising or thinking lightly of the Authority and Conduct of the Trustees

4. That the Students are seen a great deal too often in Town

5. That some of the Students seem to pay too much [58r] Respect of their Attainments in Literature; rather than to those Divine Gifts and Qualifications that most eminently fit and furnish a Person for the Ministry of the Gospel.

Resolved, That in order to apply such Remedies to these Evils as may be the Grace and Blessing of God be rendered effectual The Afternoon of Wednesday next the 25th inst. (being the day on which the publick Examination is to be held in the Forenoon) shall be a Visitation: that the Students shall be ordered to attend in the Chapel of the College at half past Three, and the Ministers then present, or one of them, by desired to give them a Lecture.

1. Concerning the worldly minded Spirit. This we consider as a very dangerous and destructive Evil that will eat as doth a Canker, and if not eradicated will blast all our hopes of the future Usefullness of those who are infected with it. If this Spirit which has manifested itself on several occasions is not check'd and subdued in the Students without having recourse to this expedient, the Trustees have determined that none

of [58v] them shall preach any where but at the College, and will thus cut off from them all expectation of Gain or Emolument while they continue in College.

2. That with regard to Lady Huntingdon's Connection whatever faults they may find with it, or whatever Opinion they may have of it, none of the Students will be thought worthy to be employ'd in it, who does not appear to be simple hearted, divested of worldly views, and having a single Eye to the Glory of God and the Good of Souls.

3. That however they may affect to despise the Authority of the Trustees, they should know that the Trustees have power to turn every one of them out of the College and that they will exercise this Power if it shall be needful respecting any one or more that shall behave improperly.

4. That the Students be enjoined to abide at the College, and not permitted to come to Town except on particular occasions, and then not without leave of the President.
[59r]
5. That all their Attainments in Literature are designed by this Institution only to be subservient and conducive to the great and important Work of preaching the Gospel, and not for Them to Glory in or to be puffed up by. If their Learning is not sanctified to them and used faithfully by them to the Honor of Christ their Divine Master it will prove a Curse to them instead of a blessing.,

Lastly That no Testimonials will be given to any whose Conduct in the foregoing Respects or any other is reprehensible.

Wednesday 25 May 1796
Publick Examination at the College [17]

Present: Revd Dr Haweis Examiner, Revd David Jones, Revd William Francis Platt, All the Trustees, Five of the Assistant Committee, and a few others.

The Students were examined, the Junior ones in English, the next in Latin, and the three Senior ones, Kemp, Jones and Winter, in Latin, Greek and Hebrew. Kemp shew'd himself a good Scholar, Jones and Winter not equal to him. With respect to the others Dr Haweis did not think so great a proficiency appear'd as did last Year.

In the Afternoon the Visitation was held. Mr Oldham, by the desire of Mr Platt, read the Minutes of the 5th and 20th instant, and then Dr Haweis stood up and address'd the Students, which in some measure [59v] frustrated the design of the Trustees which was that Mr Platt should give the Students an admonitory discourse. Mr J. Bryan impudently stood up to vindicate the Students and so did Mr Nicholson. Mr Platt spoke very properly, and Dr Haweis concluded with Prayer.

THE

First Anniversary

OF

BETHEL CHAPEL,

HERTFORD,

WILL BE HELD

ON TUESDAY, SEPTEMBER 28, 1819:

WHEN TWO

SERMONS

WILL BE PREACHED:

THAT IN THE MORNING, BY THE

Rev. Wm. Kemp, of Swansea:

AND THAT IN THE EVENING, BY THE

Rev. John Rees, of Rodborough.

Service will begin in the Morning at half past 11, and in the Evening at 6 o'Clock precisely.

———————————

A DINNER WILL BE PROVIDED AT THE BULL INN, AT A MODERATE EXPENCE.

AUSTIN, PRINTER, HERTFORD.

Plate II: Rev. William Kemp (Student 1791–96; Resident Tutor at the College 1821–31), preaches at Hertford, 1819 *(Cheshunt archives, C9/14/6)*

At a Meeting of the Trustees
held on Tuesday Evening,
the 31 May 1796

Present [Messrs] Oldham*, Weatherill, Dupont, Hodson, Astle, Langston

Resolved, 1. That the Midsummer Vacation commence on Thursday the 30 June; and end Monday 25 July.

2. That Messrs Jones, Kemp and Winter having compleated their four years do leave the College at the Commencement of the said Vacation.

3. That Mr Bickerdike having been indulged with a three months Residence at College on Account of his Health be desired to leave at the same time.
[60r]

4. That Mr Jones having behaved improperly on the 25th inst. at the Visitation of the Trustees be not permitted to deliver any Oration at the ensuing Anniversary: but that Orations be delivered by Messrs Horn, Chamberlain, Winter and Kemp.

5. That the Trustees invite Mr Nicholson to a friendly Conference, in order that perfect Harmony and Unanimity may be established between them in all matters relating to the good government of the College; And in order to have this Conference free and uninterrupted they all dine together at the Castle and Falcon on Wednesday the 8th of June at 2 oClock.

6. That a new Edition of the Rules and Regulations be printed, and that a Copy thereof be given to the President, and one to each of the Students, and also to every one that shall be admitted in future.

Mr Hodson was desired to write to Mr Nicholson by the Post.

Mr Astle concluded with Prayer.

[60v]

Monthly Meeting, 1 June 1796

Present Messrs Cooper, Dupont, Rowton, Astle, Weatherill, Oldham*, Langston, Butcher, Holmes, Hodson, Walsh

Read and confirm'd the Minutes of the last Monthly Meeting.

Read a Letter from Mr Robertson at Annan in Scotland to Lady Anne Erskine giving an account of his removal to that place from York, and requesting of the Trustees the favor of Books.

Agreeably to the Resolution of the Society to allow to the Value of 40 shillings Lady Anne was requested to say in her Letter to him, that he might draw on Mr Hodson for that Sum and lay it out in Scotland.

Read Mr Drummonds Bill for Trees etc. planted, and for Gravel and Labour amounting [61r] in the whole to £41-8-4. The Bill was rather unpleasant as it exceeded our Ideas: he having planted more Trees and Shrubs than ordered.

Referr'd to Mr Hodson to settle it in the best manner he can.

Mr Hodson reported that the public Examination was held at College on Wednesday last:

> Present The Revd Dr Haweis, Examiner, The Revd David Jones, The Revd William Francis Platt, All the Trustees, Five of the Assistant Committee, And a few others

That the three Senior Students, Jones, Kemp and Winter are to leave the College immediately after the Anniversary, having staid their full time.

That the Vacation is to take place the 30th inst. and end the 25th of July.

And that the Stewards for the Anniversary have fix'd for the Dinner to be at Enfield, as the Additions [61v] made at the Green Dragon are not perfectly dry; nor can the whole Company be accommodated there.

Quarterly General Meeting
6 July 1796

> Present Messrs Weatherill, Pontin, Bell, Cole, Langston, John Cooper, King, The Revd Mr Platt, Messrs Astle, Butterworth, Butcher Senior, Fyffe, Butcher Junior, Hodson, Holmes, Compigne, Oldham*, William Jones, Benjamin Bryan, Rowton, Edmund Gouldsmith, William Hall, The Revd Dr Haweis.

The Revd Mr Platt began with Prayer.

Read and confirmed the Minutes of the last Quarterly General Meeting. Read the Minutes of the Monthly Meeting of the 4th of May, and of the Special Meeting of the 20th.

[62r]

Mr Langston reported that the Examination of the Students for this year, was on the 25th of May. The Revd Dr Haweis, Examiner, the Revd Mr Platt was also present, and says the Students in general exceeded his expectations.

The Anniversary was held the 29th of June, and was well attended. The Revd Matthew Wilks began with Prayer: four of the Students delivered Orations Viz: Winter on Nature, Chamberlain on Providence, and Horn on Grace, These in English and Mr Kemp in Latin on Humility. They all acquitted themselves very well Winter especially was much admired for his Composition on Nature. The Revd Mr

Platt preached an excellent Sermon on Romans the 1st and 16 and the Rev John Towers concluded with Prayer.

The Dinner at Enfield, was exceedingly good, but unhappily the Company was divided, many staying at the Green Dragon; so that there were not many more than 50 at Enfield.

Read the Revd Mr Nicholson's Quarterly Report in which the attainments of Messrs Kemp, Winter and [62v] Jones were particularly mention'd, especially the first, and the diligence of the other Students commended, and their being in general devoted Men.

Read the Revd Dr Haweis recommendation of Mr John Coanes Aged 19, who being present, was called in and ask'd a few questions respecting his conversion and Call to the Ministry. When it was ordered that he attend the next Monthly Meeting with Testimonials in his favor, and in the mean while to be present at the Sunday Morning and Monday evening Exhortations conducted by Mr Weatherill.

The Chairman moved that the Thanks of this Meeting be given to the Revd Mr Platt, for his excellent Sermon, and to the Gentlemen Stewards for their attention in providing an excellent and plentiful Dinner.

The Revd Dr Haweis concluded with prayer.

Monthly Meeting 3 Aug. 1796

[63r]
 Present Messrs Weatherill, Hodson, Langston, Astle, Butcher, Bell, Oldham*, Burnell, Walsh

Read, and confirm'd the Minutes of the last monthly Meeting. Read also the Minutes of the last Quarterly Meeting.

Read a Letter from Mr Nicholson respecting a young man of Newcastle upon Tyne, Mr George Lee, whom he met with on his late Journey into the North, and recommends as a proper Person to be admitted into the College.

Read Mr Nicholson's report of Mr John Brich, whose time of Probation being expired, attended and was admitted fully as a Student.

Mr John Williams, who in February last made application to be admitted as a Student in the College, attended: and on his being examined respecting his call to the Ministry answered "that his diffidence was great as the [63v] work was great, of speaking in the name of and for God," and seem'd rather to relinquish his immediate admission to the College; and this conduct being approv'd of, he had to leave to come again in February ensuing, with advice to commit himself unto God in the matter.

Mr John Coanes attended and was fully examined respecting his conversion and call to the Ministry. He declared that the preaching of Christ with all that may attend it was preferable to him before a prosperous state in any worldly Business; but not sufficiently and plainly shewing the work of the Spirit, he was encouraged to continue attending Mr Weatherill's Meetings, to be earnest in Prayer and to come again at the Monthly Meeting in November.

Mr George Lee, aged 22, being come from Newcastle in consequence of a Letter from Mr Hodson, attended, and giving a very clear and satisfactory account of his Conversion and Call to the Ministry, he was admitted a Probationer.
[64r]
Mr William Upjohn, aged 22½ years, attended, was minutely examined respecting his Conversion and Call to the Ministry. The same plainly appearing he was admitted a Probationer; but being a Servant wish'd (and also was advised) to give his Master proper Notice, and leave him in a handsome manner. Mr Jonathan Carr was referr'd to as to Mr Upjohn's moral Character, he having enquired the same of his Master and of the People where he lodges, who all concur in giving him the best of Characters.

Monthly Meeting 7 September 1796

Present Messrs Rowton, Langston*, Cooper, Astle, Bell, Hodson, Newcomb, Compigne, Burnell, Weatherill, The Revd Mr Platt, Mr Walsh

Read and confirm'd the Minutes of the last Monthly Meeting.
[64v]
Mr Hodson reported that three Sermons had been preached for the benefit of the College at Spa Fields Chapel, the 14th of August. Those in the morning and evening by Mr Richard Povah, and that in the afternoon by Mr Cooper, and that the whole Collection amounted to £90-11-9.

Read Mr Nicholson's Quarterly Bill and Receipts amounting in the whole to £107-13-8½.

Mr Hodson reported that half a Years salary was due to the Secretary, which was ordered to be paid, and a gift of a guinea to be given to him, in consideration of his additional Trouble in summoning the Committee to the Monthly Meetings, and his increased Family.

Read a Letter from the Committee of Gainsbro' in favour of Mr Bradley's Ministry during his residence there.

Read a Letter from Lady Anne Erskine [65r] informing of Mr Bradley's going to Ireland; also recommending Mr Benjamin Callens, aged 25 years, as a Candidate for the College, who being present was examined respecting his Conversion and call to the Ministry - Being a member of the Revd Mr Wills's congregation he was desired to procure Testimonials from Mr Wills, or some of that congregation, and to attend Mr Weatherills Meetings: also to acquaint his parents of his intention, and to come again at the November Meeting.

The Revd Mr Platt concluded with Prayer.

Quarterly General Meeting
5 October 1796

Present Messrs Cooper, Long, Weatherill, Hodson, Samuel Bridgman, William Bridgman, Astle, Butcher Junior, Langston*, Bell, Butcher Senior, [65v] King, Rowton, Walsh Junior, Walsh Senior, Tutt, Emerson, Dupont, Newcomb, Mousley

Read and confirm'd the Minutes of the last Quarterly General Meeting. Read also the Minutes of the Monthly Meetings of August and September.

Read a Letter from the Committee of Gainsbro' to Lady Anne Erskine in favour of Mr Bradley, and Mr Bradley's Letter to that Lady from Ireland.

Read a Letter from the Committee of Kingsbridge to Lady Anne in favour of Mr Winter.

Read Mr Nicholson's Quarterly Report, which contains a favorable account of the Students, and of the Probationer Mr George Lee.

Read the Account of the attendance of the Assistant Committee since October last, when it was found that Messrs Pontin, Duthoit, Francis [66r] and Rowton have attended the fewest times, Mr Rowton being present said he should have attended oftner but was prevented by Illness. It was resolved therefore that the three former go out and Messrs Tutt, Long and Burridge were chosen in their Room.

Mr Hodson reported that five of the Trustees, viz. all but Messrs Oldham and Batley, went to the College on Monday the 26th of September, where they were met by Mr James Carr - The business they went upon was to consider what was best to be done with the Coach-house and Stables, which are out of Repair. The following Proposals were suggested namely
1st To make the same into a Chapel, at as little expence as may be
2nd To make Students Rooms
3rd To make them into a Study and Library [66v] the present Room used for that purpose being too close and warm in Summer.

In considering these different proposals, the Trustees survey'd all the present Students Rooms, and found that no more than 13 Students can be accommodated, even with 3 Beds in one of the Rooms and 2 in another or two. The two last Proposals were objected to by Reason of the Building being detach'd from the House. The first therefore was adopted, namely the Chapel; and to make a Study of the present Chapel, and when there shall be occasion[,] to run a Partition across the present Study, and so make two good Students Rooms. This matter was agreed to stand over 'till the January Meeting and to be put in the Notices.

Mr Hodson reported that Mr Nicholson requested a Copper and a Mash-Tub for the purpose of Brewing; being much put about in procuring of good Beer.
[67r]
Resolved that the same be provided.

Mr John Styles, recommended by the Revd Mr Kirkman, attended to be admitted into the College, when on examination it was found he was only 15 years of age, and an apprentice with his father a Carpenter, He was therefore exhorted to mind his business and serve his father faithfully; being too young either for himself or us to form a right Judgement respecting his present desires of going into the Ministry.

Monthly Meeting: 2 November 1796

Present Messrs Langston, Weatherill, Cooper, Astle, Butcher, Oldham*, Hodson, Bell, Tutt, Bridgman, Rowton, Newcomb, Walsh, Revd Mr Platt, Messrs Long, Burridge
[67v]
Read and confirm'd the Minutes of the last Monthly Meeting.

Read Mr Nicholson's Letter respecting Mr George Lee, a probationer, whose time of probation being expired, he was finally examined, approved and admitted a Student.

Mr John Coanes attended, and was very particularly and fully examined as to his experience of a work of Grace, but not manifesting any more clearly Gods work on his heart, than at the first, He was exhorted in the most tender manner to commit himself to God, and to come again in February, but not to forego any opportunity that might be presented in the mean time of settling himself in any line of Life that might be eligible to him.

Mr Benjamin Callens attended, but not bringing any Testimonials or recommendations he was desired to procure the same and to come again at the next Monthly Meeting.

[68r]

Read a Letter from the Committee of Annan to Lady Anne Erskine in favor of Mr Robertson as a Minister and a Christian conducting himself with great propriety in a suffering state.

And a letter from Mr Bradley to that Lady shewing favorable circumstances attending the Cause of Christ in Dublin.

Read Mr Nicholson's Quarterly Bill and Receipt for £81-5-2. And sundry Bills paid at Cheshunt, when the Trustees were there in September.

Mr Hodson reported that Mr James had recovered in a great measure of his ill state of health and was this day gone to College.

The Revd Mr Platt concluded with Prayer.

Monthly Meeting 7 December 1796

Present Messrs Langston, Hodson*, Weatherill, Cooper, Newcomb, Walsh, Bridgman, The Revd Dr Haweis

[68v]

Read and confirm'd the Minutes of the last Monthly Meeting.

Resolved that the ensuing Vacation commence on Friday the 16th instant and expire on Monday the 9th of Jan. 1797.

Mr Benjamin Callens attended according to the order of last Meeting and brought with him Testimonials much in his favor; and having been before examined respecting his Conversion and Call to the Ministry; he was universally approv'd of and admitted as a Probationer to go to the College as soon as possible after the Vacation.

Mr Richard Turnbull, Clerk aged 25, attended and offered himself as a Candidate for the College, recommended by a Mr Allen of the Mulberry Gardens, who being present declared Mr Turnbull to [69r] be an exemplary Christian, and very likely to be useful in the Church of Christ as a Minister. He was therefore examined respecting his Conversion and Call to the Ministry and gave general satisfaction: but thinking it right to give his Employers three months Notice, his admission as a Probationer is postponed only 'till he is at Liberty to do.

Mr William Pierpont aged 18 years recommended by Dr Haweis attended and offered himself a Candidate; but being an Apprentice or Articled for 3 years to come with [a] respectable Tradesman, He was exhorted to conduct himself as a Christian in that state he was in, with the utmost diligence and fidelity for that he would be quite soon enough for the College at the expiration of his Time, if he then should have the same Views as at present and should be approv'd.

The Revd Dr Haweis concluded with Prayer.

[69v]

Quarterly General Meeting
4 January 1797

Present Messrs Hodson, Langston*, Bell, Cooper, William Knight, Astle, King, Burnell, Weatherill, Long, Butcher, Butcher Junior, Dupont

Read and confirm'd the Minutes of the last Quarterly General Meeting; Read also the Monthly Minutes of November and December.

Read Mr Nicholson's Account of Mr Upjohn as a Probationer which being very satisfactory he was fully admitted as a Student.

Read Mr Nicholson's Quarterly Report which notwithstanding the satisfaction those periodical Reports have given This was thought to exceed.

Mr Butcher Junior and Mr William Knight were chosen Auditors for the Examination of the [70r] Treasurers Accompts for the last Year.

Read an Extract of a Letter to Lady Anne Erskine from Messrs Johnson and Howard, dated Dublin 3 Nov: 1796, in favour of Mr Bradley's Ministry in that City.

Read the Collectors Accompt of 1796 shewing the new Subscribers - those that are dead - and those who decline: The Subscriptions on the whole being £5-10-0 Less than the preceding Year.

The Chairman reported that Mr Kemp had preached at Swansea with acceptance, and the People there having been desirous of his Ordination that they might have the Sacrament administred to them, he was ordained at Bristol the 20th day of December by the Revd Messrs Young, Waring and Jones.

[70v]

Monthly Meeting 1 February 1797

Present Messrs Langston, Cooper, Bell, Weatherill, Astle, Long, Holmes, Dupont*, Hodson, Compigne, Butcher, Oldham, Tutt, Walsh

Read and confirm'd the Minutes of the last Monthly Meeting. Read also the Minutes of the last Quarterly General Meeting.

Mr Langston reported that Mr Richard Turnbull was left his Employers in a becoming manner and last Friday went to College.

Read a Letter from Mr Benjamin Callens who was to have gone to College immediately after the Vacation, But his mind having been intense on the important

Work of the Ministry and from his diffidence of himself, beg'd to relinquish it at present.

Read Mr Nicholson's Quarterly Bill, [71r] amounting to £103-12-9. And Mrs Cole's bill for Washing £5-14-7.

Read Mr Parke's bill for Collecting, amounting to £19-4-9.

Read Mr Knightly's bill when the same was ordered to be paid.

Mr Hodson reported that he had received the balance of Mr Leighton's account for old Lead £13-8-5.

Mr Hodson reported that a Students Gown having been ordered for Mr Brich, the same had been sent of too great value and was therefore by consent of the Trustees made into a Ministers Gown and presented to Mr Nicholson, And a more suitable one got for Mr Brich. The bill being produced for both was ordered to be paid.

Read Messrs Hughes and Walsh's bill for Printing, Paper, etc. Amount £7-15-2 which was ordered to be paid.
[71v]
Read a Letter from Mr Nicholson recommending a Mr Finlay, a young Man of the Congregation at Enfield as a Candidate for the College.

Mr Dupont was desired to acquaint him that he might attend the next Monthly Meeting.

Mr Hodson reported that Mr Povah having been taken ill at Brighton, Lady Anne Erskine had applied to the Trustees for Mr Horne (a Student) to have leave to be absent from College to officiate for Mr Povah during his indisposition; And that the same was granted as it was a Case of great Emergency, There being no Minister at Liberty to go down on the occasion.

Monthly Meeting 1 Mar: 1797

Present Messrs Hodson*, Langston, Cooper, The Revd Mr Glasscott, Messrs Bell, Astle, Lang, Weatherill, Burnell, Dupont, [72r] Compigne, Butcher, Holmes, Burridge, Walsh

The Revd Mr Glasscott began with Prayer.

Read and confirm'd the Minutes of the last Monthly Meeting.

Read a Letter from Lady Anne Erskine, returning thanks to the Trustees, for permitting Mr Horne to go to Brighton, in the room of Mr Povah, and the thanks of that Church for him, who is now return'd to College.

Read Mr Clement Barker's Bill for Repairs etc. when the same was order'd to be paid Amount 5-12-0.

Mr John Finlay, aged 20 years, attended, and was examined respecting his Conversion which appears clear, but his Call to the Ministry not being so evident, he was ordered to well persue the Rules, see Mr Nicholson, commit himself to God, and to attend the Monthly Meeting in May.
[72v]

Read a Letter from the Revd Dr Haweis, recommending a Mr William Thomas of Anglesea, aged 26 years, as a Candidate for the College. He attended, was examined respecting his Conversion, which plainly appeared, and his heart truly melted by divine Grace. His Call to the Ministry was not very dubious; but the Lord having been pleas'd to make him a blessing to the family he lives in, namely Mr Habgood, in Friday Street, it was thought best to desire him to continue as God had Call'd him, and to attend the May Meeting, when it might more plainly appear both to the Trustees and himself, what is the Will of the Lord concerning him.

Mr Richard Owen, aged 24 years of Haverford West attended and was examined respecting his conversion, when a Letter was read from Mr Straiten, the person he lodged with, and a Letter from Mr Oliphant, belonging to Mr Willis's Church, as [73r] Testimonials of his walking as a Christian, and likely to be useful in the Church as a Minister. He was therefore unanimously approved of, as a Probationer, The Rules were given to him to peruse, and he was ordered to attend Sunday sen'night (at which time he thought he should be at liberty to go to College) when his order would be given to him.

The Revd Mr Glasscott concluded with Prayer.

Quarterly General Meeting 5 April 1797

Present Messrs Hodson, Cooper, Jonathan Carr, Andrew, William Knight, Oldham*, Butcher Senior, Butcher Junior, Astle, Walsh Senior, Tutt, Burnell, Gavillier, Jacob Jones, Compigne, Emerson, Cock, Dupont.

Mr Jonathan Carr begun with Prayer.
[73v]
Read and Confirm'd the Minutes of the last Quarterly General Meeting. Read also the Monthly Meetings, of February and March.

Mr Hodson reported that Richard Owen went to College the 14th of March.

Read Mr Nicholson's Quarterly Report, which was very satisfactory on the whole; and greatly in favour of some of the junior Students.

Mr Hodson reported that four of the Trustees, and Mr John Cooper, visited the College on Wednesday last, and found all things very much to their satisfaction.

Read a Letter from Mr Winter, at Kingsbridge, late a Student; setting forth an afflictive dispensation of God towards him, being in a very ill state of health; but expressing his resignation to the Will of God, whether for Life or Death.

The Chairman read the State of the College Accounts for last Year, as signed by the Auditors: Balance in [74r] favor £30-0-3 1/2.

The Chairman reported: that God had been pleas'd to take Mr Richard Rowton; but that he had remembered the College and School, by leaving to the same an House, situate No. 2, New Ormond street, producing a net Rent of £21 per Annum, whereof £5 per Annum for the School and the Remainder for the College; for the Term of a Lease of which 24 Years are unexpired.

The Examination of the Students is fix'd for Thursday the 4th of May. And the Anniversary for the 29th of June.

Mr Hodson reported, that the Copper was fix'd, and the brewing Vessels nearly finish'd, for the purpose of Brewing for the Family and Students.

The Chairman concluded with Prayer.

[74v]
Monthly Meeting, 3 May 1797

Present Messrs Astle, Cooper, Hodson*, Bell, Butcher, Weatherill, Compigne, Burnell, Bridgman, Dupont, The Revd Mr Haweis, Messrs Walsh, Langston.

The Revd Dr Haweis began with Prayer.

Read, and confirm'd the last Monthly Minutes. Read also the Minutes of the last Quarterly Meeting.

Read a Letter from Mr Nicholson greatly in favor of Mr Richard Turnbull, whose time of Probation is expired. He was therefore unanimously admitted a Student.

Read a Letter from Mr Nicholson respecting Mr John Finlay, wherein is shew'd that he had attended to those enquiries the Trustees had enjoined respecting Mr Finlay, and all things appearing clear [75r] he was therefore unanimously admitted a Probationer; but not to go to College, until after the ensuing Vacation, which is to commence the 30th of June, the day after the Anniversary, and to expire on Monday the 24th of July.

Mr William Thomas attended and was further examined; and every thing respecting him appearing satisfactory; he was unanimously admitted as a Probationer to go to the College on the 24th of July, if he can decline his Master's Service with repute: he having been a blessing to him, in having the order of family prayer, bringing him under the word, and seemingly in the way to everlasting life.

The Revd Dr Haweis concluded with Prayer.

Monthly Meeting, 7 June 1797

Present Messrs Hodson, Bridgman, Bell, Butcher, Burnell, Astle*, Tutt, Weatherill, Newcomb

[75v]

Read and confirm'd the Minutes of the last Monthly Meeting.

Mr Hodson reported that the Public Examination was held on Thursday the 4th of May. Present the Revd Dr Haweis, the Revd Mr Roby, Messrs Oldham, Weatherill, Dupont, Hodson and Astle, Trustees, Messrs Butcher Senior and Junior, Mr John Cooper, Mr Tutt, and Mr James Walker. The Students went through their Examination much to the satisfaction of all present.

Mr Parry's full time being nearly expired, and Lady Anne Erskine having a place where she can employ him immediately; it was settled that he shall embrace the opportunity, and that Messrs Chamberlain and Horn leave the College immediately after the Anniversary.

[76r]

The company dined at the Green Dragon, and the Trustees engaged the large Room lately erected there for the Anniversary; and Agreed with Ives the Landlord that He shall provide the Dinner at 3s. 6d. per head; exclusive of Wine, Ale, etc.

Mr Hodson reported that the Trustees had ordered a Gate, to prevent Mr Nicholson's Children going into the Garden, as three of them have been in danger of drowning, by getting through the Garden to the Water. And that an examination of the Windows, Doors and Iron-work; it was necessary that they should be painted, in order to preserve the same; When it was unanimously agreed, that the same be painted immediately.

Mr Hodson reported that he had waited on The Revd Matthew Wilks, respecting his preaching the Anniversary Sermon, but he being engaged at that period at Bristol; it devolved on the Revd J.A. Knight, who had expressed his readiness to preach on the Occasion.

[76v]
Quarterly General Meeting 5 July 1797

Present Messrs Langston*, Butcher Senior, Butcher Junior, Astle, Burnell, Hodson, P: Duthoit, Weatherill, Dupont.

Read and confirm'd the Minutes of the last Quarterly General Meeting: Read also the Minutes of the Monthly Meetings of May and June.

Read Mr Nicholson's Quarterly Report, which was very agreeable.

Resolved that the Thanks of the Society be given to The Revd Joel Abraham Knight for his Sermon on the Anniversary, by a Letter from the Secretary expressing the same.

Read a Letter from Mr Nicholson respecting Richard Owen, whose time of Probation is expired. Mr Owen attended, and the Letter being an entire approbation of him, he was unanimously admitted a Student.

[77r]

The Chairman reported that the Anniversary on Thursday last was well attended, notwithstanding the day was showery; That three of the Students delivered Orations, Mr James on Prosperity; Mr Chamberlain on Adversity; and Mr Horn on Gratitude; and that they all acquitted themselves well and gave satisfaction to the Company; as likewise did the Accommodation at the Green Dragon where 46 dined.[18]

The Chairman further reported, that Mr Horn and Mr Chamberlain have now left College and are going, the former to Ireland, the latter to Kingsbridge. Also that Mr Thomas, admitted a Probationer and intending to go to College immediately after the Vacation, has been obliged to go to Wales, on account of the Death of his Father and a Brother, but proposes to return as soon as convenient, and go to the College.

There being no other business before this Meeting the Trustees examined a Candidate for the College, a young Man from Bristol [77v] Mr Thomas Walsh, aged 20 years, who brought a recommendation sign'd by the Revd Messrs Young, Wilkins and Phillips. He gave a very clear and satisfactory account of his conversion and call to the Ministry; and was therefore unanimously admitted a Probationer, to go to College immediately after the Vacation.

CHESHUNT COLLEGE

Monthly Meeting 2 August 1797

Present Messrs Langston, Hodson, Weatherill*, Bridgman, Bell, Dupont.

Mr Hodson reported that Mr Finlay went to College on the 24th ult: and Mr Walsh the 25th.

Mr Hodson reported that he had paid the following sums, viz. to Mr Nicholson £101-14-1, Mrs Cole for washing and mending £6-5-7, Messrs Horn and Chamberlain the usual [78r] allowance of £2-0-0 for Books.

Read a Letter from Mr Winter, late a Student, expressive of great resignation to the will of God, in his present indisposition, and requesting his Ordination, which was the unanimous opinion of all present, might take place, by the order and direction of Lady Anne Erskine.

Read a Letter from a young man nam'd William Ross of South Shields to Lady Anne requesting his admission to the College. The Letter contained a pretty full Account of his Experience, and mentions his having seen two of the Students who have been into the North the last Vacation: viz. Messrs Lee and Mather, who are to be spoken to by the Trustees when convenient about him.

Mr Ross is at present under an Engagement which will not expire in less than eight months. His Age 20 this day. Lady Anne was requested to write him an encouraging Letter.

Mr Nicholson having forgot to mention to the Trustees on the Anniversary that a Post [78r] in the Brewhouse, which is the main support of the Rooms over the same, was become rotten, and consequently dangerous; thought of it that day before Mr Dupont was gone, and told him; also of a Wall, that was wanting, instead of the old decay'd Wood-Fence, at the Dunghill. Mr Dupont having communicated these matters to the other Trustees, they requested him to go to the College, and view the Premises, and give such Orders as he thought best. Mr Dupont now inform'd this Meeting that he had order'd a strong Oak Post, and whatever else was to be done, he had given the particulars of in writing.

Resolved, That as many Persons are out of Town in the Month of August, the Collection for the College be deferred 'till October and that Mr Bickerdike be applied to to preach in the Morning and the Minister at the Chapel [79r] for the time being in the Evening, And that the same be advertised in two of the daily Papers.

Monthly Meeting, 6 Sep: 1797

Present Messrs Gaviller, Weatherill, Langston, Hodson*, Butcher, Astle, Bell, Oldham, Burridge, Holmes.

Read and Confirm'd the Minutes of the last Monthly Meeting.

The Chairman reported that Mr William Thomas, who was admitted as a Probationer in May, to go to the College after the Recess, but was prevented by being obliged to go into Wales, on account of the death of his Father and two Brothers, is now return'd, and intends going to the College on Friday next.
[79v]
The Chairman also reported that Mr George Lee preached by desire of Lady Anne Erskine, on Sunday the 27th of August, at Sion Chapel and the Mulberry Gardens with great Acceptance.

Also that Mr Mackdonald, having been sent the last Vacation to Birmingham, and having married while there, consequently can't be admitted again to College.

Read a Letter to Mr Weatherill from the Revd Mr Wilkins in favor of Mr James Cooke of Arundel, aged 20 ½ years, brought up a Staymaker. Mr Cooke attended and was examined respecting his Conversion and Call to the Ministry; but after a long Investigation there did not appear sufficient Evidence of the latter; but a forwardness and self Confidence that argued a Mind very little impress'd with a Sence of the Solemnity and Importance of that sacred Employ, and his own Insufficiency for it. He had been in London about three months, and had preached at Kentish Town and at Barnes etc. by the invitation of Mr Crockford [80r] a young Man who attends Mr Weatherills Monday Evening Meetings. Being desired to withdraw, the unanimous opinion of all present was to postpone his admission till after the Christmas Vacation, where he might perhaps give more satisfactory Evidence of his Call, and that he be exhorted in the mean while to desist from preaching, to attend the Ministry of the Gospel as a humble Hearer, and commit himself to the Lords Direction and Guidance by earnest and fervent Prayer. Being called in and acquainted with this Resolution he appeared very much disappointed, said he could not content himself to be a Hearer, his Zeal would not permit him, and in short discovered that he came to Town with a full expectation of being admitted to the College, and was unwilling to be refused: the more so as he was now out of Employment.

The Chairman reported that half a Years Salary was due to the Secretary, when the same was ordered to be paid with 1 Guinea extra, the same as last Year.

[80v]

Quarterly General Meeting, 4 Oct: 1797

Present Messrs Hodson, Cooper, Mumford, Bell, Langston*, Franklin, Weatherill, Astle, Burnell, Moxley, Butcher Senior, King, Tutt, Newcomb, Dupont, Walsh Senior, Butcher Junior, Burridge, The Revd Messrs Platt and Caldwell.

Read and Confirm'd the Minutes of the last Quarterly General Meeting; Read also the Minutes of the Monthly Meetings of August and September.

Read Mr Nicholson's Quarterly Report, which portends much Glory to God, by the order and godly conversation of the present Students.

Read a Letter from Messrs Powell and Johnston, Deacons of the Church in Plunket Street, Dublin, very much in favor of Mr Bradley, who is removed to Sligo; and of Mr Horn who is gone in the room of Mr Bradley.

[81r]

The Chairman inform'd the Meeting that Mr Rowton one of the Assistant Committee being deceased, and three being to go out, in course four new Members were to be chosen this Evening. On reading the Attendance of the Committee since last October, it was found that Mr Gaviller had attended only once, consequently he must be one of the Three to go out, but as there were Six who had attended each three times; it became a question, how to select properly Two out of the six; when it was thought most equitable that Those should go out who had been Longest on the Committee, who were Mr Burnell and Mr Compigne: but Mr Burnell being present and saying he had been out of Town, or should have attended oftner, and Mr Butcher saying that Mr John Long would be glad to be excused on account of some particular Engagements, it was determined that Mr Gaviller, Mr Compigne and Mr Long be the Three to go out, and Messrs Emerson, King, Mousley and John Phillips were chosen in.

[81v]

Read a Letter of Recommendation from Mr Nicholson in favor of Messrs Finlay and Walsh, whose time of Probation being nearly expired, they attended, were examined, and gave much satisfaction to all present. They were therefore unanimously admitted Students.

The Revd Mr Caldwell concluded with Prayer.

November Monthly Meeting, 1st Nov: [1797]

Present Messrs Langston, Hodson, Holmes, Bridgman, Butcher, Weatherill, Bell, Astle, Cooper, Dupont*, Tutt, Newcomb.

Read and confirm'd the Minutes of the last Monthly Meeting. Read also the Minutes of the last quarterly General Meeting.

Mr Langston reported that on Wednesday the 11th of October Five of the Trustees with Messrs John Cooper and Tutt visited the College and found all [82r] things agreeable but Mr Nicholson having a Pain in his head occasion'd it is thought by too close application had obtain'd leave to go to Sea for a week or two hoping that thro' the blessing of God it might be the means of removing the same.

Read Mr Nicholson's Quarterly Bill amounting to £93-14-0 and Mrs Cole's Bill for Washing amounting to £6-2-10 both which have been paid.

Read Mr Oldham's Bill for Copper etc. amount £32-9-0.

Read Mr Clement Barkers Bill Carpenter amount £22-8-5.

Read Mr Wollards Bill, Smith amount £11-13-4.

Read Mr Stephen Leightons Bill Plumber and Painter amount £11-3-1½. All which were ordered to be paid.

Mr Hodson reported that the Collection for the College on the 29th ult. amounted to £67 19s 5d.

Read a Letter to Mr Langston in favor of Mr James Cooke from Mr Finch of Arundel.

Mr Langston reported that Mr Chamberlain is well accepted at Kingsbridge where he was sent by Lady Anne in lieu of Mr Winter who by [82v] his continued ill state of health is rendered incapable of preaching.

Resolved that the Thanks of this Meeting be given to the three Ministers who preached the Sermons for the late Collection namely The Revd Dr Haweis, Dr Hamilton and The Revd Mr Caldwell.[19]

Sunday 12 November 1797

Lady Anne Erskine having shewed the Trustees this Morning a Letter from Mr Winter wherein he requests permission to return to the College for Change of Air and Recovery of his Health. The following Trustees met this Evening to consider of the Application Viz. Messrs Oldham, Weatherill, Hodson, Langston and Astle. Present also Messrs Cooper and Holmes of the Committee.

After reading the Letter Reference was [83r] had to the Minute of 13 March 1796 requesting Mr Bickerdike and it was unanimously resolved

That the Trustees had seen Cause to wish they had not granted the Indulgence to Mr Bickerdike And therefore, notwithstanding their good Will towards Mr Winter they are constrained to put a Negative on his Application for that the College is not designed as an Hospital but a Seminary for instructing Young Men for the Ministry and many Inconveniencies might and would arise from the Readmission of any Student who having completed his Education has left the College.

Monthly Meeting 6 Dec: 1797

Present Messrs Oldham, Weatherill, Cooper, Hodson*, Astle, Langston, Burnell, Bell, Newcomb, Bridgman, Butcher, Mousley, Walsh, King.

[83v]

Read and confirm'd the Minutes of the last Monthly Meeting. Read also the Minutes of Sunday Nov: 12th.

The Chairman reported that Mr Nicholson was return'd from the Sea: is better and desires to return thanks to the Trustees for the Indulgence.

Read a Letter from Mr Nicholson in favor of Mr Thomas whose time of Probation being expired: he attended, was further examined and all things respecting him being very satisfactory he was unanimously admitted a Student.

The postscript of Mr Nicholson's Letter intimated the Students desire to institute a Sunday School at the College, if approved of by the Trustees, who order'd Mr Thomas to bring them the whole Plan in writing at the ensuing Vacation; when they will consider the same and give their Answer.

Resolved that the Christmas Vacation commence the 21st inst. and expire Monday Jan. 25th.

Mr James having applied for a week above the time in order to go into Wales, the Trustees in consideration of his long Journey, have consented thereto.

Quarterly General Meeting, 3 Jan: 1798

Present Messrs Weatherill, Cooper, Bell, Long, Hodson*, William Jones, Butcher Senior, Astle, Newcomb, John Phillips, Thomas Wontner, Dudman.

Read and confirm'd the Minutes of the last Quarterly General Meeting. Read also the Minutes of the 1st and 12th of November and of the 6th of December.

The Chairman reported that the Lord had been pleas'd to take Mr Winter, late a Student, but that he had left a good Testimony behind him and departed this life on Thursday Dec: the 7th at Bristol.

[84v]

Read Mr Nicholson's Quarterly Report which gave a high account of the Students as good Men, and diligent in their Pursuits of Learning and in the general promising Usefulness in the Church of Christ.

Read the Collectors account of Subscribers the last Year; wherein is shewed, those whom the Lord hath taken by Death - Those who decline - and those who are newly come forward for the support of the Institution: the whole being about £8 more than the preceeding Year.

Mr Newcomb and Mr John Cooper were chosen Auditors for the Examination of the Treasurer's Accompts for the Last Year.

Mr James Cooke of Arundel who applied for admission the last September Meeting, attended again this Evening. He was much interrogated in order to ascertain the Lords [85r] dealings with him since that time, and to obtain a clear Conviction of his divine Call to the Ministry; but as he did not express himself to the full satisfaction of the Meeting, he was call'd upon to pray in the midst of all present: which made some Impression in his Favor; but as it would be a fortnight before the College would regularly proceed to business after the Vacation he was ordered to wait on the Revd Mr Platt on Friday next, and attend in the Committee Room on the Sunday after, to receive an Order for his Admission, if it should be so determined; Mr Newcomb being desired to apprize Mr Platt of it, and to request he would be very close in his Examination of Mr Cooke.

Monthly Meeting, 7 February 1798

Present Messrs Langston*, Cooper, Hodson, King, Butcher, Burnell, Astle, Bell, [85v] The Revd Mr Platt, Messrs Weatherill, Newcomb, Tutt, Dupont, Holmes, Mousley, Berridge, Emerson.

The Revd Mr Platt began with Prayer.

Read and Confirm'd the Minutes of the last Monthly Meeting. Read also the Minutes of the last Quarterly General Meeting.

Read the Revd Mr Platt's Letter to the Trustees respecting Mr James Cooke, wherein is shewed some difficulties (the same which appeared on his examination before the Trustees) yet recommended him to their favor for admittance as a Probationer. Mr Hodson reported that Mr James Cooke came for his Order on Sunday the 14th and went to College the 16th of January.

Read Mr Parke's Bill for Collecting amount £20-3-0, Messrs Langston & Co. for Sheeting amount £7-7-8, Mrs Cole's Bill for Washing amount £6-11-1, The Revd Mr Nicholson's [86r] Quarterly Bill amount £109-9-10 and Mr Mackdonald's for Books amount £2-0-0. All of which are paid.

Read Mr Knightly's Bill for Bricklayers work amount £15-0-4, Messrs Hughes and Walsh's Bill for Printing, Paper, etc. amount £9-8-2, Mr Webb's Bill for Repairs 5s. 6d. and Mr Drummond's Bill for replanting of Trees: All of which were ordered to be paid, except the latter, which being only planting of new Trees, instead of 22 which died of those planted before, and which by agreement he was to make good, it was thought he had no right to be paid.

Read a Letter from Mr Nicholson recommending Mr William Bennet of Cheshunt by Trade a Shoemaker, aged 24, who attended and was examined respecting his Conversion, which appeared plain: but his Call to the Ministry being very early after his Conversion, was very particularly and minutely enquired into: the result however was that he was admitted a Probationer.

[86v]
Monthly Meeting 7 Mar: 1798

Present Messrs Oldham*, Bell, Langston, Weatherill, Cooper, Astle, Hodson, Phillips, Holmes, Walsh, Butcher, Mousley.

Read and Confirmed the Minutes of the last Monthly Meeting.

Mr Langston reported that Mr Mather a Student at the College had requested leave to be absent from his Studies a fortnight on account of an indisposition of Body requiring a change of Air as prescribed by a Physician on which consideration the Trustees have given leave.

Resolved that the public Examination of the Students at College be fix'd for Wednesday the 21st inst. The Revd Dr Haweis being to be out of Town at that time the Revd Mr Eyre had been requested to be present but had wrote Mr Hodson he [87r] should be at Reading on that day.[20]

The Revd Mr Glasscott and the Revd Mr Platt are fix'd on to be invited and the Revd Matthew Wilks if it will suit his conveniency.

Read an Address drawn up by the Revd Mr Nicholson intended for Printing with the State of the College which requiring some alteration Mr Oldham was desired to take it with him for that purpose.

Mr Bennett from Cheshunt attended but having not quite settled his Affairs so as to be ready to enter the College desired a Fortnight longer was therefore told he might wait on the Trustees at Cheshunt on the 21st and then receive his Order for Admission.

Quarterly General Meeting, 4 April 1798

Present Messrs Cooper, Woolcott, Langston*, Butcher Junior, Butcher Senior, Astle, Bell, King, Weatherill, Walsh Senior, Burnell, Hodson.
[87v]

Read and confirm'd the Minutes of the last Quarterly General Meeting. Read also the Minutes of the Monthly Meetings of February and March.

The Chairman reported that Mr William Bennett waited on the Trustees at Cheshunt, at the late Public Examination of the Students, and received his Order for Admission into the College.

Mr Hodson reported that the Public Examination of the Students was held on the 21st ult. Present the Revd Messrs Glasscott and Platt, five of the Trustees, viz. Messrs Oldham, Hodson, Langston, Weatherill, Astle: Also Messrs John Cooper, Tutt, Daniel Owen, Earle and Mr Norton a friend of Mr Langstons. The Revd Matthew Wilks could not be present. The Examination was chiefly conducted by the Revd Mr Glasscott, and was very much to the satisfaction of all present.

Read Mr Nicholson's Quarterly Report, which was greatly in favor of the Students.
[88r]

Read the Auditors Account for last Year when there appeared a Balance of £29-11-9½ in the Treasurers hands.

Read Mr Batley's acknowledgement of a Donation of 5 guineas to the College which he had received from Mr Thomas Craddick of Tewksbury.

Read a Letter from Mr Nicholson in favor of Mr James Cooke, whose time of Probation being nearly expired, he attended and was something interrogated, respecting matters which were not perfectly clear at two former Meetings. But from his answers and the substance of the Tutors Letter, there appeared a full satisfaction to the Trustees for giving him an Order to be fully admitted a Student which was accordingly done.

Read a long Letter from Mr John Coanes, who once more attended for admittance into College. But on examining him personally there did not appear any thing more in his experience than when he applied before, so that the Trustees [88v] were embarrassed and perplexed on his Account. As however this was not the regular Meeting for the Admission of Students, and Mr Coanes had for some months assisted the Revd Mr Cottingham, both as Reader and Preacher, he was desired to bring from him a Letter of Recommendation at the next monthly Meeting, and Mr Burnell was requested to see Mr Cottingham on the business.

Read a Letter from Mr Nicholson to Mr Hodson respecting the Assessed Taxes, and Mr Hodson's answer thereto, informing very minutely how, and in what manner, to appeal before the Commissioners in Hertford.

Read a Letter from Lady Anne Erskine setting forth the good acceptance of Mr Parry at Tisbury, Wiltshire, where he is lately gone from Woodbridge.

Mr Butcher Junior mov'd that a more general knowledge of the publick Utility of the College be set forth in the best manner that can be adapted.

[89r]

Monthly Meeting, 2 May 1798

Present Messrs Hodson*, Bell, Cooper, Astle, Weatherill, Bridgman, Butcher, Dupont, King, The Revd Mr Roby, Messrs Newcomb, Holmes, Tutt, Burnell.

The Revd Mr Roby began with Prayer. [21]

Mr John Coanes attended as per order of the last Meeting; but as nothing had transpired in his favor, but a verbal recommendation from the Revd Mr Cottingham, and himself not sufficiently answering to formal enquiries, or to the questions Mr Roby now put to him, either as to his Conversion or Call to the Ministry, he was finally rejected, and advised to seek a secular employ.

Read a very humble and sensible Letter from Mr William Ross, aged 20 years 7 months a Ship Carpenter of [98v] South Shields addressed to Mr Hodson, for admission into College. Read also a favorable Letter from his Master, with whom he had been an apprentice And another from the Deacons of the Church where God had made him useful: uniting in recommending him. He was therefore unanimously admitted as his examination evinced the truth of his recommendation.

Read a Letter from Mr Nicholson respecting Mr John Strong, aged 34 years who formerly had lived with the Revd Mr Glasscott, as a Servant in the Husbandry-business; and since with Mr Dupont. He seemed very confident that he was called to preach, but on his examination there did not appear any Evidence thereof; nor was his natural Capacity (being but slender) judged improveable at his time of life. He was therefore unanimously rejected, and advised to a holy christian walk, without further thoughts of the Ministry.

Read an extract of a Letter from the Revd Mr Browning of Newcastle to Lady Anne recom[90r]mending to the College a brother of Mr William Mather, now a Student there. Lady Anne was requested to answer it that he might come up in August.

Read a few lines to the Trustees from the Revd Mr Nicholson requesting their advice concerning the present Vestry-Meetings, how, and in what manner he should conduct himself; when it was unanimously resolved that neither himself or any of the Students should enter into any military Associations.

Read a Letter from Mr William Mather to the Trustees wherein he requests further leave to be absent from his Studies for three months, which space is to be occupied in preaching two or three times a week, but not in Study as advised by a Physician. The Trustees in consideration of his health advised him leave, and Lady Anne Erskine sent him to Chichester.

Read a Bill of the Insurance Amount £3-4-9, A bill for a Mash Tub Amount £3-12-0, [90v] Mr Nicholson's Quarterly Bill Amount £103-18, and Mrs Cole's Bill for washing etc. Amount £7-3-0. All of which have been paid.

The Revd Mr Roby concluded with Prayer.

Monthly Meeting 6 June 1798

Present Messrs Hodson, Weatherill, Langston*, Newcomb, King, Burnell, Bell, Astle, Dupont, Phillips, Tutt, The Revd Mr Platt, Messrs Butcher, Burridge.

Read Mr Hodson's Letter to Mr William Rose in answer to his respecting admission to College.

Read also Mr Hodson's Letter to the Revd Mr Williams of Stepney respecting his preaching at the Anniversary wherein he modestly consents.
[91r]
Resolved that the ensuing Vacation begin Saturday June 30th and end Wednesday July 25th.

Quarterly General Meeting 4 July 1798

Present Messrs Hodson*, Cooper, Stickland Junior, Peter Duthoit, Burnell, Weatherill, Bell, Butcher Senior, Walsh Senior, Tutt, Compigne, Butcher Junior, Thomas Wontner.

Read a Letter from Mr Nicholson informing that he had received an Order from the Steward of the Court Baron of the Manor of Cheshunt to Repair immediately the Coping and Gable End of the Stable, pursuant to which the Trustees had Ordered Mr Knightley, Bricklayer, to make good the same.

[91v]

The same Letter intimated his weak state of Body, so as not to be able to preach at Spa Fields as requested. Nor to assist at the Ordination of Messrs Chamberlain and James.

Read Mr Nicholson's Quarterly Report, which was very satisfactory, as was also his Testimony in favor of Mr William Bennett, whose time of Probation being expired, he attended, was something further interrogated, and all things appearing in his favor, he was unanimously admitted a Student.

Mr Hodson reported that the Anniversary was held the 29th ult. and was well attended. Three of the Students, viz. Lee, Meffin and James, delivered Orations which were well approved, and the Revd Mr Williams of Stepney preached very acceptably.

Mr Hodson reported that Messrs Chamberlain and James were Ordained at Spa-Fields Chapel on Monday the 2nd instant by the Revd Messrs Eyre, Platt, Kirkman and Waring.

Read a Letter from Mr Parke setting forth new [92r] Subscriptions commencing at the Anniversary amounting to £13-13.

Mr Thomas Wontner beg'd leave to address the Chair respecting the New Chapel at the Mulberry Gardens being favour'd with a Student, at times to preach there. Four of the Trustees being out of Town, and only Two present, Mr Wontner was inform'd his Request would be taken into consideration when there could be a full Meeting of the Trustees.

Mr James having finish'd his Studies left the College on the 30th ult.

Mr Bennett admitted a Student this Meeting concluded with Prayer.

Monthly Meeting 1 Aug: 1798

Five of the Trustees, viz: Messrs Hodson, Langston, Dupont, Weatherill and Astle, met at half past five o'clock to consider of Mr Wontner's Request, presented at the last General-Meeting [92v] When it was resolved that the Trustees entirely coincide with what Mr Dupont says is the opinion of Mr Nicholson, namely that the seldomer the Students come to Town the better: and that their being permitted to preach periodically in any place in London might and would be hurtful to them. That therefore the Trustees think it their duty to continue the Prohibition of which Mr Hodson was desired to acquaint Mr Wontner by a Letter.

At the hour of Meeting only Messrs Bell, Bridgman, Cooper and Newcomb of the Committee were present in addition to the before nam'd Trustees.

Mr Dupont in the Chair.

Read the following Bills which are paid, viz: the Revd Mr Nicholson's Quarterly Bill amount [93r] £123-2-11, Mrs Ann Cole's for Washing etc. amount £7-17-8, Mr Samuel Search for Bedding amount £4-15-4, Mr John James allowance for Books £2-2-0.

Read Mr Nicholson's Letter in favor of Mr William Ross, whose time of probation being expired, he attended, was something further interrogated respecting his Conversion and Call to the Ministry, which appearing very satisfactory he was unanimously admitted a Student.

Read a Letter from the Church of Chichester, in favor of Mr William Mather, a Student who in his late indisposition and the vacation ministered there and was well accepted

Read a Letter from Lady Anne Erskine wherein was one enclosed concerning Mr John Mather aged 25 of Newcastle, who attended and was examined at large respecting his Conversion and Call to the Ministry, and the Revd Mr Browning attesting a very satisfactory account of him, he was [93v] unanimously admitted a Probationer.

The Chairman reported that the President requested an Assistant there being more than 12 Students on the Foundation. And he made Choice of Mr Meffen for that Office, in which the Trustees unanimously concurred, and resolved that he should have a Salary of Ten Pounds per Annum commencing from this day.

Mr William Ross, admitted a Student this evening, concluded with Prayer.

Monthly Meeting 5 Sep: 1798

Five of the Trustees, viz: Messrs Oldham, Weatherill, Hodson, Langston and Dupont, met a quarter of an hour before the usual time and conferr'd together about two special matters Viz:

Whether any Enlargement of the College should be made for the Reception of more Students and Whether the Land Tax should be redeemed.
[94r]
With respect to the former Mr Dupont proposed and it was resolved that an absolute Negative should not be given to any who should propose Themselves as Candidates, but that they should be postponed until November, and as the Trustees intended going to the College on Wednesday the 26th instant they will then see if any more Room can be made without much Expence.

With respect to the Redemption of the Land Tax it was resolved on unanimously, as it would be a perpetual Rent Charge on the Estate if it should be purchased by any other Person.

At the hour of Meeting they were met by the following Gentlemen of the Assistant Committee viz Messrs Cooper, Bell, Tutt, King, Burnell and Butcher.

Mr Oldham in the Chair.

Read a Letter from Mr Nicholson respecting a want of further conveniences of Students Rooms, together with Beds and Bedding: provided there is an augmentation of Students.
[94v]

Mr Langston inform'd the Meeting that he had answered the Letter as the Case required. Mr Hodson being unwell at the time.

Read two Letters from Mr Clement Barker relative to the proposed Quickset Hedge and the necessary Fence for the same, Estimating the charge to amount to upwards of £30, which considering present Circumstances it was thought prudent to defer.

Read a Letter from Lady Anne Erskine to the Trustees requesting a Student to preach at Tunbridge Wells the 9th and 16th instant - Three of the Trustees reluctantly sign'd an Order for Mr William Mathers going as the Case appear'd urgent: but hoped such an application would not soon be made again, as was intimated to her Ladyship.

Mr Hodson reported that half a years salary was due to the Secretary, which was ordered to be paid.

After the Meeting broke up the Trustees waited on Lady Anne to propose an immediate Collection for the Traveling Fund[22] in order to make way for the College Collection before the expiration of the Year, [95r] when it was agreed that the Revd Mr Charles should preach for the Traveling Fund the 16th instant.

A Proposal made by Mr Hodson to her Ladyship some years ago was revived, namely, To have a Collection annually at all the Chapels in the Connection: and it was agreed to on this Condition, that every third year it should be for the College and the other two years for the Traveling Fund. Mr Dupont suggested, and it was adopted, that the Collection should be at all the places as near as might be to the Countess of Huntingdon's Birthday, Viz: the 24th of August.

Mr Hodson was desired to draw up a Paper proper for a Circular Letter on the Occasion.

Quarterly General Meeting 3 Oct: 1798

Present Messrs Hodson, Astle, Langston*, Shadd, Tutt, Bell, King, Walsh Senior, Burnell, Butcher Senior.

[95v]

Read Mr Nicholson's Quarterly Report which was very satisfactory.

Mr Hodson reported That all the Trustees except Mr Batley together with Messrs Tutt and Walsh visited the College the 26th ult and found all well - Some repairs about the Tiling Lead-work and Plaistering were ordered to be done And the largest of the Students Rooms which has two Beds in it was thought very capable of holding a third, whereby Room is made for one Student more. Besides which the Hay-loft over the Stable which Mr Nicholson very readily gives up was found capacious enough to make three additional Rooms for one [96r] Student each adjoining those over the Brewhouse etc. which was ordered accordingly and thus the College may receive eighteen Students.

Read the attendance and no attendance of the Assistant Committee at the Monthly Meetings since the Quarterly General Meeting of October 1797 When it was found that Messrs Burridge, Emerson and Philips having attended the fewest times were to go out and Messrs Butcher Junior, Carpenter and William Knight were elected in their Room.

Read a Letter from Mr John Mitchell aged 29 of Gowruch near Greenoch Scotland to Mr Hodson respecting his admission into the College which Mr Hodson was desired to answer and to inform him that a Recommendation is necessary.

Read a Letter from Mr Thomas Billings to Lady Anne Erskine requesting admission into the College. Mr Billings attended and was informed he might come again at the next Monthly Meeting.

[96v]

The Chairman reported that a Letter had been received from Bristol setting forth the good acceptance of the Revd Mr James at that place.

Monthly Meeting 7 Nov: 1798

Present Messrs Bridgman, Cooper, Astle, Langston, Hodson*, King, Burnell, Newcomb, Bell, Butcher Senior, Carpenter, Walsh.

Read the copy of Mr Hodson's answer to Mr John Mitchell Gowruch, near Greenoch, Scotland, desiring a Recommendation before we could give him Encouragement to come up, to which Mr Hodson had received no Reply.

Read a letter from Mr Clement Barker to Mr Nicholson acquainting him with the [97r] Derangement of his affairs, whereby he has been prevented making the three additional Rooms at the College. In consideration of which and the days now growing short the Trustees determined to postpone the same 'till the Spring, as they do not appear to be immediately wanted.

Read a Letter from the Church of Norwich to Lady Anne Erskine expressing their satisfaction with the Revd Mr Chamberlain's Ministry at that place.

Read Mr Nicholson's Account for the Quarter ending at Michaelmas amounting to £118-2-0 as paid by Mr Hodson. The new Assessed Taxes made a part of that Sum a proportion of which belong to Mr Nicholson, but as he had by appealing on the ground of Income, reduced the demand from £70-10-0 to £8-0-0 it was resolved that the whole of the £8-0-0 be paid by us.

Read Mr Nicholson's request for Washing of the Sheets out of Doors at our expence. When it was considered that the augmentation allowed for the Board of each Student render'd any application of that nature improper: and therefore it was not acceded to.

The Chairman reported that Mr Upjohn having contracted a Debt to a Medical Gentleman of about £3 Mr Nicholson had inform'd the Trustees of Mr Upjohn's inability to discharge the same, and intimated a desire that it might be paid by the Society. This matter was discussed, And it was thought it would be establishing a bad Precedent, as it might lead to frequent and perhaps expensive Doctors Bills. It was therefore negatived.

The Chairman also reported the Students request to be allowed an additional Fire in the Winter season: having at present only one Fire allowed by Mr Nicholson, which [98r] is in the Study, and not sufficient for so many Students as are now in the College, which induces them sometimes to go into the Kitchen for warmth, contrary to the Rules. To prevent which it was resolved that they be allowed a Fire in the Dining Room during the Winter months, and that Mr Nicholson be desired to lay in two Chaldron of Coals to be kept separate for that purpose.

The Chairman also reported the Students Petition for Captain Wilson's Voyages: the consideration of which was postponed for the present.

Read a recommendatory Letter in favor of Mr Thomas Billings, but as the same came from his Master and only supporting moral Conduct, and as no other appearing in his favor from any Minister, he was not approv'd and advised rather to seek an employment, than that of putting himself in the Ministry.

Read Mr Nicholson's letter in favor of Mr John Mather, whose time of Probation being [98v] expired, he attended, and there being an entire satisfaction in the minds of all present, he was unanimously admitted a Student, and call'd upon to conclude with Prayer.

Monthly Meeting 5 Dec: 1798

Present Messrs Langston, Cooper, Hodson, Oldham*, Astle, Bell, King, Newcomb, Butcher Senior.

Read an extract of a Letter from the Church at Annan in Scotland very much in favor of the Revd Mr Robertson at that place lamenting their inability to administer even to his necessary wants.

[99r]

Mr Hodson reported that on Sunday next three Sermons will be preached at this Chapel for the benefit of the College That in the Morning by the Revd Mr Eyre [23], That in the Afternoon by the Revd Mr Kirkman and that in the Evening by the Revd Dr Haweis.

Resolved that the ensuing Vacation commence Thursday the 20th inst. and end Monday January 14th ensuing.

Mr Billings unexpectedly came when he was heard in a few things but again inform'd that having no recommendations but that from his late Master which goes no further than his moral character and Dr Haweis having refused to recommend him We could not enter into any particular Examination. He said he had written to Mr Morley for a recommendation, on which he was told that if at any future Meeting he should bring a recommendation every Attention would be paid to it that was proper.

[99v]

Quarterly General Meeting, 2 Jan: 1799

Present Messrs Hodson, Cooper, Astle, Langston, Oldham*, Stickland, Butcher Junior, King, Newcomb, Francis, The Revd Mr Platt.

Read Mr Nicholson's Quarterly Report, which was very satisfactory.

Mr Hodson reported that the Collection for the College was made the 9th of December, and amounted to £73-4-6. Also that since the last Regulation of the Window Tax the College is charg'd at £21-10 per Annum, for that and the House Tax.

The Revd Mr Platt said that he thought that [100r] the College being a Public Charity should be exempted from the Window Tax. Mr Francis said he could enquire whether the Orphan School in the City Road is exempted or not. He was desired to make the enquiry and report the Answer at the next Meeting.

Mr Francis and Mr Stickland Junior were chosen Auditors.

The Revd Mr Platt concluded with Prayer.

CHESHUNT COLLEGE

Monthly Meeting, 6 Feb: 1799

Present Messrs Langston*, Cooper, Astle, Bell, Holmes, Newcomb, King, Oldham, Walsh, Carpenter.

Mr Langston in the Chair.

The Chairman began with Prayer.

Read a Letter received from Mr Thomas Billings [100v] wherein he gives up making any further application to be admitted into the College.

Mr Langston reported that Mr Hodson had been with him this morning and inform'd him that Mr John Mitchell of Gowruck in Scotland who applied by Letter a few months ago to be admitted into the College was now come to Town and had called on Mr Hodson yesterday who gave him a written direction to the Chapel and desired him to attend the Meeting this evening. Mr Mitchell not coming as was expected Enquiry was made for him in the Chapel House but he was not, nor had been there. Notice was also given by the Clerk before Mr Cooper's preaching that if he was in the Chapel he might come into the Committee Room but no Mr Mitchell came therefore having no more business the Meeting adjourned.

[101r]

Monthly Meeting 6 Mar: 1799

Present Messrs Dupont, Cooper, Weatherill, Burnell, Hodson*, Astle, King, The Revd Mr Platt, Messrs Bell, Mousley, Tutt, William Knight, Langston, Newcomb, Walsh, Butcher Senior, Carpenter.

The Revd Mr Platt began with Prayer.

Mr Langston reported that having had it intimated by Mr Dupont that Mr John Mitchell who should have attended here the last Meeting was gone to the Academy at Hoxton, he had made enquiry and found that Mr Mitchell had offered himself there although he was not yet actually admitted there being no room at present and that 'till there was room he was gone to work with his Brother at Woolwich as a Rope-maker. The Revd Mr Platt said that Mr Mitchell had been with him before he called on Mr Hodson and inform'd [101v] him he was recommended to the Hoxton Academy [24] Mr Hodson said that when he called on him which was but the day before our last Monthly Meeting he made no mention of any recommendation to or desire for the other Seminary but seemed as if he was come to Town on purpose to be admitted into the College at Cheshunt and enquired of Mr Hodson the way to Spa Fields Chapel who gave him a written direction.

Being thus fully expected at our last Meeting and not coming nor giving afterwards any information to Mr Hodson or any other of the Trustees caused no

142

little anxiety about him. Considering the whole of his Conduct in this matter a Vote of Censure was passed on him for Duplicity and want of Uprightness and it was resolved unanimously that for this his Conduct he is declared ineligible to the College even if he should apply again for Admission.

Read a Letter from Mr William Kemp at Swansea [102r] formerly a Student at the College accompanying a Present of a Book to the College intitled Blackwall's Sacred Classics: for which on a Motion of Mr Platts it was resolved that Mr Hodson be desired to write him a Letter of Thanks.

Mr Hodson produced the following Bills paid by him Viz:

	£	s	d
Messrs Hughes & Walsh for printing	6	11	0
Mr James Duthoit for horse hair & sacking		19	11
William Webb Cabinet-maker for sundry repairs	1	0	3
Messrs Goad & Co. for Diaper for Table cloths	3	13	0
Messrs Oldham & Co. for brass Candlestick		7	6

Also Bills not paid Viz:

	£	s	d
Thomas Knightly, Bricklayer	2	12	2
Clement Barker, Carpenter	4	16	2

Mr Barker had deducted from his Bill £1-1-0 for his Subscription to the College but Mr Hodson saying he was in insolvent Circumstances, it was resolved improper to take the same and Mr Hodson was desired to pay [102v] the whole of his Bill either to himself or to whomsoever was duly authorized to receive it.

The Chairman reported that the publick examination will be held on Thursday the 28th instant.

Also that half a year's salary is due to the Secretary, which was ordered to be paid.

The Revd Mr Platt concluded with Prayer.

Quarterly General Meeting, 3 April 1799

Present Messrs Langston*, Cooper, Astle, Stickland, Bell, Butcher Junior, Tutt, Butcher Senior, Hodson, Walsh, Newcomb, the Revd Dr Ford.

[103r]

Mr Newcomb reported that Mr Francis had made enquiry at the Orphan School respecting the Window Tax, and found it is not exempted from it.

Read Mr Nicholson's Quarterly Report which gave great satisfaction.

Mr Oldham reported that the Revd Mr Goode, Rector of St Ann's Blackfriars, obliged the Trustees by accompanying them to the public Examination on Thursday last, the 28th Ult. and taking upon him the Office of Examiner. He express'd his Satisfaction of the Attainments the Students had made, and all things at the College were found agreeable.

Mr Carr was so kind as to attend and give directions for making two new Rooms (instead of three) over the Stable.

All the Trustees were present except Mr Batley, [103v] also Mr John Cooper, and Mr Tutt.

Read a Letter from Lady Anne Erskine congratulating the Trustees visiting the College on the public Examination: laying before them the necessity of Ministers being sent to Ireland, and very much in favor of the Revd Mr James.

Read a Letter from Mr Mitchell, wherein he shews his reason for not making further application to the College, and excusing himself in not apologizing before. His objections to the Church Prayers he gave as the Reason why he preferred the Academy at Hoxton.

Read the Auditors Accompts for last year, when there appears a balance of £29-19-8 in the Treasurer's hands.

Mr Oldham reported that he had seen Mr Nicholson respecting the Redemption of the Land Tax, and put it on a proper [104r] footing to be settled.

The Revd Dr Ford concluded with Prayer.

Monthly Meeting May 1st 1799

Present Messrs Cooper, Burnell, Hodson, Astle, Tutt, Bell, Newcomb, Dupont*, Walsh, Weatherill.

Read the following Bills which are paid viz:

	£	s	d
Mr Nicholson Quarterly Amount	123	3	1
Mrs Cole's Accompt for Washing	8	6	10

Monthly Meeting June 5th 1799

[104v]

At 5 o'clock four of the Trustees met, viz. Messrs Hodson, Langston, Dupont and Hodson, to consider of an Application made by the Revd Mr Nicholson, for an Increase of Salary, as by reason of his large and increasing Family, his present Income was insufficient, that therefore he was under the necessity of making Engagements to preach at Camberwell and elsewhere by way of Surplus to our Salary, in order to keep himself out of Debt, which with all his Emoluments he could hardly do.

Mr Dupont said he had opened himself with some freedom to him, had said that he did not wish to go so much from home, but that his Circumstances did require an Addition of £50 per Annum.

The Trustees deliberated on this matter, and the Result was that as they wish'd the President of the College to be more at home [105r] on the Lords-day, they would make him an Annual Present of £50, expecting him therefore to quit Camberwell, and to relinguish some other Engagements, which Mr Oldham was desired to acquaint him with.

The Trustees acceded to this Proposal the more readily as by the good Providence of God Miss Hillier, lately deceased, has bequeathed to the College £1000 3 per Cent Consols: which will bring in £30 per Annum, and Mr Cooper has devoted a Sum to the Glory of God, out of which he consents that the other £20 shall be made up.

Of the Assistant Committee

Messrs Cooper, Bridgman, Bell, Tutt, Newcomb, Burnell and Walsh attended: also Mr Astle.

Mr Oldham in the Chair.

[105v]

Resolved that the Anniversary be held on Wednesday the 26th instant when the Revd Mr Cradock Glasscott will preach the Anniversary Sermon.

Resolved that the Revd Dr Haweis, the Revd Mr Goode, and the Revd Mr Eyre be invited to the Anniversary.

Resolved that the ensuing Vacation commence the 27th inst. and expire Monday the 22nd of July.

To ask Mr Nicholson about Mr Meffen whose Term expires the beginning of September next; whether it is worth while for him to come to College again after the Vacation, as his Stay will be only a few Weeks.

CHESHUNT COLLEGE

Quarterly General Meeting 3 July 1799

Present Messrs Hodson*, Cooper, Weatherill, Bell, King, Tolkein, Astle, Burnell, [106r] Langston, Earle, Stickland, Butcher, Tutt, Walsh Senior.

The Chairman reported that Official Notes hath been received of the Legacy of £1000 3 per Cent Consols left by Miss Hillier.

Also that the Redemption of the Land Tax is contracted for.

Mr Langston reported that the Anniversary was well attended, and gave much Satisfaction.

And that Messrs William Mather and Meffen (their time being expired) have quitted the College and are gone, the former to Bristol, and the latter to Dartford.

Also that the Revd Mr Glasscott is to preach for the College on Sunday the 14th Instant, Morning and Evening.

Resolved that the Revd Mr Eyre is requested [106v] to publish an Account of the Anniversary of the Evangelical Magazine, which Mr Hodson was desired to draw up and send to him for that purpose.

The Chairman concluded with Prayer.

Monthly Meeting Aug: 7th 1799

Present Messrs Oldham*, Dupont, Langston, Hodson, Bell, Burnell, Tutt, Weatherill, the Revd Mr Charles.

Read the extract from Miss Hillier's Will.

Mr Hodson reported that the Collection for the College at Spa Fields Chapel on the 14th ult. Amounted to the Sum of £83-10. Also that he had purchased £41-13-3 in the 3 per [107r] Cent Consols, so that the Stock parted with for the Redemption of the Land Tax is only £150.

Mr Langston reported that an Account has been received of the well acceptance of Mr Mather at Bristol.

Mr Hodson brought and exhibited the following Accounts paid by him Viz:

	£	s	d
To Mr Benjamin Cherry of Hartford for his Trouble and Expences in procuring Certificates of the Land Tax	0	13	0
The Revd Mr Nicholson's Quarterly Account	127	11	10
Ann Cole's Bill for Washing and Mending	8	6	0
Thomas Wollard's Bill, Smith	0	19	8
To Mr William Mather Allowance for Books	2	0	0
Mr John Meffen Ditto	2	0	0
Ditto for 1 years Salary as Assistant Tutor	10	0	0

Three Candidates for Admission into the College attended: the First called in was Mr Hinxman late Curate at Sion Chapel, aged 18 last February.

The next was Mr Samuel Jones, aged 19. Son of the [107r] Revd Thomas Jones of Buckinghamshire: the other was George Gladstone from Newcastle upon Tyne aged 21 last February bred a Taylor recommended by our Student Mr Ross.

The Conversion and Call to the Ministry of the latter was clear and satisfactory he was therefore unanimously admitted a Probationer. But the knowledge and experience of the two former being but slender the Trustees could not obtain that satisfaction they wish'd concerning them and yet were unwilling to reject them without a further Examination and it growing late the Meeting was adjourn'd to Wednesday the 21st instant when they were both desired to attend again and in the mean time to attend the Monday Evening Meetings at the Chapel and also the Prayer Meetings on Thursday Evenings.

The Admission of Mr Gladstone making the number thirteen, the Revd Mr Nicholson requested of the Trustees an Assistant Tutor [108r] and nam'd Messrs Upjohn, Turnbull and Owen as eligible. Mr Upjohn being the Senior and withal being the best at English Pronunciation the Trustees made choice of him.

Mr Gladstone concluded with Prayer, the other two Candidates being present.

CHESHUNT COLLEGE

Wednesday 21 August 1799

Adjourned Meeting from the last Monthly Meeting of the 7th instant.

Present Messrs Dupont*, Langston, Hodson, Astle, Oldham and Weatherill, also Mr Holmes.

Mr Hinxman and Mr Jones attended for a further Examination respecting a Work of Grace on their Hearts and their Call to the Ministry, when the latter by no means appearing clear [108v] in either of them, the Trustees were under the necessity of refusing them Admission into the College for the present, but they were both desired not to consider this as a final Exclusion, for if at a later time they should make Application and give more satisfactory Evidence of their Call, they might be Admitted.

Adjourned

Special Meeting of the Trustees
29 Aug: 1799

Present Messrs Oldham, Weatherill, Dupont, Hodson, Langston, Astle.

Mr Dupont inform'd the Meeting that he had received a Letter from Mr Nicholson acquainting him that Mr Ross yesterday [109r] morning left the College improperly. Resolved therefore that he is no longer to be considered a Student.[25]

Mr Hodson acquainted the Meeting that first Mr Cook and then Mr Walsh had attended such of the Trustees as were present at the Chapel on the Lords-day, had stated their ill health and that they were advised to desist for a while from Study - therefore requested leave to try the Effect of Relaxation from Study and Change of Air which was granted.

Resolved that as Mr Dupont is shortly going on a Journey the Trustees make their Visit to the College on Monday next.

Resolved also that as the number of Students is now reduced below 12 Mr Upjohn be continued in his Office as Assistant Tutor no longer than one Quarter from the time of his Appointment unless the number of Students should again be increased.

Mr Oldham concluded with Prayer.

[109v]

Monthly Meeting 4 September 1799

Present Messrs Hodson, Weatherill, Langston*, King, Astle, Newcomb, Tutt, Bell, Burnell.

Mr Hodson reported that on account of an Information received by the Trustees they were under the necessity of visiting the College which they did on Monday last the 2nd instant, when it appeared that Mr Walsh had on the preceding Monday married a young Woman at Hertford: that he intended keeping it a secret and to have remained in the College, but a Woman called in for a Witness to the Marriage [110r] having divulged it Mr Walsh now requested of the Trustees that he might be permitted to continue in the College as his wife might remain with her Mother. This the Trustees could by no means consent to as it would be contrary to their determination to have only single Men in the College, therefore Mr Walsh was desired to quit.

Mr Ross was gone from the College to follow his own Business but none of his Brethren nor the President knew where.[26]

Mr Hodson reported that the Students returned thanks for the Donation of Coals last Winter and beg'd the like favor for the ensuing Winter which on the question being put was unanimously granted.

Read a Letter from Mr Edward Hughes of Buntingford to Lady Anne Erskine begging her interest and information relating to his Admission into College.

Understanding that he had formerly applied to the Missionary Society[27] Mr Hodson [110v] was requested to wait on the Revd Mr Wilks to enquire if the Cause of his being rejected by them.

Mr Hodson reported the ruinous State of the Coach house and Stables at the College which would require soon to be pulled down and that the Trustees at their Visitation had determin'd to set about building the long intended Chapel next Spring.

Resolved therefore that Mr Carr be requested to attend the next Meeting with the Plans he formerly exhibited. And that some Information relative to the Chapel be inserted in the next Notice.

Quarterly General Meeting Oct: 2nd 1799

Present Messrs Langston, Cooper, Hodson*, Tutt, Capell, Astle, Butcher, James Carr, Simpson Senior, Weatherill, William Knight, Bridgman, Newcomb, Burnell, Holmes, Stickland[28]

[111r]

The Chairman reported that Miss Hillier's Executors had transfer'd her Legacy of £1000 3 per Cent Consols into the Name of Messrs Oldham, Hodson, Langston and Batley, and had paid £15 for the Midsummer Dividend on the same: but the Stamp Duty amounting to £38-2-0 and the Transfer 12s. 6d were paid by Mr Hodson.

Read Mr Nicholson's Quarterly Report which was very satisfactory.

Read the Attendance and Non Attendance of the Assistant Committee at the Monthly Meetings since October last, when it was found that Mr Butcher Senior had departed this Life [111v] and that Mr Butcher Junior had not attended at all, and Mr Mousley only once: therefore instead of the three now nam'd, Messrs Pontin, John Phillips, and Tolkien were chosen.

Mr James Carr brought Plans for the intended Chapel; which were inspected and one was fix'd on. Mr Carr was not prepared for the Estimate: however a Subscription was begun in order to defray the Expence; as it is determined not to sell any of the Stock for this purpose.[29]

The Chairman concluded with Prayer.

November Monthly Meeting

Present Messrs Hodson, Langston*, Astle, Cooper, Dupont, Tutt, Weatherill, Bell, Tolkien, Pontin, Carpenter, [112r] King. Mr James Carr also attended with the Plans.

Read a Letter from Mr Nicholson respecting Mr George Gladstone whose time of Probation was expired. He was ask'd a few Questions which being answered satisfactorily he was admitted a Student.

Read Mr Nicholson's Quarterly Account to Michaelmas Amount £112-10-11. Read Mrs Cole's Bill for washing Amount £7-4-10 both paid by Mr Hodson.

Mr James Carr produced the fix'd on Plan with some alterations also another new Plan which appear'd to him more eligible. The same [112v] being approved of the Estimate was desired to be brought forward the next Monthly Meeting.

December Monthly Meeting

Present Messrs Weatherill, Hodson*, Bell, Langston, Holmes, Newcomb, Astle, James Carr, Cooper, Tolkien, Phillips, Walsh Senior.

Mr Carr produced the Plans, but had not made out the Estimate.

The Chairman reported that he had paid Mr William Upjohn £2-10-0 for a Quarters Salary as Assistant Tutor, which Office had ceased for the present, the number of Students being reduced below twelve.
[113r]
Read a Letter from Mr Bradley late a Student, containing a Copy of one from Mr Newman, who is desirous of being admitted into the College. Mr Hodson was desired to answer it, that he might come up and attend the February Meeting, but previous thereto might write to Mr Hodson his Experience in the Dealings of God with him relative to his desire for the Ministry.

Resolved that the Vacation at College commence Thursday the 19th inst. and end Monday January 13th.

1   The second minute book ends on 5th Jan. 1801

2   From this point the sentence 'The chairman began with prayer' has been omitted from this transcript

3   'and receipt' added later

4   This page reference is to the Countess's hymn book first published in 1780 - *A Select Collection of Hymns to be universally sung in all the Countess of Huntingdon's Chapels...* (Hughes & Walsh, London)

5   'Newcombe' added later

6   'Platt, Astle, Towers' added later

7   'Revd Mr Tessier' added later

8   No letter book for this period has survived among the College archives

9   The notice of this Anniversary is printed below p.232

10   See the accounts in College Archives, C 9/ 1

11   John Lloyd of Bath (later of Swansea) was an old friend of Lady Huntingdon. See his letters to her in College archives F 1

12   A folio has been cut out of the volume here

13   The New River Company, which supplied water to London, was begun in 1609 and completed in 1613

14   The notes on the progress of the College given to Mr Eyre and Mr Kirby are printed below p.235

15   This entry was added later

16   Although Thomas Wills had been dismissed by Lady Huntingdon the trustees obviously harboured no grudge

17   These minutes are in a different handwriting

18   One of the tickets for this meeting is in the College archives, C 9/ 14/ 3, and is reproduced here (Plate IV; between pp.186-7)

19   The 'Hints' given to Dr Haweis are printed under 'Miscellaneous Records' below, p.234

20   A notice for this meeting is printed below pp.232-3

21   From this point the routine entries about reading the minutes are omitted from this transcript

22   The Travelling Fund was established to support the itinerating ministers. See College archives E 4/ 15, 2

23   The Notes on the progress of the College given to Mr Eyre are printed below p.235

24   John Mitchell's application for admission to Hoxton Academy on 27 Feb. 1799 is in the New College archives (418/26) at Dr Williams's Library. I am grateful to Dr Nuttall for this reference

25   Added in another hand - 'Note Mr Ross had lain with Mr Nicholson's Niece'

26   The person who noted Mr Ross's offence has added here - 'The Trustees expelled him though absent'

27   This was the London Missionary Society which was established in 1795

28   A notice for this meeting is printed below p.233

29   Subscriptions for building the College chapel can be found in the Spa Fields accounts (College archives, D 1/ 4, 1793-1805). On 16th Apr. 1800 the trustees deferred a decision until June and on 4th June they decided not to proceed as the estimates were too high

III

PLAN OF THE APOSTOLIC SOCIETY

PLAN OF THE APOSTOLIC SOCIETY

[1]   London 17th October 1787

Proposals for a subscription for the future and permanent support of the College which the Right Honourable Selina Countess Dowager of Huntingdon hath instituted, and so long and so successfully maintained, through the Lord's blessing, out of her own Income; and which she intends to maintain during her Life, as a Seminary for young men whom the Lord shall call to the Work of the Ministry of the Gospel of Christ. Also her Ladyship's Plan drawn up by her with the Articles, or confession of faith to be signed by every student previous to his being admitted as such; and also the rules and regulations of the said College; and the resolutions and restrictions in consequence of such Proposal.

Resolved

That as her Ladyship intends, the Lord willing, to build a College at Swansea in South Wales[1] (the present [College] being Leasehold) and in case a fund is formed in consequence of the Proposals now made to her, also intends to convey and assign the same, with the Library of Books and furniture, [2] and also her Chapel, and the Houses to be erected for Schools in Swansea, to seven Persons (not Ministers) as Trustees and Governors;[2] and as from the disinterestedness of both parties a mutual confidence must be supposed to subsist between Lady Huntingdon and the Subscribers towards the intended Fund; it is proposed and resolved that she shall have the nomination of the Trustees and also the liberty of filling up the number as occasion shall require during her *life, and that after her decease, in case of a vacancy, the nomination of them shall rest with the surviving Trustees for the time being; who shall from time to time at the first monthly meeting next after any vacancy unanimously nominate and fill up the number of the Trustees; and if not then done, the new Trustee or Trustees shall at the second monthly meeting after such vacancy be chosen by a majority of the old; and if an equal division, they shall then immediately chose the new Trustee or Trustees by Lot: so that* [3]there may be always seven Trustees: and so as such nomination be of men in her Ladyship's connexion; holding the doctrines contained in the following 15 Articles, and subscribing to or signing the same with what is herein contained. And in case either or any of them shall declaratively dissent from all or any of the doctrines contained in the said following 15 Articles; or shall refuse to pursue the line of Conduct laid down in the subsequent part of this Plan, he or they shall be removed by the Countess of Huntingdon in her Lifetime, and after her decease by the unanimous

155

vote of the other Trustees for the [3] Time being, and another or others be chosen and appointed in his or their room by the said Countess in her Lifetime, *and after her decease by the other Trustees unanimously, or by a majority, or by lot, at the first or second monthly meeting as above mentioned. Accordingly the said* Countess of Huntingdon hath appointed the seven following Gentlemen; and we the undersigned subscribers do approve of and agree to the same appointment; and to all the Articles and resolutions herein contained, as do also we the undersigned principal Ministers of and serving in her Ladyship's connexion; namely, the Reverend Thomas Wills, the Reverend William Taylor, the Reverend John Bradford, the Reverend Craddock Glascot, the Reverend David Jones, and the Reverend Nathaniel Rowland.[4]

That Benjamin Lyon of Bartletts Buildings, Doctor of Physic; James Oldham of Holborn, Ironmonger; Mathias Dupont of Aldersgate Street, Innholder; Thomas Weatherill of Cold Bath Square, Gentleman; William Hodson of Lothbury, Merchant; William Langston of Gutter Lane, Wholesale Haberdasher; and Henry Batley of Seward Street, Goswell Street, Druggist, be the persons appointed to receive Donations and subscriptions; and also they, and their successors for the time being, be Trustees of the Fund, and Governors of the College.

That private Donations be received, and an Annual [4] subscription opened, and that the money be laid out in the Bank in the names of four[5] of the said Trustees and to accumulate during the Countess's life.

That the accumulating Fund be for no other Purpose whatsoever than for continuing and supporting the College, after the decease of the Countess, as a Seminary already opened by her for the education of young men for the Ministry according to the Plan (of Seccession[6]) now pursued by her Ladyship. This Plan the Countess of Huntingdon was obliged to adopt in the Year of our Lord 1782, being that year (not by choice) compelled either to leave the Church established in this Kingdom; or claim her Privilege as a Peeress, by appeal to the House of Lords.[7] As a Peeress of the Realm she considered herself possessed of a Right to have as many Chapels in or adjoining to her houses, as she thought proper. But her Chaplains being cited in the Ecclesiastical Court, and prevented from preaching the pure and precious Gospel where God had evidently called them to labour; the submitting to its [5] jurisdiction might have stopped the progress of the blessed Gospel under her Ladyship's patronage; and entirely defeated her one great view and wish, which was to have the same freely, faithfully and fully dispensed, without interruption, throughout the whole Kingdom: knowing that this and this only could promote the present and everlasting good of thousands of precious souls, and be for the glory of our blessed Lord God and Saviour Jesus Christ. In order to this Lady Huntingdon quietly withdrew from the established Church under the Shelter of the Toleration Act and other subsequent Acts,[8] and esteemed it her highest honour to pursue the plan of Secession; which seemed and is best calculated for the future peace and welfare of the Congregations collected under her Patronage. For had she succeeded in the House of Lords, and her right been established; the benefit which the Congregation might draw from her privilege, could have only been during her Lifetime. After her death, they must either have broke up, or dissented and left the Church form altogether, or been exposed to the penalties of the Law. And from the success which this life of Labour in the Lord's Vineyard has ever since met with, her Ladyship has the satisfaction of experiencing, that God has most eminently owned, and abundantly blessed it. Therefore feeling her Obligations to God for such a singular favour [6] shown her; and not doubting but the Lord who has begun such a glorious work in his own way, will continue to bless and carry it on in the same way till it shall become the Praise and Glory of the whole Earth; her Ladyship's one wish and desire is that a College may be erected and endowed on this foundation, for the education of young men for the ministry according to this Plan now pursued by her, and solely under the restrictions, rules and regulations herein contained; and which we the said Countess of Huntingdon, Ministers, Trustees and undersigned subscribers do hereby resolve shall not be departed from.

That in whatever situation Lady Huntingdon shall purchase Land and build a College, she agrees, upon divers considerations her thereunto moving, to convey the same unto the seven persons above named, as Trustees, or their successors. And we the said Trustees, with the Countess, and with the Approbation of the undersigned subscribers, signified by their hereunto subscribing their names, do agree (with the advice of Counsel previously had) legally to settle, for and towards, the future support of and endowing the College opened by the said Countess in Wales, the money which may be raised as aforesaid; and in case [7] it shall not be sufficient, all future sums subscribed and given for this particular purpose: if not so settled by the Givers: such Conveyance and settlement to take effect immediately on the decease of the said Countess.

That in case a College should not be built by the Countess, and yet a Fund formed before her decease, then the Trustees to provide a place, and by Deed settle it and the Fund as herein mentioned.

That such Deed of Trust shall contain the resolutions, plan, articles, restrictions, rules and regulations herein contained; and on its being signed and delivered by the said Countess and Trustees, or by the Trustees alone, shall be duly inrolled in the High Court of Chancery.[9]

That if the Countess of Huntingdon shall hereafter find it convenient to endow the College herself, and she doth it accordingly that then and in such case she shall be freed from every engagement herein; and the Trustees shall be at liberty to apply the money, which may be raised by subscription as aforesaid, towards the support, promotion or propagation of the Gospel either at home or abroad, in her Ladyship's Connexion in any way that they shall think proper, but for no other use or purpose whatsoever.

That here shall be only one Master or Tutor of the [8] students, at a salary not exceeding fifty pounds per annum, besides board, lodging and washing; and if hereafter necessary an Assistant at a salary not exceeding *Thirty pounds per annum,* both of them to be appointed, and removable by a Majority of the Trustees for the time being. But before their Appointment such Master and Assistant to be examined and approved as to their abilities and qualifications, by one or more of the principal Minister or Ministers of, or serving in the Connexion: such approbation to be certified under the hand or hands *of such Minister or Ministers: but previously to their appointment they are also to assent to and subscribe the said following Fifteen Articles or confession of faith.*

That there be only one Housekeeper, at a salary not exceeding *Twelve* pounds per annum; and two other servants, or three at most, at salaries not exceeding six pounds each.

That Lady Huntingdon is also to leave a nomination of any number of persons not exceeding *three,* resident near the College, as general superintendents and private inspectors of the same, as well respecting the Master and Students, as the household concerns. And in case her Ladyship should not leave such a nomination at her decease, then the Governors from time to time shall nominate such persons, not exceeding *three* as they shall [9] think proper for that purpose. Which persons are from time to time, quarterly, or oftener to make their reports by letter to the Governors. But as such superintendency and inspection is also esteemed altogether a work and labour of love, no salary or other emolument whatsoever is to be paid or given on account thereof.

That it is intended that twenty young men shall be admitted on the foundation; unless it shall hereafter appear necessary to add more; such as having experienced a saving work of Grace on their own hearts, are made willing to give up themselves to the Lord Jesus Christ, to serve in the Ministry of the Gospel, in the connexion already formed by the Countess of Huntingdon and according to the Plan of Secession now pursued by her Ladyship.

That they shall be boarded and clothed; and continue four years, or two years at least, in the College before they are sent out to supply any place, not in the vicinity of the College: except they shall be judged proper to be sent out before. And on any one or more being sent out, his or their place and places to be filled up; so that there may be always twenty, or other additional number as shall be by the Trustees agreed on.

PLAN OF THE APOSTOLIC SOCIETY, 1787

That each person applying to be received as a student shall be examined by one or more principal Minister or [10] Ministers of and serving in the Connexion; or by the Master of the College; who, if they find him to be a proper person for admission, shall report the examination to the Governors for the time being, and, *if they also approve of him, they or two of them at least are to* give an Order for his Admission as a Probationer, till the time of his examination for Admission as a Student which shall also be taken and reported, and an Order given for admission as a student as above, in the case of a probationer.

That in consideration of the importance of the undertaking, a trial of three Months will be allowed before their general examination for their Admission on the foundation as students, which will depend on their being enabled conscientiously to answer the following questions in the Affirmative.

1. Whether you are experimentally convinced of the total fall of man, consisting in the imputation of Adam's guilt and the communication of his depraved nature to all his posterity? And will you faithfully maintain it according to the scope of all Scripture, and your own experience, vizt that it is so total as to need the immense price of the precious blood of the God Man Christ Jesus, for man's redemption, as so powerful a remedy as Christ's blood [11] and righteousness imputed, and applied by God the Holy Ghost for man's recovery.

2. Whether the revelation of the Holy Ghost hath made this salvation plain, and in what degree to your hearts, by the knowledge of the Pardon of your sins, and your acceptance and peace with God in and through Christ, according to the new Covenant: vizt through faith alone in the Redeemer's blood and righteousness.

3. Doth your faith work by love? and hath the knowledge of your salvation produced this genuine effect, a willing heart to be an entire sacrifice to our Saviour Christ in body, soul and spirit to all eternity - to do his pleasure - to obey his commands; and to go whithersoever his Providence shall open a way in order to promote his Glory, and the welfare of immortal Souls - always looking upon yourselves as having your lives in your hands; and to be ready to suffer the Lord's will in any thing, so as he blesses his message by you to them.

4. Have you any other views in entering this College than of being devoted to the Lord; and of attaining such a degree of necessary learning as may make you instrumentally useful in the work of the Ministry? And will you during your connection with it, willingly and constantly give up your services for the good of those who (under God's Providence) [12] shall depend on it for a supply using or not using the forms and ceremonies of the established Church, as shall be judged most profitable for the place where you may labour.

159

5. Do you trust that you are inwardly moved by the Holy Ghost to take upon you the work of the ministry? Do you feel a zeal for God's Glory? a due sense of his mercy and goodness in Christ? a wish of communicating the same to others? a concern, a compassion and tenderness for souls? a desire of having them rescued from endless misery and of pointing them to Christ, the way to everlasting happiness? a desire of dedicating your life and labours to these ends? And in order to this, will you through Grace give up your mind to the study of the Holy Scriptures and your heart to be taught by the spirit of God? These are the motives which should determine your Choice; these the qualifications required; these the desires a heart so moved and qualified should have.

You who under these circumstances can with a clear conscience before God and Man become the members of this College are expected,

1. To look at the Apostles, Prophets and Martyrs, as the only Patterns for doing and suffering your Saviour's will; laying aside all distinction of sects and parties: as this institution necessarily infers. [13]

2. To count yourselves no longer your own, but as persons bought with the Blood of Christ, to be led by his Spirit - living upon him by faith and ready to be his servants and the servants of all for his sake and for the sole benefit of his Church and People.

3. To trust Christ (as his first followers did) with your maintenance abroad, and at home. Any having duly weighed the various trials, temptations and great tributions which a life of faith must necessarily expose you to, to be ready to take up your cross and to follow Christ through good and evil report.

4. All must stand upon the same footing in this College, as pensioners on the bounty of the institution. Neither birth, fortune, nor parts, will be permitted to demand the least preference. But all will be alike looked upon, as only the servants of Jesus Christ, for his purposes in the services of the Gospel.

Lastly. These qualifications of heart and spirit must prove the absurdity of any one changing his temporal condition in this Life for any supposed superior order to what he originally was before he entered the College. On the Contrary, they the more fully bring him to be the servant of all men. Therefore a life of labour, hardship, [14] severity, temptation, and suffering is and must be his Choice and Preference, to every worldly view of honour, esteem, praise, and temporal advantage, above those from among whom he arose. This point, in this College, will admit of no relaxation, but is to be strictly followed up to the hearts and minds of the students continually, in the example of our Lord, and his Apostles, by all the Superintendants of the College.

That after their probationary trial and previously to their being entered as students, they are to be called upon, freely without mental reservation, and without compulsion from any sinister or selfish view, solemnly, jointly and severally to declare, That they do according to the word and spirit of God believe, confess, and subscribe from their hearts, as essential parts of the Christian faith, the doctrines contained in the following Articles,[10] namely –

1. OF GOD

That there is but one living and true God, everlasting, without body, parts, or passions; of infinite power, wisdom, and goodness; the Maker and Preserver of all things, both visible and invisible. And in unity of the Godhead there are three persons, of one substance, power, and eternity, the Father, the Son, and the Holy Ghost.

[15]

2. OF THE SCRIPTURES

That it pleased God, at sundry times and in divers manners, to declare His will, and that the same should be committed unto writing; which is therefore called the Holy Scripture, which containeth all things necessary to Salvation. The authority whereof doth not depend upon the testimony of man, but wholly upon God, its Author; and our assurance of the infallible truth thereof is from the inward work of the Holy Ghost, bearing witness, with the Word, in our hearts.

3. OF CREATION

It pleased God, for the manifestation of His glory, in the beginning, to create the world and all things therein; and having made man, male and female, after his own image, endued with knowledge, righteousness, and true holiness; he gave them a command not to eat of the tree of knowledge of good and evil, with a power to fulfil it, yet under a possibility of transgressing, being left to the liberty of their own will, which was subject unto change.

4. OF THE FALL OF MAN FROM ORIGINAL RIGHTEOUSNESS.

Our first parents sinned in eating the forbidden fruit; whereby they fell from their original righteousness, and became wholly defiled in all the faculties and parts of soul and body. And being the root of all mankind, the guilt of this sin was imputed, and the same corrupt nature conveyed to all their posterity descending from them by ordinary generation.

5. *OF ORIGINAL SIN*

Original sin standeth not in the following of Adam, as the Pelagians do vainly talk; but it is the fault and corruption of the nature of every man, that naturally is engendered of the offspring of Adam; whereby man is, as far as possible, gone from original righteousness, and is of his own nature inclined to evil, so that the flesh lusteth always contrary to the spirit; and, therefore, in every person born into this world, it deserveth God's wrath and damnation. Any this infection of nature doth remain, yea in them that are regenerated, yet without dominion; and although there is no condemnation to them that are in Christ Jesus, yet sin in them is evil, as much as in others, and as such receives divine, fatherly chastisement.

6. *OF PREDESTINATION AND ELECTION*

Although the whole world is thus become guilty before God, it hath pleased Him to predestinate some unto everlasting life. Predestination, therefore, to life, is the everlasting purpose of God whereby (before the foundations of the world were laid) He hath constantly decreed by His counsel, secret to us, to deliver from curse and damnation those whom He hath chosen in Christ out of mankind, and bring them by Christ to everlasting salvation, as vessels made to honour. Wherefore they which are endued with so excellent a benefit of God, are called according to God's purpose, by His spirit working in due season; they, through grace, obey the call; they are justified freely; they are made sons of God by adoption; they bear the image of Christ; they walk religiously in good works, and at length, by God's mercy, they attain to everlasting felicity.

7. *OF CHRIST THE MEDIATOR*

It pleased God in His eternal purpose, to choose and ordain the Lord Jesus, His only begotten Son, to be Mediator between God and man, the Prophet, Priest, and King, the Head, and Saviour, of His church; unto whom he did, from all eternity, give a people to be His seed, and to be by Him in time redeemed, called, justified, sanctified, and glorified. He, therefore, being very and eternal God, of one substance and equal with the Father, did, when the fulness of time was come, take upon Him man's nature, yet without sin, being conceived by the power of the Holy Ghost in the womb of the Virgin Mary; so that two whole, perfect, and distinct natures, the Godhead, and the manhood, were inseparably joined together in one person, without conversion, or confusion; which person is very God and very man, yet one Christ, the only Mediator between God and man. This office of Mediator and Surety He did most willingly undertake; which, that he might discharge, He was made under the law, and did perfectly fulfil it by an obedience unto death; by which perfect obedience and sacrifice of Himself on the cross, which He, through the Eternal spirit, once offered up unto God, He hath fully satisfied Divine Justice, and purchased not only reconciliation, but an everlasting inheritance in the kingdom of heaven for all those whom the Father hath given Him. To all of whom He doth, in His own time, and in His own way, certainly and effectually apply His purchased redemption; making intercession for them; and revealing unto them, through the Word and by His Spirit, the mysteries of Salvation; effectually enabling them to believe unto obedience; and governing their hearts by the same Word and Spirit; and overcoming all their enemies by His almighty power.

8. OF THE HOLY GHOST

The Holy Ghost is the third person in the adorable Godhead, distinct from the Father and the son; yet of one substance, glory, and majesty with them, very and eternal God; whose office in the church is manifold. It is He who illuminates the understanding to discern spiritual things, and guides us into all truths; so that without His teaching, we shall never be effectually convinced of sin, nor be brought to the saving knowledge of God in Christ. And His teaching, whether it be by certain means which He ordinarily makes use of, or without means, is attended with an evidence peculiar and proper to itself, therefore styled the demonstration of the Spirit and of power. By which divine power He not only enlightens the understanding, but gives a new turn or bias to the will and affections, moving and acting upon our hearts, and by His secret, energetic influence effecting those things, which we could never attain or accomplish by our own strength. Nor is His guidance less necessary in our lives and all our actions. Without His assistance we know not what to pray for, or how to pray aright. He confirms us in all grace; and He is the author of all holiness. It is He that assures us of our personal interest in Christ, and that sheds abroad the love of God in our hearts. He seals believers unto the day of redemption; and is Himself the earnest of their future inheritance. He administers comfort to us in our temporal and spiritual distresses, by applying to our minds seasonable promises of God in Christ Jesus, which are yea and amen; and, by receiving the things of Christ, and shewing them unto us. Thus He encourageth and refresheth us with a sense of the favour of God; fills us with joy unspeakable and full of glory, and is to abide with the church forever.

9. OF FREE WILL

The condition of man after the fall of Adam, is such, that he cannot turn and prepare himself by his own natural strength and good works to faith and calling upon God; wherefore we have no power to do good works pleasant and acceptable to God, without the grace of God by Christ preventing us, that we may have a good will, and working with us when we have that good will.

10. OF JUSTIFICATION

We are accounted righteous before God, only for the merit of our Lord and Saviour Jesus Christ, by faith, and not for our own works or deservings. Wherefore that we are justified by faith alone, is a most wholesome doctrine, and very full of comfort. And this is done by pardoning our sins, and by accounting our persons as righteous by imputing the obedience and satisfaction of Christ unto us, which is received and rested upon by faith; which faith we have not of ourselves, but it is the gift of God.

11. OF SANCTIFICATION AND GOOD WORKS

They who are effectually called and regenerated, having a new heart and a new spirit created in them, are further sanctified, really and personally, through the virtue of Christ's death and resurrection, by His Word and Spirit dwelling in them; the dominion of the whole body of sin is destroyed, and the several lusts thereof are more and more weakened and mortified, and they are more and more quickened and strengthened in all saving graces to the practice of true holiness; without which no man shall see the Lord. Works, which are the fruits of faith, and follow after justification, though they cannot put away our sins nor endure the severity of God's judgment, yet are pleasing and acceptable to God in Christ, and spring out necessarily of a true and lively faith; insomuch that by them a lively faith may be evidently known, as a tree discerned by the fruit.

12. OF WORKS BEFORE JUSTIFICATION

Works done before the grace of Christ, and the inspiration of His spirit, are not pleasant to God; for as much as they spring not of faith in the Lord Jesus Christ; neither do they make men meet to receive grace; yea, rather, for that they are not done as God hath willed and commanded them to be done, we doubt not but they have the nature of sin.

13. OF THE CHURCH

The Catholic or universal Church, which is invisible, consists of the whole number of the elect, that have been, are, or shall be gathered into one, under Christ the head thereof, and is the spouse, the body, the fulness of Him that filleth all in all. The visible church consists of all those throughout the world who profess the true religion, together with their children. To which visible church Christ hath given the ministry and ordinances of the Gospel, for the fathering and perfecting of the saints in this life, to the end of the world; and doth by His own presence and Spirit, according to His promise, make them effectual thereunto.

There is no other head of the church but the Lord Jesus Christ; nor can the Pope of Rome, in any sense, be head thereof, but is that Antichrist, the man of sin, and son of perdition, that exalteth himself in the church against Christ, and all that is called God.

14. OF BAPTISM

Baptism is a sacrament of the New Testament ordained by Jesus Christ, not only for the solemn admission of the party baptized into the visible church, but also to be unto him a sign and seal of the covenant of grace, to be continued in the church until the end of the world; which is rightly administered by pouring or sprinkling water upon the person, in the name of the Father, Son, and Holy Ghost. This sacrament ought to be administered but once to any person; and we also hold, that infants may, and ought to be baptised, in virtue of one or both believing parents; because the spiritual privilege of a right unto, and a participation of the initial seal of the covenant, was granted by God to the infant seed of Abraham; which grant must remain firm for ever, without the Lord's own express revoking or abrogation of it; which can never be proved from Scripture that He has done. --Again, they that have the thing signified, have a right to the sign of it; but Children are capable of the grace signified in Baptism. And some of them, (we trust) are partakers of it; namely such as die in their infancy; therefore they may and ought to be baptised. For these and other reasons, we believe and maintain the lawfulness and expediency of infant baptism.

15. OF THE LORD'S SUPPER

The supper of the Lord is not only a sign of the love that Christians ought to have among themselves one to another, but rather it is a sacrament of the body and blood of Christ, and of our redemption thereby, called the Lord's Supper, to be observed in His church [25] to the end of the world, for the perpetual remembrance of the sacrifice of Himself in His death; the sealing of all benefits thereof to true believers; their spiritual nourishment and growth in Him; their further engagement in, and to all duties which they owe unto Him; and to be a bond and pledge of their communion with Him and with each other as members of His mystical body. Insomuch that, to such as rightly and with faith receive the same, the bread which we break is a partaking of the body of Christ, and likewise the cup of blessing is a partaking of the blood of Christ; though in substance and nature they still remain bread and wine as they were before. Those, therefore, that are void of faith, though they do carnally and visibly eat the bread and drink the wine of this sacrament of the body and blood of Christ, yet they are in no wise partakers of Christ, but rather to their condemnation to eat and drink the sign or sacrament of so great a blessing.

That the students in rotation, shall weekly, or oftener, go out and preach in the Villages and Towns in the Vicinity of the College, not more than 30 Miles [26] distant. Places of the distance of ten miles upwards to be supplied by them only on a Sunday, and to which they are to go on a Saturday and return the next Monday Morning. But the places within ten Miles may be supplied by them on week days, as the Master shall think proper, so that they return the same evening.[11]

That previous to any student being sent out or occasionally before then, he shall be examined by one or more of the principal Minister or Ministers of and serving in the Connexion, as to his qualifications and fitness to be sent out; or as to his improvement in his studies. This Examination to be either at the college, or elsewhere, as shall be most convenient, and the Governors to be made acquainted with the result of the examination.

That the students be allowed out of the said Fund their expenses from the College to their destined and respective stations, out of its vicinity and more than 30 Miles distance, after the rate of one guinea for every one hundred Miles.

That if they see their call clear to it, they shall on their leaving their studies, in case they have attained [27] the Age of *twenty one years at least* be ordained in the Secession by two or more principal Ministers of the Connexion, according to the Plan pursued by the Countess. At the same time signing in confirmation of their first subscription the above confession of Faith, or 15 Articles.

That after every call either at home or abroad for students,[12] such as the Trustees shall think proper, is attended to and answered by their being sent out of the College, by the Trustees, in consequence of Application to them from the Countess of Huntingdon's successors, for the time being, in the superintendency and management of the work of the Connexion, for such student or students to supply such place or places from whence such call or calls may come, the Trustees shall be at liberty to permit any student or students to go into and serve in the established Church, or other Churches in case there should be openings in providence for their

admission therein (but always giving the preference to the time of Secession). And it is agreed and resolved that this as well as every thing else herein contained shall be binding on all future and succeeding Trustees as well as the present.
[28]

That in case any thing improper should arise, either as to the religious principles, or the moral and outward conduct of any of the students; or in case of disobedience to the reasonable commands of the Master according to the rules and regulations of the College, the Governors only shall have the power of expelling on a just examination into the matter.

Rules and Regulations to be
observed in the Countess
of Huntingdon's College

1. The Students are to rise at the sound of the Bell; which is to be rung at 5 o'clock - to appear in the Study at a quarter after 5, before the Master, to sing a Hymn.

2. From this time till 6 they are to retire for private prayer and meditation; and to make their Beds, and clean themselves.

3. At 6 o'clock, the morning[13] exercise begins. [29]

4. Breakfast at 7 N.B. To be over in a quarter of an hour.

5. At eight, the Academical[14] Studies begin and continue till 12.

6. Dinner at ½ past 12. N.B. Dinner to be over in half an hour.

7. At 2, the Academical Studies to begin again and continue till 5.

8. At six, the evening exercise begins.

9. Supper at 7. N.B. To be over in a quarter of an hour.

10. At nine Family Prayer.

11. At ½ past 9 all retire to their Chambers - to be in bed by 10.

12. During Breakfast, Dinner and Supper, one of the students or probationers, by rotation, must read a Chapter in the [30] Bible, which will prevent unprofitable conversation, and afford matter for meditation.

13. No Book to be taken out of the Library, without the Master or Librarian's permission. And all the Books are to be kept clean, well used, and replaced with care.

14. Every one must be ready to give an Account of the manner in which he spends his spare time. It is expected that they will do it, by using wholesome bodily exercise and profitable conversation with each other, and with their neighbours.

15. Their rooms, and the Study, are to be kept clean. And for this purpose as well as to serve their brethren at their meals, two of the students or probationers by a weekly rotation, are to take upon themselves the office of Servitors.

N.B. In case any of them break either of the above rules, he or they shall be made Servitor or Servitors, for the day on which any rule or rules is or are broken.

[31]

That two *or more* of the Governors, with or without Ministers, shall visit the College *once in every year at least;* and, if they require it, have their travelling expences from and to their respective places of residence, born out of the Fund.

That as the present Trustees and Governors generously decline every thing of the kind, no future or other Trustees or Governors, shall upon any pretence be allowed any salary or other sum of money under the name of expences, or otherwise, except their expences to and from the College at their Visitation as above.

That this Society shall be intitled or named as follows:
The Apostolic Society, instituted A.D. 1787 under the Patronage of the Right Honourable Selina Countess Dowager of Huntingdon, for supporting and perpetuating her Ladyship's College in Wales, after her decease: as a Seminary for young men, who under the influence of Divine Grace, may be [32] desirous of devoting themselves to the Ministry of the Gospel of Christ, at home or abroad.

Lastly. That the above Proposal (which originated from Messieurs Langston and Batley) with what is herein contained, be entered in two Books, in order for the signatures of the Countess, the Ministers, the Trustees and Subscribers: one Book for the Countess and the other for the Trustees and Subscribers.[15]

S:Huntingdon Seceder

William Taylor	Benjamin Lyon	
John Bradford	James Oldham Oldham	
	Mat. Dupont	
	Thomas Weatherill	
	William Hodson	
	W. Langston	
	Henry Batley	
[33]	John Fielder	J. Chambers
	Jonathan Tilney	John Hoppe
	Joseph Eyre	Robert Butcher[16]
	David Whitaker	

FOOTNOTES

1   For the chapel which Lady Huntingdon built at Swansea and the college she proposed to build there see Cheshunt College archives, E4/14.

2   In her will dated 11 Jan. 1790 she left the contents of the college to its 'Governors' (Cheshunt College archives C16/3)

3   All words shown in italics in this transcript have been added later over erasures

4   It should be noted that only Taylor and Bradford signed.

5   'The reason of only 4 being named is the Bank will not admit of more, except by Charter or Act of Parliament.' Footnote in original.

6   'By Secession, we mean a withdrawing from that Church, the discipline of which, we cannot from our consciences submit to; and adopting that plan whereby we can conscientiously pursue our labours, and be left at liberty to use, or not use, the forms and ceremonies of the established Church, as shall be thought best calculated for the good and prosperity of the place which we may be asked to labour in.' Footnote in original.

7   See R. Burns, *Ecclesiastical Law* vol.11 (London, 1763), p.159 for this privilege. See also E. Welch, 'Lady Huntingdon and Spa Fields Chapel' (*Guildhall Miscellany* Vol.4, pp.175-183)

8   See Burns *op. cit.* vol.1, pp.519-529

9   By the Act 9 Geo. 11, c. 36

10   These are the Fifteen Articles of the Connexion which were subsequently attached to the College trust deed of 1793 (see Cheshunt College archives, C16/3)

11   For this see Cheshunt College archives C 8/1 & 2

12   Some of the students had gone to North America and Asia

13   'The Morning and Evening exercises consist in singing of Hymns, praying, and preaching, which the students and probationers do in rotation, for the trial and exercise of their gifts; and their improvement in divine truths.' Footnote in original.

14   'The Academical Studies are conducted in the following Order.Classes,

First –   Learn English in the morning and afternoon.

Second – Rudiments of the Latin in the morning. Read English in the afternoon.

Third – Rudiments of the Greek in the Morning. Read Latin in the Afternoon.

Fourth – Logic and the Sciences in the Morning. Read Greek and Latin in the Afternoon.

N.B. Divinity Lectures every day.'

Footnote in original.

15   The volume from which this is transcribed was the trustees' copy which was kept with the College archives

16   Only two of the ministers named in the text (Taylor and Bradford) signed, and several of those who attended the meeting on 17 Oct. failed to sign.

IV

RECORDS OF THE APOSTOLIC

SOCIETY

RECORDS OF THE APOSTOLIC SOCIETY
Instituted A.D. 1787 for supporting
and perpetuating the Countess of
Huntingdon's College

In October 1787, the Countess then residing at Spa-Fields Chapel house, Mr William Langston and Mr Henry Batley, two of the stated Hearers at that Chapel, conferring together on her advanced Age, and the improbability of her being able to endow her College (or provide for its support and continuance after her decease); proposed to each other, and then to her Ladyship, that a Society should be formed for the supporting and perpetuating the same by voluntary Contributions and Subscriptions. The Proposal, meeting her cordial approbation, was communicated to some other friends, chiefly hearers at Spa fields Chapel; Meetings were held at Mr Dupont's, the Castle and Falcon, Aldersgate Street; a Society was formed, and a subscription begun, of which Dr Benjamin Lyon was chosen Treasurer.

The Society was named the Apostolic Society: a name which was thought descriptive of its design, viz., that of sending forth instrumentally such as have received a Divine Call to the Ministry of the Gospel.

To make the Society known and to recommend it, the following Address was drawn up and dispersed in Town and Country.

The Apostolic Society,
Instituted A.D. 1787

Under the Patronage of the Right Honourable Selina Countess Dowager of Huntingdon, for supporting and perpetuating her Ladyship's College in Wales, after her Decease, as a Seminary for young Men, who, under the Influence of Divine Grace, may be desirous of devoting themselves to the Ministry of the Gospel of Christ at Home or Abroad.

For who hath despised the Day of small Things - Zechariah 4. 10.

Highly as this Land is, and hath been, favoured with faithful Ministers of the Gospel, there is yet Reason to say, that the Harvest is truly great; and zealous disinterested Labourers are comparatively very few. There are still many Parts of this Country, of which it may with too much Propriety be said; the People sit in Darkness, and in the Shadow of Death. Add to this the Zeal, and with Pain of Heart we are constrained to say, the Success, with which those who are engaged in the cause of Error and Infidelity are [2] propagating their destructive Tenets: we can need no Apology for this Undertaking.

About the Time that the Light of the pure Gospel was again beginning to dawn in England, Wales, and elsewhere, the Lord put it into the Heart of his Servant Lady Huntingdon, to erect a College, at Talgarth, in South Wales for the Reception of serious young Men, disposed to the Works of the Ministry. And in the Year 1768, a short time after the Expulsion of the Six young Men at Oxford for their strict Adherence to the Truth, her Ladyship's College was opened by that bright shining Light, and eminent Servant of God, George Whitefield.

Her Ladyship's original Intention was to have the young Men educated at her College ordained in the Establishment; but experiencing great difficulty in obtaining Ordination for them; and that Difficulty at last encreasing, to an absolute Refusal; they for some Time preached without it.

Some of the Countess's Chaplains having been cited in the Spiritual Court for Preaching at her Chapel in Spa Fields; and her Ladyship having Respect to the Future Peace of the Congregations collected under her Patronage, more than to her Privilege as a Peeress of the Realm; after defending her Chaplains without Success, in the Spiritual Court, declined appealing to the House of Lords, and quietly withdrew from the Establishment, under the Shelter of the Toleration Act, that great Charter of religious Liberty, and the Glory of the last Reformation. [1]Since that time the Lord hath very much increased the Calls for Ministers, both at Home and Abroad, in the Line which her Ladyship has pursued; and the evident Success and Blessing attending this little School of the Prophets, render the Continuance of it an Object much to be desired.

Some of the Gentlemen who are now the Trustees of this Society, understanding that in case some Provision was not made, the Support of the College must drop with Lady Huntingdon (the Maintenance and Support of which, from the beginning to her Death, she thinks it one of her highest Honours and Privileges to be the sole Instrument of) they proposed to her and some few Friends, to open a Subscription, and form a Fund, for its future Maintenance after her Decease: to which her Ladyship, considering the Good of the rising Generation as well as the present, gave her warmest Approbation, and most willing Patronage. Accordingly a Society was formed, and an annual Subscription opened. And though, at first, but few in Number met, yet they were such whose Hearts were enlarged by the Lord; and who gave Encouragement to look forward with an Eye of Faith; and view, with anticipated Pleasure, the Mite encreasing, so as to enable the Society to perpetuate a Work so much owned and blessed of God; as a Nursery for a rising Ministry; on which as the Means through [3] the Lord's Blessing, the Success of the Gospel much depends. Therefore if any shall be inclined by the Lord to Join this Society; their Donations and Subscriptions will, with Pleasure, be received by the following Gentlemen:

Doctor Benjamin Lyon, No.23 Bartlets Buildings
Mr James Oldham, No.142 Holborn
Mr Matthias Dupont, Castle and Falcon, Aldersgate Street
Mr Thomas Weatherill, Cold-Bath Square
Mr William Hodson, No.39 Lothbury
Mr William Langston, No.46 Gutter Lane, or Colebrook Row, Islington; and
Mr Henry Batley, Seward Street, Goswell Street;

in whose or some of whose Names, the Money is to be laid out in the Bank, as the Trustees thereof, and of the College which the Lady Huntingdon is now preparing to build,[2] and intends to convey to them: The Building which she has at present being held by her only as Tenant at Will.

The Money is to remain in the Bank, and to accumulate during Lady Huntingdon's Life (which may God long preserve, if it be his adorable Will) and at her Death, it is the Intention of this Society, as the Lord shall enable them, to continue the College agreeably to the Plan pursued by her Ladyship, and the Rules and Regulations drawn up by her in consequence of this Proposal; and which may be seen by applying to either of the Trustees.[3]

A General Meeting of the Subscribers will be held quarterly, on the first Wednesday in January, April, July and October, at the Castle and Falcon, Aldersgate Street, at Five o'Clock in the Afternoon.

Persons inclined to bequeath any Legacy towards the support of this Institution, are desired to make use of the following Form.

I give and bequeath to Doctor Benjamin Lyon of Bartlets Buildings, Holborn, London, Treasurer of the Apostolic Society, instituted A.D. 1787, or to the Treasurer for the Time being of the same Society, the Sum of *[blank]* Pounds to be appropriated towards the supporting and perpetuating the Countess of Huntingdons College in Wales, after her Decease, agreeably to the Rules of the said Society; which Sum I direct to be paid to the said Benjamin Lyon, or the Treasurer for the Time being of the said Society, within Three Months after my Decease, and his Receipt shall be a sufficient Discharge.

This Publication produced very little effect; which may be attributed to two causes, first, that the Society was to have no operation till the demise of Lady Huntingdon; and secondly, that her Ladyship having chosen Laymen only as Trustees of her College, and given no share in managing the outward concerns thereof to Ministers, the Revd Thomas Wills, who had married Lady [4] Huntingdon's Niece, and was then the stated Minister of Spa fields Chapel, was offended, and did not accede to, or recommend the Plan: which occasioned a Shyness between him and her Ladyship; and having afterwards in some other matters displeased her, She on the 7th of July 1788 sent him a Letter of dismission: in consequence whereof Dr Lyon, who was much attached to Mr Wills, resigned his Offices of Trustee and Treasurer. The Countess chose Mr William Astle to be Trustee in his Room, and Mr Oldham was elected Treasurer, which he accepted, but not liking to undertake the trouble of managing the Cash concerns, Mr William Hodson was chosen to be Deputy Treasurer.

The Motto prefixed to the Society's first Publication, appeared to be very properly chosen; for the first four years were indeed a 'day of small things,' as the following account of its Receipts for those four Years evince.

Amount of Cash received in 1787	£163	1	0
Ditto	in 1788	£102	7	6
Ditto	in 1789	£ 43	14	6
Ditto	in 1790	£ 89	8	0

This Money however, as it accumulated, was invested in the 3 per Cent Consolidated Bank Annuities, first in the name of Dr Lyon, etc., and afterwards in those of Messrs Oldham, Hodson, Langston and Batley.

Friday the 17th June 1791, the Countess of Huntingdon departed this life at Spa-fields Chapel House, in the 84th year of her Age. By this event the whole care and concern of the College devolved on the Trustees, as the support and continuance did on the Society. Three objects especially claimed their attention,

1st. to increase the Annual Subscriptions,

2d. to find out a suitable place to remove the College to from Wales, somewhere near the Metropolis, as Wales was too far distant for the Trustees to have any Inspection,

3d. to provide a proper Tutor, the present one being only temporary, and by no means sufficiently qualified.[4]

In order to increase the Subscriptions, the Society sent forth into the Religious World the following Publication,

Countess of Huntingdon's College

Amongst the many Works of Faith, and Labours of Love, for the great Redeemer's Glory, and the present and everlasting Welfare of Mankind, wherein that late eminent Servant of God, SELINA Countess of Huntingdon was engaged, and to which she devoted her Life and Fortune, the College she instituted for educating and training up serious young Men for the Ministry of the Gospel, claims the highest regard from the Christian World at large; as embracing in its Views and Including [5] in its Consequences, with the Devine Blessing, the eternal Happiness of Generations yet unborn.

To Perpetuate, therefore, and support, this valuable and important Seminary must be highly acceptable to God if done in Faith and Love, with a single Eye to his Glory.

For this Purpose a Society was formed in the Year 1787, by the Committee of Spa-field, Chapel, and a few other Friends to the Cause of Christ, with the Concurrence and Approbation of her Ladyship, under the Impression that her Demise was an Event that could not be very distant; and that her Fortune dying with her, the College must drop, if a Fund was not raised to support it.

The Title assumed by this Society having given offence to some good People, it may be proper, in this Place, to say it was adopted by them as best expressing the Design of the Institution; namely, to send forth, Instrumentally, a Succession of Labourers into the Lord's Vineyard. This Explanation it is hoped, will remove the Offence occasioned by the Word Apostolic.

The Lease of the present College in Wales expired before the Decease of its noble Foundress; and the Trustees have it in Contemplation to provide a Place much nearer the Metropolis, for Convenience of frequent Superintendence and Inspection. On this Occasion they think it needful to Inform that Public, whose liberal Assistance they solicit, that it is intended to receive no Persons into the College but such as shall appear to have experienced in their own Hearts, the Power of Divine Grace: that they shall be trained up in the pure Principles and Doctrines of the Reformation, agreeably to the Holy Scriptures: and shall be kept in College a sufficient Time to acquire, by diligent Study and Application, that Competent Measure of Human Literature, which, in Subordination to the Gifts and Graces of the Holy Spirit, furnishes and fits Men for the Ministry. And that, on quitting College, they shall not be confined to minister in Lady Huntingdon's Chapels only; but will be at liberty to go into the Establishment, if they can obtain Ordination; or into any of the Dissenting Churches of Christ, where there is a prospect of usefulness, and their own Inclination leads them.

That it hath pleased God abundantly to own and bless the pious Design of his departed Servant, in opening and maintaining, at her own Expense (amounting to 500ℓ or 600ℓ per Annum) this House of Gospel Instruction, is evident from the many useful Ministers and shining Lights who have received their Education there, and who have been and now are made, by Divine Grace, eminently useful in spreading abroad the Truth as it is in Jesus, both in the Establishment and in Dissenting Churches. [6]

The Fund hitherto raised by the Apostolic Society, and the Annual Subscriptions thereof, though far from contemptible, are yet very inadequate to the Accomplishment of the desired End, viz. The continual Support and Maintenance of the College. They are therefore constrained to apply to serious Persons of Ability, for their kind Assistance herein, not doubting but sincere Christians of every Denomination will esteem it a Privilege to come forward and join their Labour of Love, either by Donation or Annual Subscription, for the future and permanent Support and Establishment of this Evangelical Nursery, whose primary Object is the Glory of God by the most extensive Spread of the Gospel of Christ.

Inspectors or Superintendants of the College, appointed by the Countess of Huntingdon

The Rev. David Jones, of Langan,
The Rev. Nathaniel Rowland,
The Rev. Dr. Ford.[5]

Trustees of the College, appointed by the same.

James Oldham Oldham, Esq., No.142 Holborn, Treasurer.
Mr. William Hodson, No.39 Lothbury, Sub-treasurer.
Mr. Henry Batley, No.9 Winchester-place, Pentonville, Secretary.
Mr. William Astle, Portpool-lane, Gray's-inn-lane.
Mr. Matthias Dupont, No.5 Aldersgate-street.
Mr. William Langston, No.2 Highbury-place, Islington.
John Lloyd, Esq., Swansea.
Mr. Thomas Weatherill, No.6 Cold-bath-square.

By whom Subscriptions or Donations will be gratefully received, and by the following Bankers;

Messrs Charles Boldero, Stephen Thurston Adey, Sir Stephen Lushington, Bart. and Edward Gale Boldero, Bankers, Cornhill.

Sir Herbert Mackworth, Dorset, Johnson, and Wilkinson, Bankers, Bond-Street.

The Apostolic Society have Four General Meetings in the Year, viz. On the first Wednesday in January, April, July and October, at the Castle and Falcon, Aldersgate-street, at Five o'Clock in the Afternoon; and the Trustees meet the First Wednesday in the other Months, at the Committee Room of Spa-field Chapel.

Persons inclined to bequeath any Legacy towards the support of this Institution, are desired to make use of the following Form:

[7]

> I give and bequeath to James Oldham Oldham Esq., of Holborn, London, Treasurer of the Apostolic Society, instituted A.D. 1787, or to the Treasurer for the time being of the same Society, the sum of *[blank]* Pounds, to be appropriated towards the supporting and perpetuating the College, late the Countess of Huntingdon's, in Wales, or wherever the same shall be carried on by her Trustees, which sum I direct to be paid to the said James Oldham Oldham, or the Treasurer for the time being of the said Society, within three Months after my Decease, and his Receipt shall be a sufficient Discharge.[6]

The foregoing Address was inclosed in the following Letter, and sent to many Persons in and about London, and to various Ministers in the Country.

> Sir, or Revd Sir, or Madam,
> The Apostolic Society for continuing and perpetuating the Countess of Huntingdon's College, having directed me to send You the inclosed Address on behalf of the same, I beg leave to recommend it to your zealous Support and Encouragement, and am with great deference and respect,
>
> Sir, or Revd Sir, or Madam,
> Your most humble Servant
> Henry Batley,
> Secretary

No.9 Winchester Place,
Pentonville
18 July 1791

Note: You will be waited on in a few days by a deputation from the Society.

Agreeably to the Note at the foot of the Letter, Deputations from the Society made a personal application to many Persons who were esteemed well affected to the Cause; and obtained a considerable increase of Subscriptions: perhaps if this had been done more generally the Success might have been greater. But it is worthy of remark that the Society was much disappointed in its expectations from great Men, such as The Earl of Dartmouth, Mr Thornton, etc., although religious Characters: not one could be found who would patronise the College notwithstanding the obvious Utility of the Institution. It appeared as if the Lord would by this teach the Trustees and Society to place their dependence on Him, whose Cause they were engaged in, and not in any Arm of Flesh. Not by might, nor by power, but by my Spirit saith the Lord of hosts.[7]

The Subscriptions, Donations, and Dividends of Money invested in the publick Funds, received in the year 1791, amounted to £376 16s.

In order to find out a proper place to remove the College to from Wales, the Society at their General Meeting the 6 July 1791, appointed Messrs Oldham, Batley, Simpson, Dupont, Banks and Hodson, to be a Committee to enquire and look out for a place from ten to fifty miles from London. They saw several Houses, one at Enfield, another at Woodford, and one at Mile-end, the Revd Mr Addington's, but they were either too small, or else there was some other objection to all they either saw or heard of, [8] until Wednesday September 14 1791, when Messrs Batley and Hodson went to Cheshunt to see the Manor House there, which was to be lett or sold with 70 Acres of Land. The House they found too large with a great number of Windows, the Taxes whereof[8] and the keeping up such a place in Repair must be very expensive; besides it could not be sold for Ever, and as Tenants we might be liable to be turn'd out. Messrs Batley and Hodson liked the Situation of the Place, and Dining at the Green Dragon near the Church asked the Landlord if there were any other Houses empty thereabouts. He inform'd them of two, one the Vicarage house close to the Church Yard and the other a house adjoining the Green Dragon with near Seven Acres of land besides a large Garden and New River [9]running through the Estate. Messrs Batley and Hodson saw both these houses. The Vicarage would not suit, but the other pleased them much, and they thought if it could be purchased on reasonable Terms it would answer their purpose extremely well. They found that it was a Freehold, the Property of a Mrs Shaw in Berkshire and that Twelve Hundred Pounds was ask'd for it. They came home with this Intelligence to their Brethren, and on Friday November 11th the Trustees went to see it, and were unanimously of Opinion that it was a very eligible Spot and convenient for the purpose, there being a very large and handsome Parlour which might be used as a Chapel, and a good many sleeping Rooms or what might be made such for the Students. It was therefore resolved that Mr Oldham manage the business and purchase it on the best Terms he could not exceeding Eleven Hundred Pounds.

Mr Oldham undertook this business and managed it so well that he compleated the purchase for Nine hundred and fifty Pounds.

October 19 1791 Notice was given to Mr Hughes the Landlord of the House at or near Trevecka in South Wales, which is the present College, that We should quit it at Midsummer next, or at Ladyday if he wish'd it, which in reply he informed us he did.

And now, the Lord having helped thus far, the next great Care of the Trustees, and the most important of all, was to provide a proper and suitable Tutor: a Clergyman of the Church of England was most desirable, but he must be a converted Man, a good Scholar, of unexceptionable moral Character, and of good teaching Abilities. To obtain such a one, an Advertisement was drawn up by Mr Oldham and inserted in the Oxford, Cambridge, York and Leeds Papers, also in the Whitehall Evening Post and another Evening Paper. To these Advertisements Mr Oldham received many Answers, which were read in the society, but none of the Gentlemen seemed to come up to the Character described in the Advertisement. [9]

December 21 1791. The business of the Society requiring a Secretary, Mr George Best, late Secretary of the Countess of Huntingdon, was chosen, with a Salary of Ten Pounds per Annum.

No Tutor having been obtained by the Advertisements, several Gospel Ministers in the Country were written to on the subject: and Mr Oldham had an interview with the Revd Dr Illingworth, who promised him that if at Lady day we should not be provided with a proper Tutor, he would undertake the office till we should be suited with one. This was acceptable, and Notice was sent to Mr Jones, Tutor in Wales, that we should have no further occasion for his Services after Lady day next.

1792

Although the Estate at Cheshunt was purchased, it was not yet paid for; and the whole Fund of the Society was not sufficient to make the Payment: therefore at the first General Meeting this year, Viz., January 4th, a Book was opened for Donations towards the said Purchase, and the Sum received for that purpose was £587 10s.[10] Besides this the Society sold out £650 3 per Cent Consolidated Annuities at the high price of 95, and thus effected the payment on the 1st of March, and on the 3d Mr George Best, the Secretary, deputed by Mr Oldham who was the ostensible Purchaser, took possession of the Estate on behalf of the Society, by having the Keys delivered to him on the premises, in the presence of three Witnesses, by Mary Greatwood and Edward Blanks, in pursuance of Mrs Anne Shaw's Order to them dated 2 March 1792.

Hereupon Mr William Cardale of Bedford Row, was employed to draw up a proper Trust Deed, vesting the Estate in the present Trustees and their Successors, and explaining at large the nature and design of the Institution.

The Ministers written or applied to respecting the Tutorship, were the following, Viz.

> The Revd John Williams in Wales, who had been formerly Tutor,
> The Revd William Alphonsus Gunn, of Farnham, Surrey,
> The Revd William Love, Borough,
> The Revd J. Glazebrook, Warrington,
> The Revd Thomas Robinson, Leicester,
> The Revd William Day, Dewsbury, Yorkshire,
> The Revd J. Millner, Hull,
> The Revd D. Griffith, Llwyngwair,
> The Revd R. De Courcy, Shrewsbury,
> The Revd G. Pattrick, Aveley,
> The Revd C. Simeon, Cambridge,
> The Revd Thomas Charles, Bala, North Wales: and several others.

The Revd Thomas Robinson recommended the Revd Thomas Rogers of Ravenston in the County of Leicester, who came up to London; had an Interview with the Trustees, and appeared to them to be very well qualified for the Office; but wanted more security for its permanency than the Trustees were able to give. [10] 1792 March 20 Mr Rogers being returned home, wrote to Lady Anne Erskine, who resided at Spafield Chapel house, where the Trustees of the College had had their interview with him, accepting the Tutorship on condition he was not desired to preach out of the Establishment: but on the 22d he wrote another Letter to her Ladyship, and on the 26th one to Mr Hodson, that a very singular and unexpected Event had taken place, which obliged him to lay aside all thoughts of the College. On the 19th of April in another Letter to Mr Hodson he said, if the Trustees could have given him any certainty of the Tutors yearly stipend and of his Continuance, he certainly should not have left Town till every thing had been finally concluded upon.

It should be observed here, that the Trustees being themselves uncertain as to the Success of the Institution; could not assuredly promise its permanency. They told him they trusted in God for his Blessing upon it, and He must do the same. They also promised to increase their own Subscriptions in case there should be a falling off of others, but this was not satisfactory.

Mr Rogers's Acceptance and then Refusal of the Office, brought the Trustees into an awkward predicament: for on his acceptance they declined the services of Dr Illingworth, and on his refusal they were left destitute, even of a temporary Tutor.

And Dr Illingworth, who had made some preparations and arrangements for going to Cheshunt, was rather offended and disappointed, when informed he should not be wanted.

But now the kind Providence of God began to appear in answer to the many earnest Prayers both publick and private which had been offer'd up for a Tutor: for the Revd Mr De Courcy in a Letter dated 29 March 1792 recommended very strongly the Revd Isaac Nicholson, Curate of Coddington near Chester, as a person in whom the Trustees would not be disappointed could they prevail on him to relinquish his sequester'd situation, as a Country Curate; for a more conspicuous sphere of action. In consequence of this recommendation, Mr Hodson wrote to Mr Nicholson the following Letter.

London 7 April 1792

Revd Sir !
    As it is well known in the religious world, I presume that you are not unacquainted, that the late Countess of Huntingdon of Blessed memory had a College in Wales for training up serious young Men for the Ministry of the Gospel. And there are now in and about this Metropolis, and in various parts of the Country, many eminent Servants of God, and some in America, the fruits of her pious Zeal, and Blessings to the Church of Christ in the present day. An Institution so useful and beneficial to the everlasting Interest of immortal Souls did not expire with its noble and venerable foundress; but is carried on and design'd to be perpetuated, by a Society of friends to The Gospel, set on foot some Years previous to her Ladyship's decease. The [11] Situation however of the College is changed: instead of being in Wales it is removed to a place called Cheshunt in Hertfordshire about 13 Miles from London where the Society has purchased a commodious and delightful Freehold consisting of a roomy House with convenient Offices, good Garden and pleasant Field of 7 Acres of rich Land, the New River running thro' the Estate between the Field and the Garden. The Countess bequeathed a good Library and appointed Eight Trustees (of whom the writer hereof is one) to conduct the affairs of the College: and when any one of the Trustees dies the Successors are to chuse another so as to keep the Trust always full.

The Library and some Furniture are just arrived from Wales and the House is about to undergo some small Repairs. But we have not brought the Tutor from Wales, as he was only a temporary one and not a Minister of the Church of England as we earnestly wish our Tutor to be.

Knowing that God is the bestower of every good and perfect gift we have besought him to provide us a Tutor: and as we must use means in connextion with prayer, we have made enquiry amongst our friends in the Ministry and others, and have providentially heard of you. Grace and Learning are the two Qualifications we look for, and we are inform'd both these Qualifications reside in you: and that your Engagements in the Country are such as may be relinquish'd without much difficulty.

The Grand Argument I shall make use of is the Glory of God, as connected with that Sphere of Usefulness the present address Invites you to, <u>You</u> need not be Inform'd that Faith cometh by hearing. But how shall they hear without a Preacher, and how shall they Preach except they be sent. We wish to receive none into our College who do not appear on examination to have received their Commission to preach from the Holy Ghost: and our design is only to fit them by a competent measure of human Literature in conjunction with sound Divinity, to go wherever the Lord shall call them, at home or abroad, to carry the glad tidings of Salvation to poor Sinners through the Blood and Righteousness of the Son of God.

A secondary Argument is the agreeable and comfortable Situation in which you will be placed, and the Emoluments of the Office which is no contemptible Living. We propose that the Tutor shall keep House and board the Students. That his Salary shall be a clear £100 per annum and that he shall be allowed £20 per annum for the board of each Student. On the Tutor's part it is expected that he will ground the young Men in English, Latin and Greek, and that he shall as much as in him lies make them able Ministers of the New Testament. These [12] are the great Outlines of our Plan and Proposals and I trust you will find my Brethren and Fellow Trustees such Men as you will like to live in Friendship with. I desire to press the matter on your mind as a call to a very useful Employ; and shou'd it appear to you as a Call from God I know you dare not disobey it. I hope you will cheerfully accept it: if so I shall request to be inform'd how soon you can make it convenient to come as we wish to open the New College as soon as possible. Waiting the favour of your Answer, I remain, Revd Sir,

Your most humble Servant
W.H.

To this Letter Mr Nicholson returned the following Answer

Dear Sir !

I have perused your Letter, considered its Contents, and made your Proposal the subject of solemn frequent and ardent Prayer to God, the result of which is a strong disposition to embrace your offer. Several reasons constrain me to believe that your Call is the Voice of God addressing me in his own Words used on a peculiar occasion. The passage to which I allude is Jehovah's address to Abram, Get thee out of thy Country and from thy Kindred, etc. [11]From the moment I had read your Letter my Conscience was arrested: I had no power to resist your Invitation So evidently did it at the first appear to be of God, and so clearly does it still, that I have yet no doubt but that it is a Duty absolutely incumbent upon me to comply with your Request. However, before I give my final and decisive Answer, it is deemed necessary by my judicious friends, that all the Minutiae respecting the College, etc., should be laid before me: on which account it is judged expedient for me to come up to London. Accordingly I purpose, God Willing, to be in the Metropolis on Friday Evening next.[12] I am, Dear Sir,

> Yours truly,
> J. Nicholson

Coddington
April 21. 92

Mr Nicholson came to Town and the Trustees took him to Cheshunt: they approved of him and wish'd him to determine immediately; but as he had promised Mrs Nicholson not to make an absolute Engagement till his return he said he would send a definitive Answer in a week.

May 12. Mr Nicholson wrote to Mr Oldham the following Letter.

My dear Sir !

Your Call still evidently appears to me to be the Voice of God in his providence: in consequence of which I dare not refuse to come up. Had not this been the case, the many Ties that are here, the strength of which I now feel, would have indissolubly chained me in my present situation: but God's Word, like Alexander's Sword cutting the Gordian knot, breaks every bond asunder, and severs me at once from an affectionate People, dear Relatives, respected and respectable Connections. I consider myself as God's Servant, and [13] therefore bound in Conscience to go wheresoever He pleaseth; nay, to fly at his Command. You see then my design is not barely to accept your offer, but to engage heartily in the Work to which I am providentially called.

In consideration of which Service, is it not your intention (I ask not the following questions for my own solely, but principally for the satisfaction of Mrs Nicholsons friends) to allow me £100 per Annum, with the House, Offices, Garden and Meadow, clear of Rent, Repairs or Taxes ? Is it not your design that my Continuance in the said Office of Tutor in your College shall be permanent ? My Friends protest against my leaving my present Situation for one precarious and uncertain. Is it not your purpose that I should be allowed £20 per Annum for the Board of each Student, exclusive of Washing ? Answers in the affirmative to the three foregoing questions will remove every objection on the part of my friends, and at once fix my Resolve to come up. A Reply will be gratefully received by

Your obedient Servant
J. Nicholson

Mr Oldham, on behalf of himself and the rest of the Trustees, answered Mr Nicholsons three questions in the affirmative, whereupon he wrote the 25th of May, that in the fullest Confidence that God's Will and ours were one in this instance, he was bound in Conscience to obey our Call. 'Wherefore', says he, 'You may expect Us at Cheshunt the last week in June, or the first in July.' Some intervening Circumstances, however, delayed his coming exactly at that time; and it was not till

Friday July 13 that Mr Nicholson and his Family arrived at Cheshunt. The Library and some of the Furniture of the old College were brought from Wales: some Furniture Mr Nicholson brought from Cheshunt; and the Society purchased for his Use several articles of Furniture which he had not, and which were deemed necessary.

Several Students who had commenced their Studies in the old College, were ready to enter into the new: but some of Mr Nicholsons family being ill with a putrid sore Throat, it was judged prudent to stay till the danger of Infection was over before any were admitted.

Those who had been in the old College entered at Cheshunt in the following order, Viz.

August 1	William Jones,
	William Kemp,
6	William Robertson,
16	John Bickerdike,
	Thomas Bevan Winter,
18	Robert Bradley,
23	John Davies.

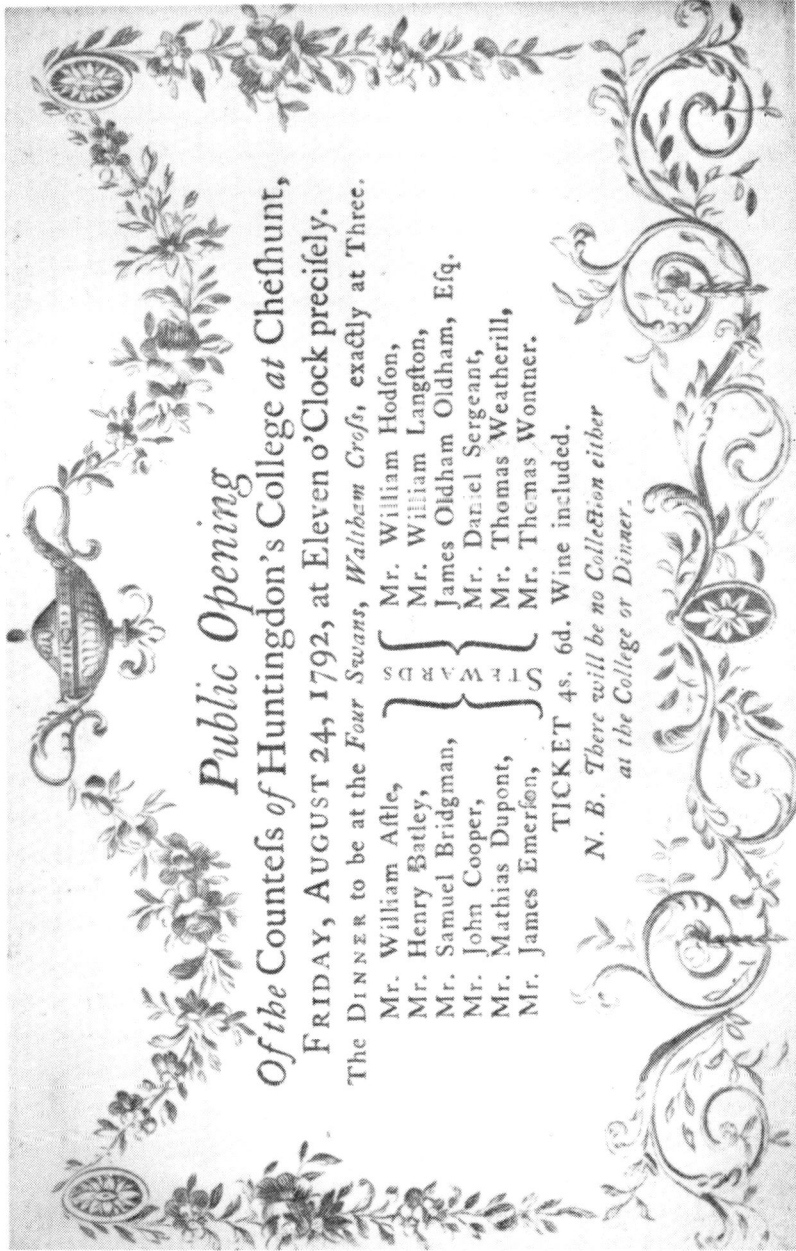

Public Opening

Of the Countefs *of* Huntingdon's College *at* Chefhunt,

FRIDAY, AUGUST 24, 1792, at Eleven o'Clock precifely.

The DINNER to be at the *Four Swans,* *Waltham Crofs,* exactly at Three.

STEWARDS

Mr. William Aftle,
Mr. Henry Batley,
Mr. Samuel Bridgman,
Mr. John Cooper,
Mr. Mathias Dupont,
Mr. James Emerfon,

Mr. William Hodfon,
Mr. William Langfton,
James Oldham Oldham, Efq.
Mr. Daniel Sergeant,
Mr. Thomas Weatherill,
Mr. Thomas Wontner.

TICKET 4s. 6d. Wine included.

N. B. There will be no Collection either at the College or Dinner.

Plate III: Invitation to the Opening of the College, 24th August 1792
(*Cheshunt archives, C9/14/3*)

Besides these, Thomas Hutchings was admitted as a Probationer the 10th August, a new Candidate, but not liking to submit to the Rules of the College, he quitted the same unhandsomely on the 21st for which he had a Vote of Censure passed on him.

[14]

Friday 24 August 1792. The College at Cheshunt was solemnly and publickly opened:[13] on which occasion the large Parlour intended to be used as a Chapel was filled with Company, as was also the Hall, and a great number were in the Court yard, where seats were erected for their accomodation. The order and manner of opening the College being published at the request of many of the Congregation,[14] a brief Account thereof may suffice here.

At Eleven o'Clock the Service began by singing the first four Verses of the 245th Hymn in the Countess of Huntingdon's Collection, page 373.[15] The Revd William Francis Platt, Minister of Holywell Mount Chapel, in London, then dedicated the House, the Institution, and all concerned therein, by solemn and fervent Prayer to God. After which two of the Students, Kemp and Winter, read Verse by Verse alternately, O come let us sing unto the Lord, etc.,[16] and the Psalms selected for the occasion, Viz. Psalms 19, 68, 132, 133. Another Student, Jones, read the first Lesson, Isaiah 55. Kemp and Winter repeated, We praise Three, O God, we acknowledge, etc. Jones read the second Lesson, Eph. 4 to the end of Verse 16th. Kemp and Winter repeated, O be joyful in the Lord, all ye Lands, etc. Then were sung the first and third Verses of Hymn 112, Page 172.[17]

The Revd Ant. Crole, Minister of Pinner's Hall Meeting, Broad Street, London, then delivered a Charge to the Students, President and Trustees, wherein he required their Assent and Consent to the 15 doctrinal Articles drawn up for this Connection, which he read, and to which they signified their Assent by holding up the right hand. Then were sung the 1st and 3d Verses of the 45th Hymn, Page 68.[18]

While this was singing the Revd John Eyre, Minister of Homerton Chapel, Hackney, went into the Pulpit, and as soon as the singing ceased, after a short Prayer, preached an excellent Sermon on Rom. 12, 13, 14, 15. In the Introduction to his discourse he remarked, that this was the Birthday of the late Countess of Huntingdon, who was born 24 Aug. 1707, and that it was the Anniversary of opening her College in Wales, being the same day in 1768. After the Sermon the last Verse of the 76th Hymn was sung.[19]

Then the Revd King Lemuel Kirkman, Curate at Spa Fields Chapel, concluded with a fervent and affectionate Prayer, for the success of the Gospel in general, and for the College in particular: which was followed by singing, Blessings for ever on the Lamb, etc.

The four Ministers who engaged had all been Students at the College in Wales.

It was nearly half past Two when the Service ended. Seven or eight hundred Persons were computed to be present, many of them very respectable, and much satisfaction was expressed. Indeed a divine Unction was evidently both upon the Ministers and the Congregation.

There being no house near where a large Company could be accomodated at Dinner, the Trustees, Ministers, and upwards of one hundred more dined at the Four Swans at Waltham Cross, about a Mile from the College in the London Road. The rest dined in different Parties at different houses.
[15]
In September 1792 an anonymous Letter was sent to Mr Nicholson of which the following is a Copy.

Sir,
    If the Coledge is not Already Insured (from Fire) its recommended to have it, soon done; as there is a greater Spirit of Envy against it, then is suspected, Concealed.

The Premises were already insured, but the Trustees and Society thought it right to increase the Sum: and two of the Students slept below Stairs for some time, having a Lamp burning, and a large Bell to ring in case of any Alarm. No attempt however was made. Praised be God.

In October Mr Nicholson was so extremely ill, as to cause serious apprehensions and fears for his valuable Life. They had a Prayer Meeting at the College; and pleaded with God earnestly and fervently for his Recovery; and it pleased the Lord in Mercy to restore him.

November 7. Mr Jedidiah Thompson, recommended by the Revd Mr Haweis, as a Candidate for the College, was examined, but there not appearing sufficient evidence of his Conversion and Call to the Ministry, the Trustees could not admit him: on which occasion Mr Hodson, by desire of his Brethren; wrote to Mr Haweis the following Letter.

London 13 November 1792

Revd and dear Sir !
    Wednesday last was the Monthly Meeting of the Trustees and Committee of the College; and the examination of the young Man from Brighton (Mr Jedidiah Thompson) was by particular desire postponed till

then. I am sorry to say that we could not obtain any clear and satisfactory evidence of his being divinely enlighten'd, or having experienced that saving work of Grace on his Soul, which must be the sine qua non of admission into the College: and therefore, desirous as we were of receiving him, we could not in conscience do it at present. As he informed us he did not mean to return to Brighton, we encouraged him to come on Sunday mornings and Monday evenings to Mr Weatherill's School of the Prophets, [20]where; if he has any real acquaintance with divine things, and Gifts for publick work in the Lord's service, he will have opportunities of exercising them, and may at some future time be admitted into the College.

Mr Nicholson, through Mercy, is so well recovered, that he preached last Lord's day, at Sion Chapel[21] in the Morning and Spa-fields in the Evening, with much Life and Zeal. We have received a very liberal Donation of Fifty Pounds from Mr Mulford of Basingstoke. We trust the Lord, who thus sends Money to support the Institution, will also send us young Men to fill it.

I hope Mrs Harris and Yourself are well and enjoying much of the Lord's Presence, and remain with the kind Christian Respects of all my Brethren in the Trust,

Revd and dear Sir,
Your devoted Servant in the best of Causes
W.H.

[16]

1792 November 28. Six of the seven Students admitted in August as Probationers, were now examined afresh and admitted fully as Students: but Mr Robertson having been complained of for some behavior of a pert and domineering nature towards Mrs Nicholson, was reproved by the Trustees, and his Admission suspended till the first Wednesday in February, when the President was to report concerning him.

The amount of Monies received in the year 1792, besides the £587-10 mention'd in page 9, as raised by Donations towards the purchase of the Estate at Cheshunt, was as follows, Viz.

Subscriptions	£322	17	0
Collection at Spa Fields Chapel	54	5	6
Dividends on 3 per Cent Consols	15	15	0
	392	17	6

1793 January 1. The President, in his Letter addressed to Mr Hodson, containing his Report of the state of the College, says, 'I feel it my duty to return my unfeigned Thanks to the Gentlemen in Trust and the Assistant Committee, for their spirited

Conduct manifested at our meeting at the Spa, in the support of the good government of the College, by the Suspension of Mr R. I was conscious that Punishment was necessary. I perceived its salutary tendency, and it has produced the desired Effect. Its Influence has been universal. From that time their Conduct in toto has been unexceptionable.'

January 23. Mr Nicholson wrote the following Letter, addressed to the Trustees.

Brethren,
As my temporal Affairs necessarily require my presence in Cheshire the first Wednesday in February tis utterly impossible for me to appear at Spa Fields at the time to which Mr Robertson stood suspended: therefore I thought it my duty to bear my Testimony in the present mode to the propriety of his Conduct from the time of his Suspension to be present. Am happy to have it in my power to assure you, that during the time of his Probation his Conduct has been becoming.

I am, Brethren, with Respect,
Your Servant
J. Nicholson

This Letter was written at the Castle and Falcon, Aldersgate Street, just as Mr Nicholson was on the point of setting out for Cheshire: and was I believe the first and only notice he gave the Trustees of his intended Journey: which occasioned the following Letter to be written to him by Mr Hodson.

London 4 February 1793

Revd and dear Sir,
I hope this will find You and Mrs N. safe returned from Cheshire, and all well at the College. I wish it had occurr'd to you that there would have been a Propriety in your addressing a particular Letter to the Trustees [17] on the subject of your going, acquainting them how long you intended to be absent, and what dispositions were made for conducting the College till your return. This would have been satisfactory to the Trustees, to whom it was really unpleasant to find themselves ignorant of these Circumstances concerning which you was quite silent in your Letter; that only announcing that you was going. As the Trustees are desirous on all occasions to shew every Respect to You, I trust you will think Them entitled to the same, and am persuaded the present omission was without design.

Something has been said about preaching at Waltham, but no regular information has been communicated on this head to the Trustees, who certainly ought to be consulted respecting any new Place, antecedent to a Student's preaching there, and their Concurrence had in Writing.

In a word, the Trustees wish it to be understood, that They are to be considered as standing in the place of the late Countess of Huntingdon, in all the affairs of the College, and that their direction is in all things to be looked up to.[22]

We are happy that your Report concerning Mr Robertson is such as encourages us to admit him fully as a Student, which I suppose will take place at our monthly Meeting on Wednesday next. Two or three more young Men are talked of as Candidates for the College, of whom we know but little as yet: but hope the Lord will direct us to receive only such as are of his sending. I remain, Revd and dear Sir,

> faithfully yours,
> W. Hodson

Wednesday February 6 1793. Mr Robertson was fully admitted as a Student.

March 1. Mr Thomas Witham, Master of Spa-fields Chapel School, was chosen Secretary in the room of Mr Best, who resigned on account of his going to reside at Richmond. But the Business of the Secretary being much less now the College was settled; than it had hitherto been, a Salary of Four Guineas per Annum was thought sufficient, and was accepted.

March 20. Mr W. Finnis of Dover wrote to Lady Anne Erskine concerning Mr Hutchings. The following is an Extract from his Letter.

> This morning I waited on Mr Child (our Minister) with a Letter I received from my Son Newman Finnis at Rye in Sussex, who with the Members of the Church wish to be informed of the true Character of the present Minister Mr Thomas Hutchings, who says he was at Lady Huntingdon's College under Tuition. Mr Child refer'd me to your Ladyship for information, and I hope you will be pleased to favour me with a line so soon as possible, as the said person is proposed to be ordained over them in about a fortnight.

Lady Anne gave this Letter to the Trustees, by whose direction the following Answer to it was written and sent.

CHESHUNT COLLEGE

To Mr Newman Finnis, Shoemaker at Rye

25 March 1793

Sir,

Lady Anne Erskine has received a Letter from your Father relative to Mr Thomas Hutchings, who it seems is proposed to be ordained [18] as your Minister. As the Letter respects the College, of which I am one of the Trustees, Lady Anne desires me to answer it.

I must therefore inform you, that if Mr Hutchings, by saying he was at Lady Huntingdon's College, would have it understood that he was a Student there for any considerable time, that he acquired a competent share of Literature, and that he left the College with approbation and with Testimonials of his Abilities, good Character and good Behavior, it is a gross Imposition. Mr H., it is true, was admitted into the College as a Probationer in August last, where he staid but a few days, and left it in so unhandsome a manner as to occasion the following Censure to be unanimously passed on him by the Trustees and Committee of the College which Censure stands upon Record in their Minute Book and was publickly read to all the Students in the College by their President.

Resolved, 26 September 1792

That the Disingenuity and Duplicity which Mr Hutchings was guilty of, were such as are diametrically opposite to that Uprightness of Character a Professor of Christianity and a Candidate for the Ministry ought to ever sustain. That the Trustees and Committee conceive that it merits their decided Disapprobation and Censure: to express which it is resolved that the said Mr Hutchings shall not at any future time be admitted either into the College or into that Connection where Humility and Sincerity must be always expected in the Servants of the Lord.

It should be explained to you that the Conduct thus censured was this. Mr H. on the 21st of August said he was not at all well and desired leave of me to go for a few days to his Friends. I wished him to defer going till after the Publick Opening of the College which was to be the 24th. He replied he should return in time to be present at the Opening: whereas he intended no such thing, for I learnt afterwards that he had sent off his Box and intended coming no more.

Having related the above facts concerning Mr H. in compliance with what I conceive to be my duty on such an important occasion, I leave the matter to the great Shepherd and Bishop of Souls, whose Prerogative alone it is to send Labourers into his Vineyard, and who has by his Apostle Paul said to the Under-Shepherds in all Ages then to come: 'Lay hands suddenly on no Man.' I remain, Sir, Your very humble Servant

> William Hodson

Letter to Mr Cardale complaining of the long delay of the Trust Deed, dated 24 April 1793.[23]

Dear Sir,

The Trustees of the College hoped the Deed would have been compleated before the last Quarterly Meeting of the Society: and they are greatly disappointed that they have not yet been called together to execute the same. We are really ashamed to meet the Committee and Subscribers who begin to be very impatient, wondring what can possibly impede and protract the business to such a length of time. Do, dear Sir, I beseech you, let it be finished out of hand, otherwise we are in danger of losing Subscriptions to a considerable Amount. I am, Dear Sir, etc.

> W.H.[24]

FOOTNOTES

Records

1   i.e. the Glorious Revolution of 1688
2   This was the college building which Lady Huntingdon proposed to erect at Swansea
3   See the *Plan* printed above
4   The temporary tutor was a Mr Jones - who has not been identified
5   It is not known exactly when Lady Huntingdon appointed these inspectors, but it was probably after she ceased to visit the College in old age.
6   A copy is in the College archives - C 9/ 8/ 5
7   Zechariah 4: 6
8   The window tax had been increased in 1784 and was to be still further increased in 1802 and 1808
9   The New River was excavated to supply water to London in the early seventeenth century. It can still be seen in the former College grounds
10   See the College archives, D1/ 2, ff. 24 & 25
11   Genesis 12: 1
12   April 27th
13   This continued the Trevecka tradition of opening the College year on the anniversary of the Countess's birthday
14   *The order observed at the Opening of the Countess of Huntingdon's College, at Cheshunt...Embellished with a neat Engraving of the College. Published at the Request of Several Persons Present...* (Edw. Hodson, London, 1792)
15   Jesus, where'er thy people meet,
     There they behold thy Mercy-seat
16   Psalm 95
17   Peace be to this congregation
18   Captain of thine enlisted host,
     Display thy glorious banner high
19   Fly abroad, thou mighty Gospel
20   Mr Weatherill was a trustee of Spa Fields chapel, but nothing is known of his 'school'
21   Sion chapel at Mile End Old Town had been opened for the Connexion two years earlier
22   A line has been drawn against this paragraph at a later date
23   The College trust deed was dated 1st Feb. 1793 and had to be enrolled in Chancery within six months. It was not enrolled until 3 July
24   The last few lines of this account have been crammed into the bottom of the page

V

LIST OF SUBSCRIBERS

SUBSCRIBERS TO THE COLLEGE
1787 - 1799

This catalogue was compiled from Cheshunt archives C5/ 3 which lists all the subscribers from the foundation of the Apostolic Society until 1816. All 382 subscribers before 1800 are arranged here in alphabetical order. The address given is the first, where it changed later this is indicated by an asterisk after the address. The house number is also in brackets after the address. The amount subscribed is almost always in guineas (£1-1s.0d). A few potential subscribers are not recorded as paying anything.

An attempt has been made to identify those subscribers who were members of the Connexion chapel in London. Those for Spa Fields (SF after the name) are taken from the Spa Fields Minute book (printed in my Two Calvinistic Methodist Chapels, London Record Soc., 1975, pp.44-87) and the registers (Public Record Office, RG4/4536, 4316). Those for Mulberry Gardens (MG in list) from the register (P.R.O., RG4/ 4165).

Year	Name	Address	Amount
1793	Adderley, Thos	Stoke Newington	1
1795	Addiss, Wm W	Whitechapel	1
1793	Agace, Daniel esq	Gower St (26)	2
1796	Alers, Wm esq	Fenchurch St (7)	1
1797	Allies, Jas	Worcester, Broad St	1
1797	Allies, Richd	Worcester, tanner	1
1794	Andrews, Peter	Henry St *	2
1791	Andrews, Thos	Bank of England	½
1793	Anon	Mr Butcher	1
1797	Anon	Rev Mr Nicholson	1
1795	Anon	Mrs Hill	2
1796	Anon	Mr Weatherill	1
1798	Anon	Mr Parke	½
1792	Anon F A	Mr Tutt	1
1795	Anon Lady	Cheshunt	1
1793	Anon P J	Mr Duthoit	1

1794	Anon R I	Mr Duthoit	1
1791	Ashton, Isaac	Billiter Lane (23)	1
1787	Astle, Wm SF	Grays Inn Lane *	3
1796	Ayscough, Mrs	Cripplegate *	1
1792	Ayscough, Wm	Cripplegate	1
1793	Bailey	Royal Exchange	½
1795	Bailey, Mrs	Hackney Grove (6)	1
1799	Bailey, Thos	St Pauls Churchyd (8)	5
1793	Bainbridge, Matthew	Goswell St (137)	1
1791	Banks, Benjamin	Holborn, Middle Row	0
1795	Barker, Clemt	Cheshunt	1
1799	Barlow, Peter	City Rd *	1
1787	Barns, Thos	Islington, 6 High St	1
1798	Bates, Benjamin	Upper Thames St	1
1787	Batley, Hy SF	Pentonville, Winchester Pl	5
1799	Bawtree, Saml	Minories, 8 Cresc	2
1792	Baxter, Mrs G.	Cheshunt	2
1796	Baylie, Eli	Rosomans St (39)	3
1795	Beaufoy, Rev. Saml	Kent, Sutton	1
1791	Bell, Wm	Laystall St	1
1787	Bensley, Thos	Fleet St, Bolt Court	0
1791	Bickley, Wm	Oxford St, Berners St *	1
1797	Biggerstaff, John	Islington	1
1797	Bishop, Mrs	Spa Field (23)	1
1791	Blain, Archbald	Great Sutton St (42)	½
1798	Blakesley, Benjamin	Friday St. (47)	1
1792	Blundell, Major	Holborn Bridge (70)	1
1792	Bond, John	Charterhouse St (5)	1
1794	Bostock, Mary	Half Moon Passage (10)	1
1792	Bott, Thos	Limehouse *	2
1791	Bressingham, Wm	Drury Lane, 6 Craven Bldgs	½
1792	Brewer, Rev Saml	Stepney	2
1791	Bridgman, John	Goodmanfield, Leman St (88)	1
1791	Bridgman, Saml	Turmmell St (2) *	1
1791	Bridgman, Wm	Whitechapel, New Rd	1
1792	Broady, Joseph	Whitechapel (83)	1
1793	Brooke, Mrs	Great Saffronhill (121)	1
1791	Brooks, Jas	Millman St (5) attorney	2
1791	Brown, Elizabeth	Goswell St, 12 Bullyard	1
1794	Brown, Thos	Goswell St, 12 Bullyard	1

1792	Bryan, Benjamin	Holborn, 39 Red Lion St *	1
1792	Bryan, Rev Edw	Essex, Newport	1
1794	Bryan, Rev John	Newgate St (27) *	1
1792	Bulmer, Joseph	Whitechapel (144)	1
1791	Burnell, John	Golden Lane (111) *	1
1791	Burnett, Jas	Furnival Inn (4)	1
1794	Burridge, Geo	Shoreditch *	1
1792	Burridge, Sarah	Goswell St *	1
1799	Butcher, John SF	Snow Hill, 10 Kirby St	1
1787	Butcher, Robt	Spa Field, 18 Braynes Row	1
1791	Butcher, Robt jun.	Spa Field, 18 Braynes Row	2
1787	Butterworth, Richd	Holborn Bridge *	5
1791	Byfield, John	Constitution Row (2)	1
1792	Caldwell, Rev Robt		1
1792	Cannon, Rev Thos	Grub St	1
1792	Capell, John	Royal Exchange	1
1792	Carpenter, Thos	Islington Rd (5)	1
1787	Carr, Jas SF	City Rd, 29 York Place *	2
1794	Carr, Jonathan	Spafield, 9 Braynes Row	1
1798	Chamberlain, Rev John		1
1787	Chambers, Jarvis	Gutter Lane (46) *	2
1792	Charles, Rev Thos	North Wales, Bala	1
1792	Clark, John	Whitechapel, 6 Red Lion St	1
1797	Cock, Ambrose	Lower Shadwell (65)	1
1792	Cole, Wm	Hatton Wall (31)	2
1791	Colebrooke, Geo	Islington, Colebrooke Row	1
1792	Collambell, Nath	Goswell St (11)	1
1791	Compigne, Jas	Pentonville, Pleasant Row *	1
1787	Cooke, John SF	Holborn (120)	1
1795	Cooke, Mrs Eliz	Leadenhall St (73) *	1
1792	Cooper, Edw	St Johns St (127)	1
1791	Cooper, Jas	Liquorpond St (28)	1
1791	Cooper, John	Goswell St (94) *	5
1795	Cooper, Mrs Mary	Goswell St (94) *	2
1791	Cope, Jacob	Upper Thames St (111), glazier	1
1797	Cowdell, Mrs	Islington	2
1798	Cowie, Robt esq	Lime St (50)	2
1792	Cowley, Wm	Islington, 19 Gwyns Bldgs	1
1791	Coxhead, Geo	Holborn (115)	2
1793	Cragers, John	Finch Lane (7)	1
1791	Crole, Rev Ant.	Islington	1

1796	Cumber, Isaac	Pentonville, 13 John St	1
1792	Curtis, Wm	Ivy Lane (14)	1
1791	Daling, Richd	Bromley, Middx *	10
1792	Davies, David	Cheshunt	1
1792	Davies, Hugh	Piccadilly (227) *	1
1794	Davison, Wm	Grays Inn Lane, 3 Swinton St	1
1792	Dexter, John	Mile End, Saville Place	1
1797	Dobee, John	St Georges East, New Rd	1
1791	Dornford, Thos	Philpot Lane (14)	1
1793	Druce, Jas	Newcastle St, Fleet Mkt	1
1791	Dudman, John	Wapping, 5 Harrison St	1
1787	Dupont, Mathias SF	Aldersgate St (179) *	2
1792	Duthoit, Jas SF	Old Broad St (9) *	1
1791	Duthoit, Miss	Highbury Place (34) *	1
1791	Duthoit, Peter SF	Highbury Place (34) *	2
1792	Earle, Joseph	Watling St (92)	1
1791	Ebden, -	Wapping, slopseller	1
1791	Elliott, Richd	Spafield (29) *	1
1792	Ellis, Wm	Fenchurch St (126)	1
1792	Ellis, Wm	Upper Rathbone Place (17)	1
1791	Emerson, Jas MG	Whitechapel Rd (33)	1
1787	Erskine, Ly Anne A	Spafield	10
1791	Evans, Thos esq	Knightsbridge	2
1791	Everard, Wm	Whitechapel Rd (188)	2
1794	Ewer, Thos	Newgate St (50)	1
1797	Exshaw, Mrs	City Rd, Nelson Terr	1
1787	Eyre, Joseph	Cornwall, Bodmin	0
1787	Eyre, Rev John	Homerton *	1
1793	Fell, John	High Holborn	½
1791	Flint, Joseph	Hermitage (362) *	1
1791	Flower, Adam	Whitechapel, 11 Mulberry St	1
1791	Fogg, Thos	Cypress Bldgs (14) *	1
1792	Ford, John	Minories (110)	1
1791	Ford, Rev Dr	Highbury Place (21)	5
1792	Foyster, Saml esq	Tottnhm Ct Rd, 36 Tottnhm St	2
1791	Francis, Edward	Shoreditch (161) *	2
1791	Franklin, John	Islington, Paradise Row *	½
1796	Fuller, Robt	Wormwood St (32)	2
1787	Fyffe, Hy SF	Holborn (313) *	2
1795	Gage, Mrs	Bath	2
1787	Galpin, John esq	Twinham	5

1794	Gaviller, Geo	St Georges East, 3 New Rd	2
1794	Gaviller, Miss	St Geo East, 3 New Rd	1
1795	Geale, John	Pentonville, 8 Henry St	1
1794	George, John	Strand, 18 Holywell St	1
1792	Gilbert, Edward	Whitechapel (139)	1
1794	Giles, Mrs	Water Lane (20) *	1
1797	Giles, Thos	Water Lane (19)	1
1791	Giles, Wm	Tower St, 20 Water Lane	1
1793	Glasscott, Rev C	Devon, Hathersleigh	1
1799	Gooch, Thos SF	Coppice Row (23)	1
1792	Goudge, Alexr	White Lyon St (24)	1
1792	Gould, Wm	High Holborn (57)	1
1793	Gouldsmith, Edmund	Aldergate, 9 Cast St	1
1795	Gouldsmith, Jesse	Love Lane (9) *	1
1791	Gray, Mich.	Bishopsgate Without (5)	1
1792	Green, Francis	Denmark Hill	1
1793	Green, John	Mile End	1
1792	Griffin, Mrs	Islington, Tyndall Pl *	1
1791	Griffin, Wm	St Johns Lane *	1
1791	Groves, John esq SF	New Palace Yard, Westminster	10
1797	Habgood, Jas	Friday St (49)	1
1787	Hall, Luke	Gutter Lane	1
1796	Hall, Stephen esq	Fenchurch St (6)	1
1794	Hall, Wm	Spital Fields, Steward St	1
1797	Hammond, Geo	Whitechapel (145)	1
1793	Hammond, Mrs	Upper Wimpole St (15)	1
1798	Harryman, Wm	Highbury Place (24)	1
1798	Hartis, Miss Lydia	Northants, Aldwinkle *	10
1791	Haweis, Rev Tho		1
1791	Hayter, Thos	Mark Lane (58)	5
1792	Hervey, Lady Caroline	Brighton	20
1792	Hervey, Lady Emily	Brighton	20
1792	Higgs, Wm	Bloomsbury, 49 Broad St	1
1792	Hillier, Miss	Pancras Lane (56)	2
1791	Hilton, Richd	Rosoman St (40)	1
1792	Hinde, John	Whitechapel (134)	1
1792	Hippuff, Chas	Birchin Lane (26)	1
1795	Hitch, Mrs	Ratcliffe Highway, Princes Sq	1
1792	Hobson, Margt	Spa Field (8)	1
1792	Hodgkinson, Enoch	Stamford St, Surry	2
1791	Hodgson, Thos	St Johns Lane, Georges Court	1

1792	Hodson, Dr Jas	Hatton Garden (29) *	1
1791	Hodson, Thos	Mark Lane (58)	1
1787	Hodson, Wm SF	Lothbury (39)	3
1791	Hole, -	Benjamin St	5s
1791	Holmes, Joseph Thos SF	Newgate St (50) *	2
1794	Holmes, Miss	Newgate St (50)	1
1787	Hoppe, John	St Pauls Churchyd (32)	2
1791	Horsley, John sen	Hoxton, Haberdashers Walk	1
1794	Hughes, Robt	Chandos St (62)	1
1792	Hughes, Thos	Inner Temple Lane	1
1799	Hughes, Thos	Monmouth, Usk	1
1794	Huntly, Jepthah	Royal Exchange	1
1792	James, Rev Morgan		1
1793	Johnson, Mr	Reading	1
1794	Johnson, Mrs	Rev Mr Nicholson	1
1796	Jones, Jacob	Finsbury Sq (10)	1
1791	Jones, Mrs		1
1791	Jones, Rev David		1
1797	Jones, Robt	Curtain Rd (42)	2
1792	Jones, Wm	Spitalfields, Brick Lane	1
1794	Joseph, Richd	New St Sq	2
1792	Kebbell, Jas MG	Duckend, Park Lane	2
1799	Kemp, Rev. Wm	Swansea	1
1798	Keys, Saml	Cheshunt	1
1791	King, John SF	Islington Rd (29)	1
1799	King, Philip esq	Camberwell Green	1
1793	Kirk, Jas	Limehouse *	1
1791	Knight, Rev. J A	Tottnhm Ct Rd, 5 Sells Row *	1
1791	Knight, Wm	Pentonville, Anne St	1
1795	Lambe, Miss	Homerton	1
1795	Lambe, Miss	Homerton	1
1792	Langston, Stephen esq	Watling St (92)	1
1787	Langston, Wm SF	Highbury Place (2) *	5
1795	Lawton, Saml	Newcastle on Tyne	1
1796	Leaver, Robt	Chick Lane, Durham Yard *	1
1793	Leaver, Saml	Chick Lane, Durham Yard	1
1793	Lee, Ephraim	Beach St *	½
1791	Lee, Jas	Aldgate (21), stationer	½
1795	Lettsom, John C, MD SF	Basinghall St, Sambrook Ct	2
1791	Lloyd, John esq	Swansea	1
1798	Locke, Mrs	Wilts, Devizes	1

1791	Locke, Thos esq	Wilts, Devizes	1
1798	Logston, -	Cheshunt	1
1792	Long, John	Rosomans St (39)	1
1791	Long, Nathl	Grays Inn Lane (97)	2
1797	Macdonald, Rev Wm	Bath *	1
1793	Mandell, John esq	Southampton Place (11)	1
1792	Marriott, Wm	Hoxton Sq (55)	1
1787	Mason, John	Fleet St (152) *	2
1794	Mather, Mrs	Clapton *	2
1796	Matravers, Philip	Godmansfield, Mill Yard	1
1794	Matthew, Wm	Newgate St (63)	½
1795	Matthews, Walter	Newgate St (50)	2
1792	Meyer, Rev Mr		½
1792	Miller, John	Thames St, 2 Broken Wharf	½
1792	Mitchell, Wm	Ratcliff Highway, 3 Princes Sq	1
1797	Monds, Thos W	Whitechapel	1
1792	Moore, Jas	Tottnhm Ct Rd, 7 Howland St	2
1797	Moreland, Mrs Ann	Old St (18)	2
1787	Morris, Thos esq	Camberwell *	10
1792	Mousley, Robt	Goswell St (103)	1
1797	Moxley, Wm D	Kings Row (2)	1
1791	Mum, Hy	Goodmanfields, 12 Alice St	3
1796	Mumford, Danl	Hatton Gdns, 10 Greville St	1
1791	Nesbitt, Thos	Bank of Kingsland	1
1796	Nevill, John	Vineyard Walk (4)	1
1791	Newcomb, Wm	White Lion St (17)	1
1795	Nisbett, Saml	Kingsland Place (14)	1
1797	Noeth, Valentine	Limehouse, Narrow St	2
1787	Oldham, Jas O esq SF	Holborn	5
1787	Omer, Jas	Ratcliff Row (18), St Lukes	1
1787	Owen, -	Spa Place, 6 Wood St	5s
1792	Owen, Danl	Essex, Chingford	1
1787	Owen,Richd	Leadenhall St (87)	1
1794	Page, Mrs	Goswell St, 9 Pear Tree St	1
1792	Painter, John	Wilderness Row (10)	1
1791	Parker, Thos	Wilderness Row (17)	1
1793	Payne, Geo	Newgate St (80)	1
1796	Peddon, Christopher	Eyre St Hill	½
1794	Peeram, -	Lawrence Poultney Lane (10)	1
1798	Perram, Mrs	Cheshunt	1
1795	Philips, Chas	City Rd, 7 Winkworth Bldgs	1

1795	Phillips, Geo	City Rd, 7 Winkworth Bldgs	1
1791	Phillips, John	Cold Bath Sq (1)	1
1796	Phillips, Mrs	Cold Bath Sq (1)	1
1792	Phillips, Wm	Shoreditch (16)	1
1793	Phipps, Thos	Gutter Lane (40)	1
1791	Pinkney, Geo	Newgate St	1
1798	Plant, Thos	Finsbury Place	1
1791	Platt, Isaac	Islington, 9 High St.	1
1794	Platt, Mrs	Tindall Place	1
1791	Platt, Rev W F	Holywell Mount *	1
1798	Plummer, Thos esq	Fenchurch St (32) *	5
1791	Pontin, John SF	Clerkenwell, Red Lion St	5s
1791	Pontin, Wm SF	Turnmill St (22), City Rd	2
1791	Powell, Mary	nr St Lukes Workhouse	2
1795	Prettyman, Wm	Idol Lane (6)	1
1799	Price, Elijah	Islington, Lower St	2
1791	Price, Sep.	Leadenhall St (150)	1
1793	Pugh, Richd	Islington, 10 Barnsbury Pl	½
1791	Pulleye, Saml	Saffron Hill (21)	1
1795	Ravenshear, Mrs		1
1791	Ravenshear, Wm	Saffron Hill	½
1797	Rawlins, Jas	Wilderness Row (4)	1
1792	Raynier, John	Hackney, Well St	1
1795	Roberts, Mary	Eyre St	½
1791	Roberts, Mrs Eliz	Islington, Lower St	1
1791	Robson, Miss M A	Mr Tilneys	1
1791	Rowell, Edward	Compton St (18)	1
1791	Rowton, Richd	Lambs Conduit St (24)	1
1799	Rusby, John	Surrey Rd, nr Obelisk	1
1791	Rusby, Thos	Leather Lane	1
1793	Russell, Hugh	Theobalds Rd (39) *	1
1791	Rust, Wm	Hull	1
1797	Savage, Jas	St Georges East, 2 Sampsons Yd	2
1787	Sawrey, Miles	Plymouth	2
1791	Scutt, Miss Hannah	Brighton	1
1798	Sergrove, -	Enfield, Baker St	½
1791	Serjeant, Danl	Old Gravel Lane, coal mcht	1
1792	Sevier, -	Bristol	2
1791	Shadd, Fra.	Aylesbury St, 1 Bishops Ct	1

1793	Shannan, Wm	Bishopsgate Without (54)	½
1791	Sharman, -	Bishopsgate Without (54)	½
1791	Sharratt, Joseph	Great St Helens (26)	½
1793	Short, John	Bedford St, 3 Liquorpond St	1
1787	Silver, Joseph SF	Hatton Garden (28)	2
1793	Simmons, John	Little Warner St, Coach & Horses	1
1799	Simpson, Chas	Newgate St (21)	1
1794	Simpson, Miss Lydia	Ratcliff Highway (133)	1
1791	Simpson, Miss Sarah	Ratcliff Highway (133)	1
1791	Simpson, Wm	Ratcliffe Highway (133)	3
1791	Simpson, Wm jun	Burr St *	1
1791	Smales, Richd	Walworth, Chatham Place	1
1799	Smith, Geo	Paternoster Row, Lovels Ct	1
1787	Soames, Hy	Cateaton St (21)	2
1787	Soames, Mrs	Holborn St (68)	2
1787	Soames, Nathl	Ludgate St (9)	2
1797	Spittle, Jas	Black Friars, Broad Way *	1
1798	Spragg, Matthew	Shoreditch (21) *	1
1791	Stanley, Miss	St Johns Walk	2
1794	Stickland, John jun	Newgate Market	2
1791	Stockton, Richd	Whitechapel (79) grocer	1
1797	Strickland, Thos	Worcester, Shambles, butcher	1
1799	Sumner, Wm SF	Clerkenwell Close (1)	1
1792	Tabberer, Geo	Hatton Gardens (110) *	2
1792	Tabberer, Hannah	Hatton Garden (110) *	1
1792	Thompson, Saml	Whitechapel (113)	1
1787	Tilney, Jonathan	Holborn (120)	1
1798	Tolkien, John Benjn	Pentonville, 79 White Lion St	2
1795	Tomkins, Miss Rebecca	Whitechapel (142)	1
1792	Tooley, Mrs	Eyre St Hill 15	½
1794	Tooth, Saml	City Rd (20)	½
1798	Towers, Eliz	Cold Bath Fields, 4 Little Warner St	1
1787	Towers, Geo SF	Cold Bath Fields, 4 Little Warner St	2
1798	Towers, John	Cold Bath Fields, 4 Little Warner St	1
1792	Towle, Nathl H	Bank	1
1791	Trovey, Chas	Cold Bath Fields, Durrington St	½

1791	Tutt, Thos	Royal Exchange	1
1792	Underwood, Rev. Stephen	Leicester Sq, 35 Martin St	1
1793	Urling, Geo esq	City Rd next Chapel	2
1793	Uwins, Thos	Hoxton, 7 Haberdashers Walk	½
1791	Vidgen, John	Tower	1
1795	Wakeman, Thos	Hackney, Mare St	1
1791	Walker, Edward	Moorfields, Paul St	1
1796	Walker, Jas SF	Shoe Lane, 26 Harp Alley	1
1796	Walker, Mrs Jas	Camberwell, 8 Denmark Row	1
1787	Walsh, Francis	Inner Temple Lane *	2
1792	Walsh, Francis jun	Bartholomew Close (57)	1
1792	Warham, Randle	Aldgate High St (24)	1
1798	Warren, Saml esq	Kentish Town, Grove House *	5
1797	Waters, Wm	St Georges East	1
1791	Watson, Miss	Clerkenwell Green	2
1787	Weatherill, Thos SF	Cold Bath Sq (7)	1
1796	Webb, Mrs	Greenhill Rents (24)	1
1787	Webber, J P	Whitechapel Rd (15)	1
1799	West, Geo H	Holborn *	2
1794	West, Mrs Wm	Islington	1
1794	Wheeler, Joseph	Shoe Lane (53)	1
1787	Whitaker, David	Hackney	2
1797	Whitchurch, Jas	Islington, 7 Pullens Row	1
1792	Whitridge, Joseph	Clapham Rd *	1
1795	Whittingham, Rev R	Beds, Potton	2
1792	Wilcoxon, Arthur	Lombard St (58)	1
1793	Wilde, Wm	Compton St (55) *	1
1791	Wilkinson, John	Penton St (14)	1
1792	Wilks, Rev Matthew	Wellams Bldgs (2) *	1
1792	Williams, Rev Thos	Stepney	1
1792	Wilson, John esq	Islington	2
1793	Wilson, Joseph	Milk St	1
1799	Wilson, Matthew	South Molton St (31)	1
1795	Wilson, Mrs Thos	Highbury Place (12)	1
1795	Wilson, Mrs Thos	Highbury Place (12)	1
1795	Wilson, Thos SF	Birchin Lane	1
1787	Wilson, Thos esq	Highbury Place	2
1787	Wilson, Thos jun	Wood St (124) *	1
1791	Wollaston, John SF	Holborn Bridge (1)	1
1792	Wontner, John	Minories (125)	1

1792	Wontner, Thos SF	Minories (115)	2
1791	Wood, Spencer	Bridewell Precinct	1
1791	Wood, Thos	Bridewell Precinct	1
1792	Woodhouse, Mrs	South Molton St (57)	1
1792	Woolcott, Thos	Clerkenwell, 26 Compton St *	1
1798	Wright, John	Norwich	1
1791	Wright, Roger	Goswell St (103)	1

VI

LIST OF STUDENTS

STUDENTS, 1791-1799

No complete register of students for either Trevecka or Cheshunt has survived and probably none was ever kept. Dr Nuttall has provided a list of Trevecka students with additional details and references (*Trans. Hon. Soc. of Cymmrodorion*, session 1967, pt II, pp. 269-277), and Dr Orchard's *Cheshunt College* [1968] (pp. 21-25) gives a list of alumni with dates of admission to Cheshunt. Rev. Charles Surman supplied the college with copies of all his Cheshunt cards from his monumental index of Congregational ministers (now at Dr William's Library).

All three lists were produced before the college archives were collected together and arranged so that they now need to be supplemented with the additional information which has been discovered. This list could not have been compiled without the help of all three, but it incorporates extra material. However it is certainly incomplete and may contain mistakes caused by the duplication of names and the use of obituaries written long after the events described.

Henry Atley Admitted to Trevecka, c. 1789. Admitted to Cheshunt, 29 Aug. 1792. Minute of admission rescinded, 7 Nov. 1792
Minister of the Postern chapel, Newcastle upon Tyne, 1791
Minister of Farnham (Surrey), [1792]-1795
Minister at St Albans (Herts), 1795-96
Licenced meeting houses at Redbourn (Herts), 1796
Minister of Hornchurch Lane chapel, Romford (Essex), 1796-
Conducted a boarding school at Stepney and ran a mission for lascars
Letters in Cheshunt College archives
Died 15 July 1822, aged 56
Father of Henry Atley, a Cheshunt student

William Bennet Admitted 7 Feb. 1798
Inhabitant of Cheshunt
Possibly the minister of Bethel chapel, Leeds, 1802
Minister at Dursley (Gloucs), 1804-23
Classical tutor of Cheshunt College, 1823-24
Died 24 Jan. 1830, aged 54

John Bickerdike Admitted to Trevecka, n.d. Admitted to Cheshunt, 28 Mar. 1792. Left June 1795
Born London, 1774
Ordained at Spa Fields chapel, 23 Feb. 1808

Itinerant minister (Woolwich, Reading, Derby, Faversham, Cheltenham)
Kept a school
Removed to Kentish Town
Died 20 June 1858

Robert Bradley Admitted to Trevecka, n.d. Admitted to Cheshunt, 28 Mar. 1792. Left 4 Feb 1795
Minister of Birdport St Chapel, Worcester, 1799-[1801]
Minister of Chichester, 1801-3
Minister of St George's chapel, Great Newton St, Manchester, 1807

John Brich Admitted 17 Mar. 1796. Left 19 Dec. 1799
Born High Leigh (Ches), Mar. 1770

Benjamin Callens Admitted 7 Dec. 1796. Refused the place, 1 Feb. 1797

John Carnson Admitted a probationer in 1795, but not admitted a student
Born in Ireland c. 1775. Father minister of Annan (Dumfries)

John Chamberlain Admitted 4 Dec. 1793. Left 30 June 1797
Born Titchfield (Hants), 1760
Ordained at Spa Fields chapel, 2 July 1798
Minister at Newhaven (Sussex), 1803
Minister at Bath

James Cooke Admitted 7 Feb. 1798

John Davies Admitted to Trevecka, 1791. Admitted to Cheshunt, 22 Aug. 1792. Left June 1795
Born Llangyfni (Carms), 30 Aug. 1769
Ordained at Spa Fields chapel, 1796
Minister at Handsworth (Staffs), Tetbury (Gloucs) and Ludgershall
Minister at Whitstable (Kent), 1824-29
Minister at Bracknell (Berks), 1830-44
Died at Bracknell, 2 Mar. 1861

John Finlay Admitted 1 Mar. 1797. Left 25 June 1801
Born Ridge, near South Mimms (Herts), 13 Jan. 1776
Ordained at Enfield (Middx), 1801
Minister at Cork, 1801-3
Minister at Worcester, 1804
Minister at Chichester, 1804-6
Minister at Tunbridge Wells, 1809-49
Died Mar/Apr. 1853

George Gladstone Admitted 7 Aug. 1799
Born Newcastle upon Tyne, 16 Feb. 1778

Itinerant minister (Alfriston, Sussex; Hull)
Minister of Zion chapel, Lincoln, 1804–49
Died 4 Sept. 1857

Andrew Horn Admitted 1 Jan. 1794. Left 30 June 1797
Born Edinburgh, 1768
Ordained at Sion chapel, London, 13 June 1797
Minister of Plunkett St chapel, Dublin, 1797–1803
President of Cheshunt College, 1803–7
Minister of High Wycombe (Bucks), 1807–

Thomas Hutchings Admitted 8 Aug. 1792. Left of own accord, 21 Aug. 1792
Inhabitant of Portsmouth

John James Admitted 4 Dec. 1793. Left 30 June 1798
Born at Marross (Carms), 6 Jan. 1768
Ordained at Spa Fields chapel, 2 July 1798
Itinerant minister (London; Tunbridge Wells; Bristol; Ebley, Gloucs; Worcester; Brighton; Chester; Congleton, Ches)
Resident tutor of Cheshunt College, 1814–21
Minister at Enfield
Died at Enfield, 1830/31

William Jones Admitted to Trevecka, 1791. Admitted to Cheshunt, 28 Mar. 1792. Left 30 June 1796
Ordained 1799
Minister at Nantwich (Ches), 1798–1800
Two, or three, persons of this name were students at different times

William Kemp Admitted to Trevecka, n.d. Admitted to Cheshunt 28 Mar. 1792. Left 30 June 1796
Ordained Bristol, 20 Dec. 1796
Itinerant minister
Minister at Swansea, 1796–
Resident tutor of Cheshunt College, 1821–31
Correspondence in Cheshunt College archives, C 9/ 6/ 8, 13, 31
Died 6 Mar. 1831, aged 56

George Lee Admitted 3 Aug. 1796
Inhabitant of Newcastle upon Tyne
Minister of the Postern chapel, Newcastle upon Tyne, 1801–4
Minister at Wallingford (Berks), 1807–12
Minister of the Tabernacle, Roch's Lane, Exeter, 1812–

William Macdonald Admitted 4 Dec. 1793. Left, having married, 1797
Minister at Lincoln and Enfield
See Cheshunt College archives, F/ 2382
Died 3 Dec. 1824, aged 58

John Mather Admitted 1 Aug. 1798
Born Newcastle upon Tyne, 20 Jan. 1773
Ordained at Spa Fields chapel, 17 May 1803
Itinerant minister (Hull, Sleaford, Canterbury, Gloucester, Bristol, Ebley, Folkestone, Faversham)
Minister at Beverley (East Riding), 1807-43
Died 21 Mar. 1852. Brother of William Mather

William Mather Admitted 2 Apr. 1795. Left 29 June 1799
Born Newcastle upon Tyne, 13 July 1769
Ordained at Holywell Mount chapel, London, 13 June 1797
Itinerant minister
Minister of Zion chapel, Dover, 1804-23
Died 20 May 1825, aged 55. Brother of John Mather

John Meffen Admitted 4 Sept. 1795. Left 27 June 1799
Born Norwich, 23 June 1776
Itinerant minister (Dartford, Folkestone, Norwich)
Minister at Odiham and Sutton (Hants), 1816-[19]
Minister at Great Yarmouth, 1819-66
Died 5 Apr. 1870

David Morgan Admitted 29 July 1793. Left Christmas 1794

Richard Owen Admitted 1 Mar. 1797. Left 28 Mar. 1801
Born Walton West, Haverfordwest (Pembs), 1777

John Parry Admitted 5 June 1793. Left 12 May 1797
Born Denbigh, June 1762

William Robertson Admitted to Trevecka, n.d. Admitted to Cheshunt, 1 Aug. 1792. Left June 1795
Itinerant minister (York)
Minister at Blyth (Northumberland)
See Cheshunt College archives, F 1/ 763

William Ross Admitted 2 May 1798. Expelled Aug. 1799
Born South Shields, 2 Aug. 1777
Minister at Shadwell (London), 1800-8
Died 23 Dec. 1808

William Thomas Admitted 6 Sept. 1797

Richard Turnbull Admitted 7 Dec. 1796. Left 7 Nov. 1800
Born Morpeth (Northumberland), 1771

William Upjohn Admitted 3 Aug. 1796

Thomas Bevan Winter Admitted to Trevecka, n.d. Admitted to Cheshunt, 16
Aug. 1792. Left 30 June 1796
Minister at Kingsbridge (Devon), 1796-97
Died at Bristol, 7 Dec. 1797

VII

MISCELLANEOUS RECORDS

A: MISCELLANEOUS ACCOUNTS
1792

[1] Donations to the Society for supporting and perpetuating the Countess of Huntingdon's College - towards paying for the House and Premises purchased at Cheshunt in Hertfordshire.

1792				
Revd T. Haweis		10	0	0
Revd Dr Ford		10	0	0
J. Oldham Oldham		20	0	0
T. Weathcrill		10	10	0
W. Hodson		10	10	0
W. Langston		10	10	0
N. Dupont				
H. Batley		10	10	0
W. Astle		10	10	0
A Friend		50	0	0
Mr Duthoit		10	0	0
Mr Rowton		5	5	0
Mr Butterworth		10	10	0
[2]				
1792				
Jan. 4	Mr Silver	10	0	0
	Mr Tutt	5	5	0
	Mr Thomas Wontner	5	5	0
	Mr Holmes	10	0	0
	Mr S. Bridgman	2	2	0
	Mr W. Griffin	1	1	0
	Mr Butcher Senior	3	3	0
	Revd Mr Platt	2	2	0
	Mr Towers	10	0	0
	Mr Serjeant	1	1	0
	Mr Francis	2	2	0
	Mr R. Butcher Junior	2	2	0
	Mr Emerson	5	5	0
6	Mr Pulleyn	5	5	0

7	Mr Darling	20	0	0
	Mrs Darling	10	0	0
	Mr Groves	25	0	0
8	Mr Leaver	1	1	0
	Strangers		5	0
	Ditto		2	6

[3]
1792

Jan. 8	Mr John Long		2	6
10	Mr Cooke	5	5	0
	Mr Simpson	5	5	0
11	A.T.	1	1	0
13	Mr Galpine	10	10	0
18	Lady Mary Fitzgerald	1	1	0
	A Stranger		1	0
19	A Friend per Mr Holmes	3	3	0
20	Miss Hill	42	0	0
25	Mr Crowing, Sion Chapel	1	1	0
	Mr Compigne and Friend	5	5	0
29	Mr Edmund Gouldsmith		10	6
Feb. 20	Thomas Burne Esqr	50	0	0
Apr. 4	Mr Bell	5	5	0
	Mr Nathaniel Long	2	2	0
May 2	Mr Were	10	0	0
July 4	Mr Thomas French	6	6	0
	Mr Edmund Gouldsmith	1	1	0
	Mr Pontin	2	2	0
Aug. 5	Mr & Mrs Hansard	2	2	0
24	Mr Jasper Holmes Senior	25	0	0
	A Friend per Mr J.T. Holmes	5	5	0

[4]
1792

Aug. 30	A Friend per Mr Tutt	1	1	0
	Mr Edwards per Mr Charles	1	1	0
31	Mr Samuel Adams	1	1	0
Sept. 7	Mr Gabr. Nichols	5	5	0
9	Mr Silver and Friend	1	1	0
26	Miss Hillier	10	0	0
Oct. 3	Lady Car. Hervey	20	0	0
	Lady Emily Hervey	20	0	0
5	Mr Geale	1	1	0

Nov.	2	A Friend at Glocester per				
		Mr Dupont		2	2	0
		Mr Broadby			2	6
	12	J. Mulford Esqr of				
		Basingstoke		50	0	0
Dec.	11	E.M.		1	1	0
	14	John Gould		1	1	0
				£587	10	0

Laus Deo

[Cheshunt archives, C 9/ 5/ 2 v.]

---

[1]

Tickets delivered for the Dinner at the Opening of the College 24 August 1792

No. 1	Mr Weatherill	4	6
2, 3, 4	Mr Towers	13	6
4, 5	Mr Langston	9	0
7	Mr William Jones	4	6
8, 9	Mr Butcher	9	0
10	Mr Butcher Junior	4	6
11	Mr S. Bridgman	4	6
12, 13	Mr Emerson	9	0
14, 15	Mr Compigne	9	0
16, 17	Mr Batley	9	0
18, 19	Mr Astle	9	0
20	Mr Owen	4	6
21	Mr Tabberer	4	6
22	Mrs Tabberer	4	6
23	Revd Mr Platt		
24	Mr William Giles	4	6
25	Mr Francis	4	6

26	Mr Burridge (per Mr Platt)	4	6
27	Revd Mr Crole		
28	W. Hodson	4	6
29	Revd Mr Eyre		
[2]			
30, 31	Mr Phillips	9	0
32, 33	Miss Stanley	9	0
34	Mrs Powell	4	6
35-37	Mr King	13	6
38	Mrs Woolcott	4	6
39	Mrs Painter	4	6
40	Mrs Blain	4	6
41	Mrs Biggerstaff	4	6
42, 43	Mr Pulleyn	9	0
44, 45	Dr Hodson	9	0
46, 47	Mr Pontin	9	0
48, 49	Mr Cooper	9	0
50	Mr Bride	4	6
51, 52	Mrs & Mrs Brown	9	0
53	Mr Holmes	4	6
54, 55	Mr Serjeant	9	0
56, 57	Mr Keeble	9	0
58, 59	Mr Burnell	9	0
60	Mr Duthoit	4	6
61	Miss Duthoit	4	6
62	Mr Franklin	4	6
63-68	Mr Wontner	1 7	0
[3]			
69	Mr Knight	4	6
70	Mr Bridgman	4	6
71	Mr Oldham	4	6
72	Mr Dupont	4	6
73, 74	Mr Flower	9	0
75	Mr Broady	4	6
76	Mr Owen	4	6
77	Mrs Fisher	4	6
78	Mrs John Butcher	4	6
79	Mr Phillips per Mr Platt	4	6
80	Mrs Robson	4	6
81	Mrs Swithin	4	6
82	Mr Munn	4	6

83, 84	Mr Dudman	9	0
85, 86	Mr Evans	9	0
87	Mr Brown	4	6
88	Mr Sutton	4	6
89	Capt. Wilson	4	6
90	Mrs Deven	4	6
91	Mr Thomas	4	6
92	Mr Anth. Aviolette	4	6
93	Mr John Short	4	6
[4]			
94	Mr Butterworth	4	6
95, 96	Mr Weatherill	9	0
97	Revd Mr Charles		
98	Revd Mr Caldwell		
99	Revd Mr Kirkman		
100	Revd Mr Nicholson		
101, 102	Mr Maudsley	9	0
103-5	Mr Tutt	13	6
106	Mr Capel	4	6
107	Mr Batt	4	6
108	Mr Blain	4	6
109	Samuel Foyster Esqr	4	6
110	Mr Jas Moore	4	6
111	Mr Slade per Mr Platt	4	6
112	Mr Griffin	4	6
113	Mr Best		
114	Mr Dulley	4	6
115-7	Mr Fyffe	13	6
118	Mr Morris	4	6
119	Mrs Atkins	4	6
120, 121	Mr King	9	0
122, 123	Mr Ramsden	9	0
124	Mr Parker	4	6
125	Mr Gouldsmith	4	6
126	Mr Anthony	4	6
[5]			
127	Mr Roberts	4	6
128	Mr Campion	4	6
129	Mr Eyre and friend	9	0
130	Revd Mr Munn		
131	Mr Burridge	4	6

132	Mr Morris		4	6
133, 134	Mr Oldham		9	0
5, 6, 7, 8	Sundries		18	0
139	Mr Wills		4	6
		£29	9	6
140	Mr Emerson		4	6
		£29	14	0

[6]
Steward's Account
1792

Aug. 24	To R. Moore at the 4 Swans Waltham Cross			
	for 148 Dinners at 3s.	22	4	0
	9 Ditto at 1s.		9	0
	Ale and Porter	2	9	4
	Tobacco		1	0
	46 Bottles Wine at 2s. 6d.	5	15	0
	6 Ditto to the College		15	0
	Brandy and Rum		8	9
	The Waiters	1	0	5
		£33	2	6
Oct. 10	To J. Lake for 200 Tickets		14	0
	To a bad Shilling taken by one of the Doorkeepers for a Ticket		1	0
		£33	17	6

[7]
Contra
1792

Aug. 24	By 132 Tickets sold at 4s. 6d.	29	14	0
	By Cash of Mr Oldham		7	0
	By Ditto of Mr Weatherill		6	9

By Ditto of W. Hodson		6	9
By Ditto of Mr Dupont		7	0
By Ditto of Mr Langston		7	0
By Ditto of Mr Batley		7	0
By Ditto of Mr Astle		7	0
By Ditto of Mr Cooper		7	0
By Ditto of Mr Bridgman		7	0
By Ditto of Mr Emerson		7	0
By Ditto of Mr Serjeant		7	0
By Ditto of Mr Wontner		7	0

£33 17 6

[Cheshunt archives, C 9/5 /2 r.]

12 August 1/92
For the College

Morning	Gold	8	8	0
	Silver	20	6	6
	Copper		11	9
	More		2	6
		29	9	0
Evening	Gold	3	3	0
	Silver	11	11	0
	Copper		10	6
		44	13	6
Supplement	Gold	8	18	6
	Silver		11	0
		£54	3	0
	More		2	6

[Cheshunt archives, C 9/ 10/ 1]

Postage of Letters, etc

[1r]

1792	Paid by George Best as Secretary of the Society for the support of the Countess of Huntingdon's College		
Jan 28	Letter from Mr Morgan of Glasbury		7
30	Ditto Mr Jones Tutor		7
Feb. 16	Ditto Ditto		7
25	Ditto from Mr Robinson		6
27	Ditto from Mr Jones		7
Mar. 1	Horse hire to and from Cheshunt to examine whether the fixtures and other things bought in, were left	8	6
3d	Ditto to take possession of the House and premises	8	0
	Letter from Mr Milner		7
		19	11

[1v]

Mar. 14	Letter from Mr Morgan			7
19	Ditto Mr Griffiths			7
20	Ditto Mr Morgan			7
30	For my Coach hire to and from Cheshunt and Expences for a week to receive the goods, etc. Most part of the time at the Inn. Including ale to the men on unloading the goods, and a teapot, etc. left for Mrs Powell	1	3	0
Apr. 12	Letter to Mr Simson			4
	Ditto to Mr Coulthurst			6
	Ditto to Mr Richardson			6
	Ditto to Mr Pentycross			4
14	Ditto from Mr Charles			7
17	Ditto from Mr Simeon			5
May 21	Ditto from Mr Morgan			7
		2	7	11

[2r]

May 21	Letter from Mr T. Davis		7
	A quire of writing Paper	1	2
June 13	Letter from Mr Webb,		
	Cheshunt		3
	A Letter		1
July 20	Ditto		1
Aug. 1	Ditto respecting Mr Robinson		6
Nov. 16	With 6 Letters		6
28	Letter from Mr Brewer		1
1793			
		2 11	2
	Paid 19 February 1793		
Feb. 10	A Letter from Mr Jenkins		5
15	Ditto from Mr Moore		

[Cheshunt archives, C 9/ 5/ 1]

B: COUNTESS OF HUNTINGDON'S COLLEGE, Instituted 1768, At TALGARTH IN SOUTH WALES; Removed 1792, To CHESHUNT in HERTFORDSHIRE; And Supported by VOLUNTARY SUBSCRIPTIONS.

The Rev. ISAAC NICHOLSON, President

The late illustrious and truly honourable Countess of HUNTINGDON, animated by a fervent Zeal to spread the Knowledge of a Redeemer, and diffuse the Savour of his Grace, among other Institutions intended to effect so desirable an End, founded and supported a College in Wales, at her sole Expence; from whence many Ministers, eminent for Usefulness and Fidelity, have gone forth, to teach and preach Jesus Christ.

Had her Ladyship's Ability been equal to her Zeal and Benevolence, the Continuance of this Seminary would have been at her own Expence, as nothing lay nearer her Heart than the Support of it.

Apprehensive of her Removal in Consequence of her advanced Age; and sensible her Support would cease with her life, her Income being only a Jointure; several Friends to the Cause of God and his Gospel, offered themelves, in the Year 1787, to form a Society for the Continuance and Support of her College, when it should be deprived of her fostering Hand. The Design was highly approved by her Ladyship, as well as the Rules meant to be established, and she was pleased to annoint the Persons hereafter-named, as Trustees, whenever her Decease should call such a Trust into Exercise.

That afflictive Event having happened, and the College in Wales being only held on a Lease, which is expired, the Persons nominated by her Ladyship have endeavoured to carry into Effect the Trust reposed in them. A convenient and commodious Freehold, well adapted for the Purpose, has been purchased, pleasantly situated at Cheshunt, in Hertfordshire, where the original Design of the noble Foundress, namely, that of educating gracious young Men for the Ministry, is in future to be carried on.

As the Society is disinterested in its Views, disclaiming all Party, and desiring only to be the happy Instruments, in the Hand of the great Head of the Church, in preparing Labourers for his Vineyard, who may approve themselves able Ministers of the New Testament; with the fullest Confidence of deserving Support, they solicit all real Christians to join zealously in assisting to perpetuate this truly Evangelical Institution;

The Outlines of which are,

That every Candidate for Admission, must produce to the Trustees, Testimonials of his exemplary Morals, and give the fullest Satisfaction of his Faith in the Christian Doctrines contained in the Articles of the Church of England: and as we mean to obtain a better Conviction of this than any mere Subscription can afford, one or more of the Ministers who labour among us, shall examine into the Candidate's Knowledge, Views, natural Endowments, and Attainments; intending only to admit such, whose Promise of Ability as Speakers, is as clear, as the Evidence they produce of the Soundness of their Faith and the Purity of their Conduct is undoubted.

The more effectually to be satisfied in both these Points, every one admitted will be considered for Three Months as a Probationer; and if then approved for Diligence, Fidelity, and Improvement, he will be fully admitted, educated, and boarded freely, at the Expence of the Society, till his Education shall be judged by the President, and one or more of the principal Ministers in the Connection, sufficient to qualify him for the Work of the Ministers.

The Appointment and Removal of the President, and the Admission or Expulsion of Students, are vested solely and exclusively in the Trustees.

On the demise of a Trustee, the surviving Trustees are to elect a Successor, on or before the second monthly Meeting after his Decease.

There is an Assistant Committee of fourteen, chosen out of the Subscribers at large, who, together with the Trustees, meet the first Wednesday in every Month (except when the general Meetings are held), at the Committee Room, Spa-Fields Chapel, from Six o'Clock till Eight, to transact the Business of the Society. Three of the Assistant Committee to go out every Year, at the General Meeting in October, and three others to be chosen in their room.

There are also two Auditors chosen every Year, at the general Meeting in January, who are to examine the Accounts of the preceding Year, and make their Report at the next Quarterly Meeting.

The Society have Four General Meetings in the Year, viz. the First Wednesday in January, April, July and October, at the Castle and Falcon, Aldersgate-Street, to which every Subscriber of One Guinea per Annum or upwards is summoned: at these Meetings Information is given by the Trustees, of the State of the College, and of all incidental Occurrences.

There is a Secretary, who is to attend all the Meetings of the Trustees and Society, and take Minutes thereof; to keep a regular Book of Students admitted, and when they leave College [1]; to write Letters under the Direction of the Trustees and Committee; summon the General Meetings, &c., &c.

The Treasurers are always to be of the Trustees, and chosen by them. They are to keep fair and regular Books of all Receipts and Disbursements, and to balance the Accounts of every Year, so as that the same may be audited previous to the General Meeting in April next following.

The Plan of Education intended to be pursued.

I. To improve the Students in the Knowledge of the Scriptures, and to instruct them in the Method of communicating that Knowledge in the most able and pleasing Manner.

II. To teach them the Latin and Greek Languages, so far at least as to read the Classics and the Greek Testament readily; and to those who are most advanced, the Hebrew. We wish also to procure one French Student, who may be able to qualify others in that Language, in order to endeavour at introducing the pure Gosepl of Christ into the Countries where the French Tongue is generally spoken.

III. To initiate them in the first Principles of Mathematics, in order to teach them to reason accurately.

IV. To give them some general knowledge of History and Geography.

Lastly, to exercise them in English Composition on sacred Subjects every Week, in order to habituate them to Regularity of Discourse in Writing, that when they enter on their Ministry, they may express themselves with Energy and Propriety, as well as Fluency.

Subscriptions or Donations in Support of this Institution are received by

> James Oldham Oldham, Esq. No. 142, Holborn, Treasurer,
> Mr William Hodson, No. 39, Lothbury, Deputy-Treasurer,
> Mr Mathias Dupont, No. 5, Aldersgate-Street,
> Mr Thomas Weatherill, No. 6, Cold-bath Square,
> Mr William Langston, No. 2, Highbury Place, Islington,
> Mr Henry Batley, No. 9, Winchester-Place, Pentonville,
> Mr William Astle, No. 23, Portland-Lane, Gray's-Inn-Lane,
> John Lloyd, Esq.
> Mr George Best, No. 13, near Spa-Fields Chapel,
> Secretary.
> Mr William Parke, No. 109, Gray's-Inn-Lane, Collector.

Persons desirous of contributing to the Support of this truly valuable Institution, by any Legacy in their last Will, are requested to make use of the following Form, viz.

I give and bequeath to James Oldham Oldham, Esq. in Holborn, or the Treasurer for the Time being, of a Society for supporting and perpetuating the Countess of Huntingdon's College, formerly in Wales, but now removed to Cheshunt, in Hertfordshire, the Sum of to be paid by my Executor, in Months after my Decease, out of (here mention the Money out of which it shall be paid) *in Trust to apply the same to the Support of the said College, and his Receipt shall be a sufficient Discharge.*

Note. All Ministers who subscribe to this Institution, are deemed Visitors of the College, and may inspect the same at their Pleasure.

It is intended there shall be one or more public Examinations of the Students every Year, Notice thereof will be sent to the Subscribers.[2]

[Cheshunt archives, C 4/ 26]

FOOTNOTES

[1] The record of students is to be found in C9 /9 1.
[2] A list of subscribers was printed on the third page of this circular.

C: NOTICES OF MEETINGS

The ANNIVERSARY of opening the COUNTESS of HUNTINGDON'S College at CHESHUNT, will be held on Wednesday, the 27th Instant, at the College: the Sermon to be preached by the Rev. THOMAS HAWEIS, Rector of Aldwinkle. Service to begin exactly at Eleven o'Clock.

The Dinner, for the Sake of better Accommodation, will be at the KING'S HEAD, ENFIELD: to be on Table at Three. Tickets to be had of the Secretary, or at the Committee Room of Spa-Fields Chapel, till the 22d Instant exclusive.

Thomas Witham,
Secretary.

Rosoman's Street, Clerkenwell,
August 4, 1794

Note, On Sunday, the 24th Instant, Two Sermons will be preached at Spa-Fields Chapel, for the Benefit of the College. That in the Morning by the Rev. William Francis Platt, Minister of Holywell Mount Chapel; and that in the Evening by the Rev. Anthony Crole, Minister of Pinners Hall Meeting.

The Quarterly General Meeting of the Society for supporting and perpetuating the Countess of Huntingdon's College, will be held at the COMMITTEE ROOM of *Spa-Fields Chapel*, on Wednesday next, the 4th of January, at Six o'Clock precisely.

THOMAS WITHAM,
Secretary.

Rosoman's Street
December 29, 1796

Note, The Design which the Trustees have in Contemplation, of erecting a Chapel at the College, on the Scite of the Coach-house and Stables; and making the large Parlour, at present used as a Chapel, into a Library and Study; is postponed till their Finances shall be better able to bear the Expence.

On *Wednesday* the 21st Instant, there will be a Public Examination of the Students, at the COUNTESS OF HUNTINGDON'S COLLEGE, CHESHUNT, to begin at Eleven o'Clock precisely.

The Trustees, Ministers, &c. will dine at the GREEN DRAGON next to the COLLEGE, at Two o'Clock: if you intend to be present, and to dine with them, they request you will please to inform me on or before the 17th Instant.

The QUARTERLY GENERAL MEETING of the SUBSCRIBERS will be held at the COMMITTEE ROOM of *Spa-Fields* Chapel, on *Wednesday* the 4th of April, at Six o'Clock precisely.

T. Witham,
Secretary.

Rosoman's-Street, Clerkenwell,
12th March 1798.

Note. The Anniversary this Year will be the 29th of June, of which particular Notice will be given in due Time.

The Quarterly General Meeting of the Society for supporting and perpetuating the Countess of HUNTINGDON'S College, will be held at the COMMITTEE ROOM of *Spa-Fields' Chapel*, on *Wednesday* next, the Second of *October*, at Six o'Clock precisely.

THOMAS WITHAM,
Secretary

ROSOMAN-STREET,
26th September, 1799

Note. At this Meeting PLANS for a CHAPEL at the College will be brought for Inspection, as the Out-building, where the Chapel is intended to be erected, is become so ruinous it must be taken down.[1]

[Cheshunt archives, C 9/ 10/ 1]

A few Remarks relative to the Collection for the College August 16 1795

1. It has been found needful to have a Collection once a Year towards its support, as the Annual Subscriptions have not been sufficient without this Aid.

2. The number of Students a few Months ago was Thirteen and the Trustees were under the necessity of augmenting the Allowance for Board and Washing, on Account of the Advanced Price of Provisions, etc.

---

[1] All four notices are printed. Most of these copies have been re-used for memoranda.

3. At the publick Examination held the 27th of May some of the Students were thought fit to be sent out: - and accordingly there have been four sent to enter upon their publick work in the Lord's Vineyard - namely

> Mr Bickerdike who is now at Derby
> Mr Bradley at Newark
> Mr Davies at Ashborne
> Mr Robertson at York

4. The number of Students now in the College is Nine, and as it will appear by a Letter received lately from Dublin which I shall read to You, that more Labourers are wanted, I hope you will earnestly pray to the Lord, not only that He would incline his People's Hearts to support the Institution, but that He would also send us more young Men, such as He has appointed and intended for the Ministry of the Gospel. We have no Objection to receive half a dozen or half a Score of the right Sort.

[Cheshunt archives, C9/ 10/ 1]

Hints for the Revd Dr Haweis
Oct. 29 1797

1. The College is, thro' the good hand of God upon us, in a prosperous Condition: there are 11 young Men in it, all of whom we hope and trust are gracious Men, and of promising Abilities for Usefulness. And 11 are gone out into various parts of the Lords Vineyard, in England, Scotland, Ireland, and Wales.

2. The Annual Subscriptions do not themselves maintain the College. It requires a further Aid. And this Year, besides the current Expences, there have been some considerable Extraordinaries, for Repairs and Accomodations for the Family, to defray which we want to collect this day £100.

3. We have been disappointed this Year of a very handsome Legacy, bequeathed to the College by a Friend to the Institution who was a member of this Congregation. He left the Rent of a house (which amounts to about £21 per Annum) for [ ] years to come to the College and School but the Statute of Mortmain which renders void either Houses or Lands left to charitable Uses deprives us totally of the intended benefit. Therefore if any of you wish to remember the College in your Will let it be in Money.

4. It is well known that in this Chapel there are fewer Collections than in most other places. We have had but one Collection this Year, and that was for the winding up of the Chapel Repair. We therefore hope for your Liberality on the present Occasion.

[Cheshunt archives, C9/ 10/ 1]

For the Revd Mr Eyre December 9 1798

1. That there are now 14 Students in the College being the largest number we ever had.

2. That we have had no Legacy or large Donation this Year: and the Annual Subscriptions alone did not amount to a Sum sufficient for the Support of the College.

3. That above £200 out of our £700 3 per Cents must go for the Redemption of the Land Tax.

4. That there has been no Collection made in this Chapel throughout the whole Year, except one for the Traveling Fund.

5. One Student only, having compleated his Studies, has quitted the College this Year, namely Mr John James, who has enter'd upon his ministerial Labours with great Acceptance.

[Cheshunt archives, C9/ 10/ 1]

APPENDIX
COLLEGE INCOME AND EXPENDITURE

1787	Donations	66	9	0			
	Subscriptions	96	12	0	163	1	0
1788	Donations	28	2	6			
	Subscriptions	68	5	0			
	Interest	6	0	0	102	7	6
1789	Donations	0	0	0			
	Subscriptions	33	12	0			
	Interest	10	2	6	43	14	6
1790	Donation	5	5	0			
	Subscriptions	71	8	0			
	Interest	12	15	0	89	8	0
1791	Donations	136	12	6			
	Subscriptions	223	18	0			
	Interest	16	5	6	376	16	0
1792	Donations	587	10	0			
	Subscriptions	322	17	0			
	Interest	15	15	0			
	Spa Fields	54	5	6	980	7	6
1793	Donations	14	16	6			
	Subscriptions	418	1	6			
	Interest	15	0	0			
	Spa Fields	61	0	0			
	Books sold	7	7	0	516	5	0
1794	Donations	6	6	0			
	Subscriptions	429	13	6			
	Interest	15	0	0			
	Spa Fields	60	0	0			
	Legacy	20	0	0	530	19	6
1795	Donations	15	15	0			
	Subscriptions	451	7	0			
	Interest	15	15	0			
	Spa Fields	62	14	6			
	Legacy	100	0	0			
	Old lead sold	13	12	9	658	9	3
1796	Donation	1	11	6			
	Subscriptions	445	17	0			
	Interest	21	0	0			

	Spa Fields	91	12	9			
	Legacy	10	10	0			
	Trees sold	5	5	0			
	Timber sold	2	2	0	577	18	3
1797	Donations	6	6	0			
	Subscriptions	469	9	6			
	Interest	21	0	0			
	Spa Fields	67	19	5			
	Old lead	20	4	0	584	18	9
1798	Donations	15	5	0			
	Subscriptions	466	15	6			
	Interest	21	0	0			
	Spa Fields	73	4	6	576	15	0
1799	Donations	10	10	6			
	Subscriptions	467	17	0			
	Interest	36	0	0			
	Spa Fields	83	10	0	597	17	6

Expenses were usually very close to annual income:

Year						
1791	104	7	1	(376	16	0)
1792	84	13	2	(980	7	6)
1793	485	0	7	(516	5	0)
1794	543	2	6	(530	19	6)
1795	525	12	0	(658	9	3)
1796	564	11	6	(577	18	3)
1797	585	7	5	(584	18	9)
1798	576	7	1	(576	15	0)
1799	702	11	11	(597	17	6) [32]

This information is summarised from the College accounts (C9/ 1).

INDEX

The names of subscribers (alphabetically listed pp. 197-207) and incidental names are not included in this index.

Addington, Dr., house of, 18, 20
Alarm clock presented, 68, 74
Aldridge, Rev. Mr., 17
Aldwinkle (Northants), vi, x, 201
Andrews, Mr., 17
Anglesey, 122
Annan (Dumfries), 95, 113, 119, 141
Apostolic Society, formed, v, ix, 4, 173
     plan of, 14, 153-168
Arminians excluded, 65
Arson at College, 50, 187
Arundel (Sussex), 90, 91
Ashbourne (Derbys), 104
Assistant Committee formed, 19, 20
Astle, John, 26
  William, trustee, xi, 11, 176
Atley, Henry, 49, 211
Ayre, Rev. Mr., 8

Baker, John, 17
Bala (Merioneth), 32, 199
Banfield, Mr., 4
Baptists excluded, 26, 47
Barker, Clement, carpenter, 62, 68, 86, 92, 102, 122, 129, 138, 140, 143
Barnard, Rev. Mr., 3
  Rev. Thomas, vi
Barton, Rev. Mr., 27
  John, 16
Bath, x, 200
Batley, Henry, trustee, xi, 3-150, 156, 168, 173, 175, 179
    secretary, 22
Beaching, Charles, 64
Beasley, Mr., 23, 25, 26
Beccles (Suff.), 29
Bennett, Mr., 8
  William, student, 132, 133, 136, 211
Bensley, Mr., 14
Best, George, 3 58
  secretary, 26, 58, 181, 191, 226
Bickerdike, John, student, 35, 36, 48, 51, 52, 55, 59, 78, 79, 80, 81, 87, 90, 91, 96, 97, 98, 104, 126, 130, 186, 211
    illness, 107, 108
Biggerstaffe, Mr., 4, 5

Billings, Thomas, 139-142
Birmingham, 127
Blanks, Edward, 34, 181
Boddily, Rev. Mr., 93, 94
Bodmin (Cornwall), x, 200
Bond, Mr., 4
Bowen, Rev. F., 26
Bowles, Mr., 17
Bradford, Rev. Mr., 8
Bradley, Robert, student, 35, 36, 48, 51, 52, 55, 59, 79, 81, 90, 91, 93, 101, 104, 116, 117, 119, 120, 129, 151, 186, 212
Brewer, Rev. Mr., 53, 99
Brich, John, student, 106, 107, 108, 115, 121, 212
Bridgeman, Mr., 17
Brighton (Brighhelmstone), x, 22, 50, 98, 121, 201, 204
Bristol, x, 32, 58, 146, 204
Bromley (Middx.), 200
Brotherton, James, 95, 97, 99
Browning, Rev. Mr., 134
Brynn, B., 15
  John, 87
Buckingham, 65
Buntingford (Herts.), 149
Burge, Mr., 58
Burnhill, Mr., 27
Burnett, Mr., 18
Butcher, Robert, 17
Butterworth, Mr., 4
Cadogan, Rev. Mr., 32
Caldwell, Rev. Mr., 47, 48, 58
Callaway, Thomas, house of, 32
Callens, Benjamin, student, 117, 118, 119, 120, 212
Cambridge, College moved to, v, vii, xii
    St. Catherine's Coll., 29
Camp, Mr. carpenter, 58
Cannon, Rev. Mr., 67
Cardale, Mr., lawyer, 27, 28, 33, 41, 61, 62, 63, 66, 76, 181, 193
Carnson, John, 90, 91, 92, 95, 97, 98, 99, 212
Carr, James, 34, 58, 61, 62, 101, 102, 144, 149, 150
  Jonathan, 116

INDEX

Chamberlain, John, student, 65, 74, 79, 82, 100, 108, 114, 124, 125, 126, 129, 212

Chambers, Mr., 8

Chapman, Mr., donation, 90, 92

Charles, Rev. Thomas, ix, xi, 17, 32, 38, 46, 48, 63, 101, 138, 182

Chatteris (Cambs.), 47

Cherry, Benjamin, 147

Cheshunt (Herts.), College *see,* College, at Cheshunt

        Green Dragon, 102, 114, 115, 124, 180, 233

        houses at, xii, 20, 21

        manor court, 135

        vestry, 135

Chichester (Sussex), 135, 137

Chingford (Essex), 203

Cirencester (Glous.), 27

Claridge, William, 65

Clark, John, 65

Clock presented, 68, 74

Coanes, John, 116, 118, 133, 134

Coddington (Ches.), xi, 45, 183

Cole, Ann, washerwoman, 97, 105, 108, 121, 126, 129, 132, 135, 137, 144, 147, 150

College, in Wales, v, vii, xii, 15, 19, 21, 26, 29, 177

    at Cambridge, v, vii, xii

    at Cheshunt, v, vii, xii, 24, 180, 197–203.

    accommodation, 28, 137, 139

    account book, 45

    accounts, 60

    arson at, 50, 187

    attack on, 77

    books at, 15, 18, 29, 36, 37, 145

    brewing at, 118, 123, 126

    chapel at, 43, 53, 57, 58, 59, 61, 62, 63, 102, 117, 149, 150, 232, 233

    collector for, 13

    communion plate, 15

    conveyance of, 31

    dinner, 221-225

    donation book, 28, 43

    fires at, 140

    furniture of, 15, 18, 26, 29, 30, 32, 36, 42, 43, 45, 58, 59, 77

    garden, 39, 100, 102, 106, 124

    gardener, 16

    gun fired at, 81

    housekeeper, 16, 27

    income of, 236

    insurance of, 50

    land tax, 138, 140, 144, 146

    legacy board, 78, 82, 83, 107

    letter book, 83

    opening of, 52, 187

    plan of, 20, 29, 155-168, 230

    President of, 7 *s.a.* Nicholson, I.

    record book, 45, 171-193

    rules for, 27, 167, 168

    senior student, 79, 137, 147

    stables, 135

    subscribers, 8, 17, 60, 219-221

    Sunday school, 130

    taxes, 134, 140

    trespass at, 86, 89, 100

    trust deed, 30, 41, 61, 63, 66

    trustees, 7

    tutor, 27, 31, 32

    washing, 40, 81, 140

    Welsh students, xiii, 64

    windows, 36, 57, 141, 143

Committee, Assistant, 19, 20

Connexion, founded, ix, 6, 156, 174

    chapels in, 9

    itinerancy in, 109, 110

Cooke, James, student, 127, 129, 131, 133, 212

    illness, 148

Cooper, Mr., 15

    donation, 145

   Mrs., donation, 31

   James, 17

   John, 42, 75

Cottingham, Rev. Mr., 17, 133, 134

Coulthurst, Mr., 37, 38

Courcy, see De Courcy

Coxhead, Mr., 17

Craddick, Thomas, donation, 133

Creswell, Rev. Edward, 29

Crichlade (Wilts.), 29

Crole, Rev. Anthony, 36, 51, 75, 79, 187

Croule, Rev. Mr., 15, 46

Cureton, Rev. Mr., 57, 67, 87

    legacy, 76

INDEX

INDEX

Hopper, Mr., 14

Horn, Andrew, student, xi, 75, 76, 79, 82, 114, 124, 125, 126, 128, 213

Hornby, Mrs. A., see Powell, Averina

Howell, Henry, 23

Hoxton Academy, 142

Hughes, Mr., 18, 40, 181

    Edward, 149

Hughes & Walsh, printers, 10, 79, 92, 121, 132, 143

Hull, x, 31, 204

Huntingdon, Countess of, v-x, 3-14, 155-157, 173, 176

    will of, 15

Hutchings, Thomas, student, 45, 46, 47, 51, 187, 191, 213

        left college, 49, 50

        censured, 90

Illingworth, Dr., 25, 31, 33, 64, 182

Ipswich (Suff.), 100

Irish, Rev. Mr., 27

Isham, Thomas, 65

James, Rev. Mr., 17

    John, student, 68, 74, 79, 82, 213

        illness, 108, 119

        ordained, 136, 137

Jenkins, Rev. Mr., 3, 14

Jones, Rev. Mr., 16, 58

    David, 63, 64, 84, 178

    Edward, 17

    J., tutor, 23, 26, 31, 32, 35, 39, 181

    Rev. Lewis, 62

    Samuel, 147, 148

    Thomas, 25, 147

    William, student, 35, 36, 46, 47, 51, 52, 59, 78, 79, 81, 90, 93, 94, 100, 108, 112, 114, 115, 186, 213

        complaints, 83, 84, 86, 87, 109, 110

Jordan, J., 17

Kemp, William, student, 35, 36, 46, 51, 52, 55, 59, 79, 87, 100, 108, 112, 113, 114, 186, 213

        ordained, 120

        gift, 143

Kennedy, Rev. Mr., 27

King, Mr., 15, 42

Kingsbridge (Devon), 117, 123, 125, 129

Kirby, Rev. Mr., 99, 100

Kirkman, Rev. Lemuel, 19, 36, 37, 118, 141, 187

Knaresborough (Yorks.), 78

Knight, Rev. J.A., 3, 125

    W., 19

Knightley, Thomas, bricklayer, 58, 78, 96, 102, 121, 132, 135, 143

Lampeter Velfry (Pembs.), 64

Lancaster, Joseph, 78

Land tax, 138, 140

Langston, William, trustee, xi, 3-151, 156, 168, 173, 175

Lee, George, student, 115-118, 127, 136, 213

Leicester, 31, 32

Leighton, Stephen, plumber, 58, 78, 92, 121, 129

Linby (Notts.), 29

Llangan (Carms.), 16

Lloyd, John, trustee, ix, xi, 14, 31

        death of, 89

London, Camberwell, 145

    Kentish Town, 20

    Mile End, 19

    Mulburry Gardens, ix, x, 15, 119, 127, 136

    Pell Street, xii

    Pentonville, 23

    Sion Chapel, ix, x, 15, 108, 127

    Spa Fields, ix, x, 3, 86, 87, 100, 108, 116, 136, 146, 232

    Stepney, 135

    Whitechapel, x

Longes, Mr., 17

Love, Rev. William, 32, 182

Lynby, see Linby

Lyne, Rev. Mr., 29

Lyon, Dr., treasurer, 4, 10, 90, 156, 173, 175, 176

Macdonald, William, student, 67, 75, 79, 82, 132, 214

        married, 127

Madan, Rev. Martin, vi

Married men excluded, 60, 127, 149

Mather, John, student, 134, 137, 140, 214

INDEX

INDEX